The Dynamics
of Sex and
Gender:
A Sociological
Perspective

The Dynamics of Sex and Gender: A Sociological Perspective

Laurel Richardson Walum
Ohio State University

Rand McNally College Publishing Company / Chicago

77 78 79 10 9 8 7 6 5 4 3 2 1

For Ben and Josh

Preface

Somehow it is fitting that my last involvement with the creation of this book should be the writing of a preface. For it is only at the end that we know where we have been; and only by ending that we can once again begin.

This book is an attempt to view the dynamics of sex and gender from a sociological perspective. That perspective links the private experiences of individuals, the structure of institutions, and the interests of the powerful. My purpose throughout has been twofold: first, to explore and understand the nature of gender dynamics in American society; and second, to engage the interest of both the novice and the professional in that understanding. Accomplishing the first goal required the integration of research from many disciplines—psychology, anthropology, linguistics, political science—as well as sociology. And, sometimes, it has necessitated bypassing traditional sociological explanatory categories and concepts. Interesting the student and the scholar has often meant the extended discussions of sociological concepts within a gender-dynamics context, the inclusion of descriptive and illustrative materials, extensive referencing, and specification of areas in need of research.

Although *The Dynamics of Sex and Gender* does not represent a particular school of sociology, it does review and integrate a wide array of research about gender and invites the reader to partake in the enterprise. Consequently, the book can be used as a major text in gender-roles and women's studies courses, as an adjunct in introductory sociology, social problems, American studies, and foundations classes, as well as in courses where the instructor wishes to include materials on gender, such as social organization, social stratification, social change, and minority relations.

The first section explores the processes by which the young are socialized into the culture through language, family processes, toys, books, and education. Section Two stresses the role which the ideas of science (biology, psychology, the social sciences, law and religion) have played in adult social control, and it examines alternative paradigms. The final section is concerned with the structure of sexual inequality as it is maintained by, and reflected in, the social organization of work, home life, and politics, including the structure and processes of sociopolitical change.

Most any book must be highly personal, but a book on sex and gender is intensely so. Each intellectual question created a "gut level" response. At times my rage sent me furiously to the typewriter; at times my sorrow froze my fingers; and at times my optimism transformed thoughts to wishes. In the final rewriting, I have tried to set aside those angers, sadnesses, and hopes. But even so, it is still not only an academic book; it is a personal one, informed and shaped by my own biography.

I am a woman and a feminist. These elements of my identity have had a crucial impact on the final structure of this book. For example, although I planned to present a balanced account of men's and women's experiences, I have not succeeded. I write more of women than of men. Given the paucity of research on the male sex role, this path to understanding was both short and narrow. And since, as a woman, I have not directly experienced the social-psychological worlds of boys and men, this avenue to sensitivity was blocked.

What I have come to fully realize through the writing of this book, therefore, is how absolutely salient gender is in our everyday lives—how differentiated and disparate are the social worlds inhabited by males and females. I am convinced—as I was not three years ago—that a complete and adequate sociology of gender requires a kind of teamwork between male and female researchers in which each is sensitized to the life experiences of the other. I hope this book will encourage researchers to undertake that venture.

Three years have passed since I first proposed this project. During that time many, many persons have helped in a variety of ways. Without the previous work of researchers and scholars, I would not be writing this preface in my lifetime. Although I credit their research in the text, I wish to thank all of them again for their dedication and inspiration.

As I review the groups and individuals directly relevant to my life while working on this book, I am overwhelmed with my good fortune. Both my Women's Group and the Women's Poetry Workshop have been there with encouragement and support. The questing and questioning of students from a half-dozen undergraduate sex-roles classes have given fresh dimensions to my work. Especially grand have been the energy and elation generated in the Graduate Sex-Roles Seminar, spring (and summer), 1976. To all the people in those groups, my deepest appreciation.

Many individuals have contributed directly to the preparation of this manuscript. Nona Glazer, Joan Huber, and Betty Frankle Kirschner, have critically reviewed the entire manuscript at various stages of revision. Adrian Aveni, Tim Diamond, Judith Di Iorio, Lucille Duberman, Jan Dunham, Russell Dynes, Harriet Ganson, Laura Gordon, George Martin, David Milder, John Seidler, Yuan Tien, and

Diane Vaughn have generously lent their expertise to critically review parts of it. Many others have helped in reviewing, editing, and general preparation in a variety of ways. These include John Applegath, Margaret Boberschmidt, Mai-Lis Dickerson, Mary Margaret Fonow, Jenny Gilbertson, Lawrence Malley, Williams Phillips, David Rust, Nancy Sundquist, Elaine Wellin, and Nellice Woltemade.

Three persons must be singled out for very special thanks. First, Ruth Branscom for coming through beyond the call of duty with skill and patience. Second, Russell Dynes who as Chairperson of the Department of Sociology, Ohio State University, facilitated the completion of my work. And last, but far from least, Betty Frankle Kirschner who has been an incredibly fine friend as well as critical sociologist—and has had the elegance to know when to be which.

Columbus, Ohio
November 8, 1976   Laurel Richardson Walum

Acknowledgements

The following have been reprinted with the permission of the publishers and the authors:

Page 9: from "Sex Role Stereotypes and Clinical Judgements of Mental Health" by Inge K. Broverman, Susan Raymond Vogel, Donald M. Broverman, Frank E. Clarkson and Paul S. Rosenkrantz, *Journal of Consulting and Clinical Psychology* 34(1970):1–7.

Page 48: from "Poems," *What Boys and Girls Can Be.* Kansas City, Mo.: Hallmark Cards.

Page 75: from "Some Female Stereotypes of Male Body Build-Behavior" by Richard M. Lerner, *Perceptual and Motor Skills* 28(1969):363–66.

Pages 77–78: from "Biology as Written in a Patriarchal Society and a Matriarchal Society" by Ruth Hershberger, *Adam's Rib.* New York: Harper and Row, 1948.

Page 84: from "Trebly Sensuous Woman" by Miles Newton, *The Female Experience,* by the editors of *Psychology Today.* Del Mar, California: Communication Research Machines, 1973.

Page 195: from "Women in American Politics: An Overview" by Naomi Lynn, *Women: A Feminist Perspective,* Jo Freeman, editor. Palo Alto, Calif.: Mayfield Publishing, 1975.

Page 198: from "A Study of Career Structures of Federal Executives" by Mary M. Lepper, *Women in Politics,* Jane S. Jaquette, editor. New York: Wiley Interscience, 1974.

Contents

Section One
Learning the Culture

In the beginning, the human foetus is female. When embryos with the XY chromosomal patterns emit the hormone androgen, they become male. The clitoris is transformed into a penis, the ovaries to testes, and the vaginal tract closes over. If the differentiation proceeds without error, the child is recognized at birth as male or female and assigned to one of these two categories, which are used universally to designate sexual differences within the human species.

Commonly, it has been assumed that everything else about the child flows naturally from its anatomy. A boy's disposition, role in child rearing, choice of sex partner, and desires for achievement are frequently viewed as naturally and normally different from a girl's. Such biological determinism has a long history in both scholarship and folklore. Part of the attractiveness of this belief has been its relative truth. Up until quite recently men have led qualititatively different lives than women. It has, therefore, seemed natural to explain these differences as a consequence of biology.

More recently, however, the research efforts of many different scientists—physiologists, psychologists, sociologists, endroconologists, ethologists, and anthropologists, etc.—have brought into serious question the import of biology for the subsequent social and sexual development of the child and adult. Researchers from disparate disciplines have come to stress the importance of *social shaping*—of learning to be a "masculine" or "feminine" person.

In the chapters that follow we will examine the processes by which children are socially shaped into "masculine" or "feminine" persons. We will be seeking answers to the question "To what extent, in what dimensions, and through what methods are boys and girls taught to be different?" We will look at the major ways in which young children acquire various aspects of the culture in which they live—through language, interaction with parents, the media, and the school. We will begin our exploration by looking at the relationships between culture, sex, and gender. What has our culture done to make certain that anatomy dictates destiny?

1

1

Culture and Gender

The year is 1984. The place is a quiet retreat off the Grecian coast. The event is the First World Congress on the Human Nature of Males and Females. Representatives from all societies are convened for the purpose of determining the natural differences between the sexes and of thereby preparing each sex to accept its destiny. The discussion is in progress.

"But *only* men enjoy playing with babies," says the Manu representative.

"Enjoyment is not the issue," counters the Toda Conferee. "It is a matter of sacred trust. And only men can be entrusted with the sacred tasks of housework."

"On the contrary," answers the American. "It is a matter of natural strength and physical power. Men have these and therefore are naturally dominant and responsible for the important matters of business and state."

"Nonsense!" retorts the Tchambuli. "Men are irresponsible and emotionally dependent. Women are naturally dominant because they are less emotional and therefore more capable of managerial functions."

"I can't imagine what you are all talking about," asserts the Mundugumor. "I knew this conference was a foul idea. There is no basic difference between men and women. Both sexes are aggressive, competitive and violent. Of course, fishing is a woman's task, but we surely cannot argue natural differences on the basis of tasks performed."

"I must agree with my colleague from Mundugumor concerning the essential similarity between the sexes," chimes in the Arapesh representative. "However, I must disagree with her concerning the nature of the similarity. All people, as I know them, are gentle, kind, protective, and loving. Aggression and violence are not natural to anybody."

And so the debate continues. Each representative has come carrying cultural baggage—the beliefs, judgments, and evaluations of his or her society. Each one sees the personalities associated with a given sex in their societies as the right,

3

natural, and appropriate ones. Not only do they disagree on which sex is more aggressive, competitive, and dominant, but they disagree on the *reasons* for making such claims, as well as on the relevance sex has as a dimension for distinguishing one person from another.

Everyone is born into a *culture*—a set of ideas shared by a group of people, ideas that are symbolically expressed in their behavior and artifacts. These ideas comprise beliefs about the nature of reality, moral judgments about what is right or wrong, and evaluations of what is desirable and attractive or disgusting and to be avoided. Some peoples take for granted, as a cultural belief, that men are naturally superior to women; some take for granted that women are naturally superior to men; and some cannot understand the dispute at all. In each case the culture is defining for its members that which is to be taken for granted as factual, inalienable, and proved.

Our cultures also give us a system of ideas for judging how things *ought* to be. For example, according to 300 cultures (out of 1170 sampled) women should be virgins at marriage. These societies have a *proscriptive norm* (a thou-shall-not rule) concerning premarital coitus. In the United States, men should be financially responsible for their families. This is an example of a *prescriptive norm* (a thou-shall rule) governing the role of men and one that has been formally institutionalized into our legal marriage contracts.

In addition, the culture includes ideas about what is preferable or enjoyable. In our society, often that which is defined as pleasureable is in direct conflict with that which is defined as right. The old shibboleth, "Everything I like is either immoral, illegal, or fattening," exemplifies this conflict. It is no wonder that we frequently experience considerable stress in making decisions.

Culture, then, is ideational. Behavior, arts, and artifacts are merely symbolic representations of the culture. Platform shoes, the all-day girdle, mascara, and pantyhose are artifacts that symbolize attitudes toward women just as the gray flannel suit, tie, and jockstrap symbolize attitudes toward men. Each of these items of attire is culturally approved and consistent with the culture's ideas about the nature of men and women, judgments about what is morally appropriate for men and women to do, and evaluations of what is attractive and desirable in each of the sexes.

Any complex society has a great number and variety of ideas, some of which are shared by only a few of its members. But despite the diversity, there does exist a cultural perspective that is unconsciously shared. For example, we believe that we really do exist and are not actors in another person's dream, that fertilization of ova are required for pregnancy, that time can be measured, and that if we drop a pencil it will fall. We have a general understanding of what a newscaster is talking about and why it is newsworthy—that is, we understand each other's words.

Sex and Gender

Similarly, there is a dominant cultural attitude toward sex and gender—a set of ideas we take for granted regardless of our own gender, ethnicity, or family

[handwritten margin notes: proscriptive norm: thou-shall-not; prescriptive norm: thou-shall]

background. For example, an adult member of our society sees the population as composed of two and only two sexes, male and female. From before the cradle to beyond the grave, a person is supposed to be inextricably and forever male or female. A distribution of traits of both sexes within one individual does not appear natural. Indeed, we refer to the sexes as opposite rather than different.

There has been a great deal of confusion in both scholarly and popular discussions concerning the meaning of the concepts, sex and gender. In this book, *sex* refers to the biological aspects of a person such as the chromosomal, hormonal, anatomical, and physiological structure. It is an *ascribed status* in that a person is assigned to one sex or the other at birth. *Gender* refers to psychological, social, and cultural components. Unlike sex, it is an *achieved status*. People learn what behaviors and attitudes they should have according to their label—male or female. Further, when a male is acting in culturally condoned gender-appropriate ways, he is viewed as *masculine,* and when a female is acting in gender-appropriate ways, she is seen as *feminine.*

[handwritten margin note: sex = ascribed status]
[handwritten margin note: gender = achieved status]

We are so accustomed to thinking of all aspects of one sex as consistent that it may be difficult to accept inconsistency. Chromosomally, a person may not have the genetic pattern of a female (XX), but have female sex organs, as was the case for some women Olympic athletes. A person's gonads—the sperm- or egg-producing organ (testicles in the male, ovaries in the female)—may not be fully developed preventing reproductive capacity; or they may be composed of both ovarian and testicular cells. Although both sexes normally have both the male hormones (androgen and testosterone) and the female ones (estrogen and progesterin), in some adults, sex hormone proportions conform more to the other sex than to their own. Similarly, both the internal sex organs (seminal vesicles and prostrate gland in males; uterus, fallopian tubes, and vagina in females) and the external ones (penis and testicles in the male; vulva including the clitoris in females), may be atrophied or ambiguous. For example, a large clitoris can be mistaken for a penis; or, testicles may not have descended at birth. Consequently, it is entirely conceivable for a child to be, say, chromosomally and hormonally a male, but anatomically a female.

Further, one's biological sex (even if consistent on all indicators) may be totally independent of one's gender identity. Although the Olympic athletes were disqualified from competition based on chromosomal analysis, they were reared as girls and continue to identify with that gender. *Gender identity* ("I am a boy" or "I am a girl") is one of our most basic self-definitions. The concept should not be confused with masculinity or femininity. A boy playing with dolls knows that he is a boy; a tomboy knows she is a girl. Few people worry about knowing what gender they are, although many struggle with whether they are feminine or masculine *enough.* Even transsexuals—persons who identify with a gender other than the one they were reared into—know what gender they are and seek the necessary medical attention to alter their sex.

Along the same lines, we are accustomed to assuming that one's sex identity is linked to one's sex-object preference. However, sexual arousal by a member of one's own sex or the other sex is independent of one's sex-identity as well as of one's masculinity or femininity. Homosexuals know what sex they are. Further, some see themselves as masculine; others, as feminine. And some see no relationship between their masculinity or femininity and their sexuality. That is, they do not differ in these regards from the heterosexual population.

In summary, sex categorization within the cultural context that everyone is (should be) either male or female is determined at birth. Anatomical differences are the basis upon which a child is placed into a sex category. This sex identification is decided by others. *Gender* identity—what it means to be male or female in terms of appropriate role performances, personality structures, attitudes, and behaviors—is not determined at birth. Nor, as we have seen, is it universally agreed upon. Rather, a child with a given anatomical structure is socialized or taught to think, feel, and act in ways considered natural, morally appropriate, and desirable for a person of that sex. These are the lessons that individuals take on in learning to achieve a given gender from their culture.

Learning Gender: The Case of "Agnes"

The case history of "Agnes," described by Garfinkel, vividly underscores the nature of achieving one's gender learning (Garfinkel: 1967). When Agnes at age 19 first appeared at the UCLA sex-change clinic, she appeared to be a very attractive, well-endowed young woman. Medical inspection revealed she possessed normal-sized male genitalia, no female genitalia, and only feminine secondary sexual characteristics (developed breasts and subcutaneous fat, pelvic girdle, lack of facial and body hair, etc.). A long series of interviews with her ensued, during which it was learned that she had been identified as a boy at birth and raised as such until she was seventeen. At that age, she decided to "pass" as female. She had come now to the sex-change clinic to have her "tumor" removed and a vagina constructed so that she could have what nature had intended all along. She insisted it was both moral and correct for her to be a female.

Her presentation of her biography underscored her insistence that she really was a female, misunderstood, and mislabeled. Any questions concerning her past identification as a boy were rejected. According to her account, she never had to line up with the boys in school, never had to undergo a physical examination with boys, etc. That is she had taken the stance of any normal adult in this culture. For her, there were only two sexes and she was female and was always meant to be female.

Once she had decided to pass as a woman (although in her terms once she had decided to *be* the sex she was always intended to be), she had to *learn* how women *are* and at the same time avoid being found out. She had to discover in the process of doing the womanly thing, what the features of the womanly thing were, and at the same time keep her genitalia and biography a secret. Put another way, the elements of natural behavior for women, the features women take as given, for Agnes became continuously problematical. The daily taking for granted of one's identity and of knowing how to present that identity to others, became for Agnes an ongoing problem. She devised certain practices for withholding information, such as evading questions, speaking in generalities or of impersonal cases, and shifting the conversation away from areas that might potentially disclose her secret. She devised a series of techniques by which she could avoid situations or conversations in which her secret might be revealed. For example, when going swimming with her friends she wore tight underpants and a skirted suit. Or, when asked for a urine sample during a physical exam for a job, she claimed an inability to urinate and later brought back her female roommate's sample.

But she also had to learn how to reveal that she was a woman. Much of her learning about the practices of womanhood were developed in the context of the claim that she already knew what they were. For example, her fiancé's mother, while teaching her how to cook Dutch-Indonesian style, was in actuality teaching her how to cook. Agnes was ostensibly learning a style of cooking, concealing the fact she lacked culinary skills, while presenting herself as someone who just didn't know the Dutch-Indonesian way. Her future mother-in-law, a seamstress, taught her how to sew and in the process taught her what styles were becoming to her figure, what colors went with her complexion, and how clothing can be used to present the desired image. Much of the learning of appropriate gender-role behavior, according to her own account, came from the lectures and behaviors of her fiancé. For example, when he arrived home and found her sunbathing in front of the apartment, he lectured to her that "nice girls" don't show off that way. She was learning that she was attractive to other men but her boyfriend wanted her pure.

In her own account of situations, each one had to be "cased out," escape routes planned, and the presentation of herself as a normal woman maintained. She reported her happiest times were those when she was "treated completely normally without any regard to my problem at all" (Garfinkel, 1967:170).

The case of Agnes, although extreme, illustrates the manner in which each of us demonstrates that we have achieved a particular gender, that we are naturally what we claim to be. Women in our culture frequently report feeling undressed without mascara or lipstick. Although they are literally dressed in their clothing, they feel undressed as women. That is, the process of "putting-on" one's face is a behavior through which some women *achieve* their gender identity. Similarly, the baggy-eyed middle-aged man can stand in rumpled pajamas and say to the mirror, "You are the chairman of the board of trustees. Be patient. I'll have you looking the part in half an hour."

We all go through a multitude of behaviors daily—from opening doors for a friend to sitting with crossed knees—that are symbolic cues to those around us that we wish to be treated as belonging to one sex or the other. And as we are cueing others about our gender, we are reinforcing our own sense of identity. Male students have reported feeling angry and castrated when a woman "purposefully beats a man to the door and opens it" (Walum, 1974); women students have reported feeling unfeminine and unprotected when they do not receive such courtesies as having doors opened for them. If one cannot perform the expected gender-role behaviors, one feels demasculinized or defeminized.

This leads us to a very important insight: gender behavior is both *prescribed* and *chosen*. On the one hand, appropriate behavior is socially shared and transmitted through the culture: people learn what is appropriate for their gender. But, on the other hand, they are constantly (whether through habit or will) choosing to present themselves as masculine or feminine persons. Therefore, persons have the option to accept or reject cultural definitions of appropriate gender behavior, and consequently the ability to change either themselves or the culture. The processes by which the culture can (and is) being changed will concern us later.

Masculinity/Femininity

Now let us look more closely at what middle-class American culture defines as natural, morally appropriate, and preferable for men and women. In a study by Broverman et al., (1970), mental health clinicians of both sexes were presented with a checklist of bipolar items presenting personality or behavioral traits. (See Table 1.1.) Each of these items had been previously found (Rosenkrantz et al., 1968) to be both stereotypically associated with gender and differentially evaluated as to social desirability. The right-hand side of Table 1.1 gives the list of attributes stereotypically associated with masculinity; the left-hand side those associated with femininity. Of these 38 items, 27 (70 percent) of those considered socially desirable are masculine items; 11 are feminine ones.

The mental health clinicians were divided into three groups, with three different sets of instructions. The first group was asked to indicate for each item the pole toward which a normal, healthy, mature, and competent man would tend; the second group was asked to evaluate a mature, healthy, normal, competent woman; and the third group a mature, healthy, competent adult (sex unspecified).

The researchers found there were no statistically significant differences in the judgments between male and female clinicians; and that there was substantial agreement as to what constituted a healthy male, a healthy female, and a healthy adult. The clinicians also agreed that the socially desirable items were those to be found in a healthy mature adult. Further, they shared the societal concensus about sex-role stereotypes and social desirability. Male-valued stereotypic items were more often ascribed to healthy males than to females. Females were associated with characteristics that, in our culture, are considered negative: submissive, easily influenced, not adventurous, dependent, feelings easily hurt, excitable in a crisis, conceited, disliking math and science, subjective. Broverman comments, "This constellation seems a most unusual way of describing any mature, healthy individual" (1970:5).

But perhaps the most significant result of the study is the differentiation clinicians make between women, on the one hand, and men and adults, on the other. These clinicians agreed that the mature adult was substantially equivalent in personality structure to the mature man. But maturity for a woman was different

TABLE 1.1: Clinical Judgments of Mental Health*

Competency Cluster: Masculine Pole is judged more socially desirable

---

Feminine Pole	Masculine Pole
Not at all aggressive	Very aggressive
Not at all Independent	Very independent
Very emotional	Not at all emotional
Does not hide emotions at all	Almost always hides emotions
Very subjective	Very objective
Very easily influenced	Not at all easily influenced
Very submissive	Very dominant
Dislikes math and science very much	Likes math and science very much
Very excitable in a minor crisis	Not at all excitable in a minor crisis
Very passive	Very active
Not at all competitive	Very competitive
Very illogical	Very logical
Very home-oriented	Very worldly
Not at all skilled in business	Very skilled in business
Very sneaky	Very direct
Does not know the way of the world	Knows the way of the world
Feelings easily hurt	Feelings not easily hurt
Not at all adventurous	Very adventurous
Has difficulty making decisions	Can make decisions easily
Cries very easily	Never cries
Almost never acts as a leader	Almost always acts as a leader
Not at all self-confident	Very self-confident
Very uncomfortable about being aggressive	Not at all uncomfortable about being aggressive
Not at all ambitious	Very ambitious
Unable to separate feelings from ideas	Easily able to separate feelings from ideas
Very dependent	Not at all dependent
Very conceited about appearance	Never conceited about appearance

---

Warm-Expressiveness Cluster: Feminine Pole is judged more socially desirable

---

Feminine Pole	Masculine Pole
Very talkative	Not at all talkative
Very tactful	Very blunt
Very gentle	Very rough
Very aware of feelings of others	Not at all aware of feelings of others
Very religious	Not at all religious
Very interested in own appearance	Not at all interested in own appearance
Very neat in habits	Very sloppy in habits
Very quiet	Very loud
Very strong need for security	Very little need for security
Enjoys art and literature very much	Does not enjoy art and literature at all
Easily expresses tender feelings	Does not express tender feelings at all

*Adapted from Broverman et al., 1970:3 with permission of authors and publisher.

from that of an adult. That is, there is a double standard of mental health. Put simply, for a woman to be considered mature and healthy as a woman in this culture, she must behave in ways that are considered socially undesirable and immature for a competent adult. There exists, then, a culturally constructed conflict situation for women. If, they choose to act in the more socially desirable and adult ways preferred by their culture, they risk having their femininity questioned. If, however, they choose to act in the prescribed feminine way, they are accepting a non-adult status.

The clinicians have not created this cultural understanding of the natural and morally appropriate differences between males and females, although they may help to perpetuate it. They, like the rest of us, carry the beliefs, judgments, and evaluations of their culture.

American Cultural Values

Core values

Ideas about gender do not occur in a cultural vacuum; they are intricately linked with the culture's *core values*.[1] Core values are central and highly salient ideas around which a culture patterns its other beliefs, judgments, and evaluations. The United States has two core values that are frequently in conflict—*achievement* and *equality*. On the one hand, we believe in individual differences and reward those who are able to achieve. On the other hand, we also believe that all persons are to be treated equally. The old draft system gave deferments to students in college—a system rationalized by the achievement value. After all, it was argued, persons who are more talented and who are struggling to be successful should be excused from the draft. The lottery system for the draft, on the other hand, was supported by the equality value. Under it, each man was given an equal opportunity to serve (or not serve) in the military. (As might be expected, the major opposition to the lottery system came from those persons, college enrollees, who had previously enjoyed a privileged position.)

Our culture's image of the mature adults places the achievement value high. Inherent in this core value are three major themes: the individual is more important than the group, the stress is on action, and the outlook is on the future.

The idea of achievement means that the individual is both responsible for success and expected to pursue it.[2] Individuals are to act as free and autonomous

---

[1] Why these values have arisen is beyond the scope of this book. Suffice it to say at this point that the values perpetuated or sustained in society service the interests of the powerful in the society (see Section Three).

[2] Although we are primarily concerned with the American value system, it should be noted that the emphasis on individual responsibility for achievement is a part of the value system of all industrialized societies (Huber, 1976, personal communication). We can suggest three major reasons for the alliance between individualism and industrialization. First, holding individuals responsible for achievement appears to be a fairly successful way of motivating them to do work valued by the society. Second, it is a rather efficient way of minimizing worker unrest. After all, if one views oneself as personally responsible for one's life accomplishments, then one blames only oneself, not society, for failure (see Chapter 9). Third, industrialized societies require a geographically mobile work force. Whereas values embracing kin and

persons, first. No male, for example, is expected to remain with his company or *achievement value*
in his home area, if a better job is available elsewhere. Other cultures place group
goals above those of the individual; the citizen who would consider personal aims
above those of the nation is considered immoral. Autonomous individualism, *1) dedication to group*
however, is not incorporated in the United States culture's definition of femininity.
Women who leave their families to pursue their own careers and identities are *1) individual pursuit of success*
subject to severe social criticism. As domestic workers—mothers, wives, and
housekeepers, women are expected to be dedicated to group, not individual goals.

The second theme of the achievement value, the accent on action, can be *2) accent on action*
traced back to the inception of this country. As a society we have been, and
continue to be interested in "getting things done." When meeting someone, our
first question is, "What do you do?" We might consider a response such as "I *3) emphasis on future*
watch the clouds and stars" weird or enticing, but not really an answer. Our
question requires an occupational answer—an answer that lets us know what
kinds of achievements we might expect from this person. In other cultures, such
a question would be impertinent or irrelevant. But we have as an ideal the "*man
[sic] of action*"—sharp, quick, hardheaded, and efficient. So activity-oriented are
we, that Nehru is credited with asking, with some degree of incredulity, "Is it *really*
true that Americans don't know how to meditate?"

The traits attributed to the woman, as we have seen, are the opposite: passivity, patience. To be properly feminine, she waits for the man to hail her a cab, pay
their lunch tab, open a door for her, lead her across an intersection, and ask her
for a date. So ingrained is the belief that women are not to be overly active that
Billie Jean King, a world tennis champion and activist for "equal pay for equal
work" in the sports world, once remarked,

> Sometimes I go up for an aggressive volley and really smash it and I find myself
> thinking, "How unladylike—but how great it feels!" Any kind of experience that is so
> close to perfection can't be bad can it? And yet, look how many women are brought
> up to think that way: "Act like a lady . . ." (*Newsweek,* September 24, 1973, p.84).

The third theme of our achievement value, the emphasis on the future, is also
one that applies only to men. They are expected to strive hard for a better
future—to work long hours, plan ahead, save for rainy days, and defer immediate
gratifications. The woman is the helpmate who praises her husband's accomplishments and lives vicariously through him. But the future promises of achievement
are those of her father, husband, and sons.

The importance of the individual, of action, and of the future combine to form
the motif of the core value achievement—a value associated with men. Women,
meanwhile, are asked to become the kind of people that this culture does not
value. To be a woman in this culture is, in a very profound sense, to be un-
American. To grow up learning, on one hand, what the dominant culture values are

---

community are inconsistent with those needs, stress on individual achievement contributes to the creation
of the kind of work force needed in industrialized societies.

and, on the other, that activities based on those values are taboo can only create in women a feeling of lesser worth, lesser value. To be asked to assume personality traits that the culture does not value highly is to be asked to see yourself as second-rate, incapable of achievement, and permanently blighted.

The consequences for the male are equally difficult. Whether he wants to or not, he is impelled to live up to society's expectations, or suffer guilt and withdrawal. To the extent he has bought the American ideal, he has to measure himself against it. If he fails to act gentlemanly or get a raise or support his family, his sense of masculinity is on the line. The sexual impotence that frequently follows the loss of job or the failure of an exam tells him in the clearest of somatic terms that he is not a man.

Implicit in the previous paragraphs is another value that must be made explicit: *patriarchalism* (also referred to as *sexism* and *male chauvinism*), or the belief in the superiority of the male. This value, although consistent with other American values, is not peculiar to American society. Rather, all industrialized societies— socialist, capitalist, democratic, and authoritarian—share this belief. Patriarchalism is to culture like a rhythm section in a band. Sometimes it overrides the melodic theme and sometimes it is hushed—but it is always there. When we have been listening to a band for hours and hours, we lose awareness of the rhythm as distinct from the totality of the music. Similarly, the principle of male superiority after hundreds of years has become so embedded in the culture that we unconsciously behave and think in ways that perpetuate it.

How is it that persons learn so thoroughly the values of the culture that they unquestionably consider them to be natural? They do so through a process called *socialization.*

2

Language: The Inescapable Socializer

"You're nothing but a silly sexpot, incapable of amounting to much in the world. You'd better get yourself a man, so you'll be somebody." All women have heard this indictment.

"Go get 'em, Tiger. Get yourself a good job, take care of your wife and family, but have a little something on the side." All men have heard this battle cry.

You may protest, "People don't expect *me* to be like that." As one woman student wrote in a journal kept for a Sociology of Women's class, "I consider myself fortunate. My parents never told me to act like a girl; they wanted me to have a career and always talked to me like I would." Or, as a male student wrote, "I don't understand what the fuss is about. My parents never hassled me about being a big career man. They just wanted me to be a good person, happy, and contented with my life."

Unfortunately, despite the protestations and claims to a gender-free rearing, it is impossible for a person who is socialized into this culture to escape the culturally prescribed gender-stereotyping. This is so because we all have learned verbal and nonverbal language that encapsulates gender-stereotyping.[1]

The world can be thought about in many different ways. The language we acquire as children provides the lens through which we see and therefore, structure the world. Language is not a piece of clothing we put on and take off at will; rather, it is more like a mold into which young minds are poured. In the process of learning the language, the child learns how to think like other members of the society.

This means that much of what we define as reality is merely that portion of life that we have learned to identify verbally. Through language, we abstract and select from the myriad of sensory impressions those elements that are considered

---

[1]For an excellent annotated bibliography, see Thorne and Henley, 1975:204–311.

relevant; by means of our categories we make sense out of the world and assimilate our experiences.

A few examples might clarify the relevance of language for the structuring of thought. In English, we take for granted such notions as causality, temporal sequence, and the existence of the individual. It is almost impossible for us to think in noncausal ways, to imagine life *without* the concept of time, or an "I" as inseparable from a "we." Yet, societies do exist where these ideas are incorporated into the language and are taken for granted. Similarly, ideas about gender are deeply embedded in our language and become non-conscious, taken-for-granted elements of our thought structure—for example, the idea that the two sexes are absolutely distinct from one another.

But more than thought patterns are reflected in language, for it determines in great part the nature of our social relations. In acquiring language both verbal and nonverbal, we are learning to be the kinds of people judged appropriate in our society.

Communication is a complex "multichanneled system. . .of behavior" (Scheflen, 1974:3) in which persons of a common culture share a common code for conveying messages. And much of communication is communication *about* the communication process itself (metacommunication) and is conveyed nonverbally through gestures, postures, and facial expressions. These are used to perpetuate or alter the ongoing communication. That is, the communication system itself transmits the culture and thereby constrains behavior. It is a "means of regulating *all* types of behavior and/or maintaining social order and social control" (Sheflen, 1974:4). With the acquisition of language we learn *how* to interact with others; without this acquisition we are noncommunicating human beings.

The life of Helen Keller, born blind and deaf, amply illustrates the point. Before she learned to communicate, she was considered incorrigible, alone in a sightless, soundless world. Through the patient work of her teacher, she not only learned how to communicate, she learned to be a social human being. And the kind of social human being she became was the one appropriate to her cultural milieu.

Language perpetuates the thought structure and social patterns by continuously reiterating them. When parents, teachers, or television programs communicate to the young, they use both the verbal and nonverbal languages of the culture; indeed, even when we dream, we communicate to ourselves in these languages. It is inescapable. And the consequence of this inescapableness is that we are perpetually being labeled by ourselves and others along gender-stereotypic dimensions.

When people are *labeled,* they are treated in accordance with that label, and consequently they learn to see themselves as persons who deserve that label and come to act accordingly (Scheff, 1966; Becker, 1970). Men and women "come to see themselves as others see them" (Cooley, 1902:151). They non-consciously apply labels to themselves; and, then, subsequently act in ways compatible with the labels.

Because verbal and nonverbal languages can be so subtle and omnipresent, we need to look closely at the ideas about gender within them. Because these ideas embedded in our languages are inescapable labels, we might also profit by exploring the consequences these labels might have on linguistic practices. And finally, we will explore the language of the black culture to discover if the language practices regarding gender are substantially the same as those in the white culture.

Verbal Communication

All members of our society—male and female, black and white, young and old, rich and poor—are exposed to the verbal language of the dominant culture. Analysis of it can tell us a great deal about a peoples' fears, prejudices, anxieties, and interests. A rich vocabulary on a particular subject indicates societal interests or obsessions (e.g., the extensive vocabulary about cars in America). And many different words for the same subject (such as *freedom fighter* or *terrorist, passed away* or *croaked, make love* or *ball*) generally shows a wide range of attitudes and feelings in the society toward that subject.

It should not be surprising, then, to find rooted in the linguistic structure differential attitudes and feelings about men and women. Although language has not been completely analyzed, six general propositions concerning inherent ideas about males and females can be made. The first five of these refer to current linguistic practice; the sixth to an historical process, "the semantic derogation of women" (Schulz, 1975).

First, in terms of grammatic and semantic structure, women do not have a fully autonomous, independent existence; they are part of man. Our language is not divided into male and female with distinct conjugations and declensions as is characteristic of many other languages. Rather, women are included under the general rubric *man*. Every grammar book specifies that the pronoun *he* can be used generically to refer to he or she. Further, *man,* when used as an indefinite pronoun, grammatically refers to both men and women. So, for example, when we read *man* in the following phrases we are to interpret it as applying to both men and women: "man the oars," "one small step for man, one giant step for mankind," "man, that's tough," "man overboard," "man the Toolmaker," "alienated man," "garbageman." Our rules of etiquette complete the grammatical presumption of inclusivity. When two persons are pronounced "man and wife," Miss Susan Jones changes her entire name to Mrs. Robert Gordon (Vanderbilt, 1972: Chapter 6). In each of these correct usages, women are a part of man; they do not exist autonomously. The exclusion of women is well expressed in Mary Daly's rather jarring slogan "the sisterhood of man." (1973:7–21).

However, there is some question as to whether or not the theory that *man* means everybody is carried out in practice. For example, an eight-year-old interrupts her reading of "The Story of the Cavemen" to ask how we got here without cavewomen. A ten-year-old thinks it dumb to have a woman postman. A twelve-year-old questions the language construction of *woman chairman.*

Linguistic Practices

"man"
1) ♂ does not suggest humanity but male images

2) pronoun usage

3) ♀ immature, incompetent + incapable ♂ mature, complete + competent

4) in practice, ♀ referred to in terms of sexual desirability; ♂ by prowess

5) ♀ in relation to ♂; ♂ in relation to world

6) neutral words for ♀ become obscene or debased; neutral words for ♂ do not

But children are not the only ones who visualize males when they see the word *man*. In a suggestive exploratory study, Schneider and Hacker (1973) asked one group of college students to bring in photographs for a forthcoming sociology book that had chapter titles such as "Society," "Urban Life," "Political Behavior," and "Economic Behavior." Another group of students were asked to bring in photos for the same text with chapter titles such as "Social Man," "Political Man," and "Economic Man." The researchers found that students assigned the chapter titles using *man* brought in pictures only of males more frequently than the other group of students. In another preliminary study, DeStefano (1976) has reported that college students choose silhouettes of males, rather than males and females, for sentences with the word *man* or *men* in them. Indeed, recently linguists have begun to question whether there actually is a semantic generic in English. Research is currently in progress to test whether sex indefinite words must have semantic markers—lady pilot, female professor—in order to include women, and further whether the use of these markers "diminish the importance of the referent" (DeStefano, 1975:2).

Man, then, does not suggest humanity, but rather male images. The consequence is the exclusion of women in the visualization, imagination, and thought of both males and females. Speculatively, I would suggest that this practice perpetuates in men both feelings of dominance over and responsibility for women, and that it has ramifications for the kinds of relationships that exist between the sexes.

Second, in actual practice, our pronoun usage perpetuates different personality attributes and career aspirations for men and women. Nurses, secretaries, and elementary school teachers are almost invariably referred to as *she;* doctors, engineers, electricians, and presidents as *he.* In one classroom, students referred to an unidentified child as *he* and then, interestingly, shifted to *she* when discussing the child's parent. In a faculty discussion of the problems of acquiring new staff, architects, engineers, security officers, faculty, and computer programmers were all referred to as *he;* maids, secretaries, and file clerks were referred to as *she.* The "he occupations" required courage or advanced training, while the "she occupations" required service orientation.

Even our choice of sex-ascription to nonhuman objects subtly reinforces different personalities for males and females. It seems as though the small (e.g., kittens), the graceful (e.g., poetry), the unpredictable (e.g., hurricanes), the nurturant (e.g., the church, the school), and that which is owned and/or controlled by men (e.g., boats, cars, governments, nations), represent the feminine, whereas that which is a controlled forceful power in and of itself (e.g., God, Satan, Tigers) primarily represent the masculine.

Third, linguistic practice defines females as immature, incompetent, and incapable and males as mature, complete and competent. Apparently, the words *man* and *woman* tend to connote sexual and human maturity. Consequently, we find in common speech, organizational titles, public addresses, and bathroom doors, that *lady* is frequently substituted for *woman.* Simply contrast the different connotations of *lady* and *woman* in the following common phrases;

Luck, be a lady (woman) tonight.
Barbara's a little lady (woman).
Ladie's (Women's) Liberation Movement.
Ladie's (Women's) Air Corps.

In the first two examples, the use of *lady* desexualizes the contextual meaning of *woman.* So trivializing is the use of *lady* in the last two phrases that they sound wholly anomolous. The male equivalent, *lord,* is not used; and the synonym, *gentleman,* is not used nearly as frequently in common speech. That is, there are fewer occasions in which it is seen as necessary to desexualize or repress masculinity. When *gentlemen* is used, the assumption seems to be that certain culturally condoned aspects of masculinity (e.g., aggressivity, activity, and strength) should be set aside in the interests of maturity and order as exemplified in the following phrases:

A gentlemen's (men's) agreement.
A duel between gentlemen (men).
He's a real gentleman (man).

Rather than requiring males to set aside the stereotypes associated with man, the opposite occurs frequently. The contextual connotation of *man* places a strain on males to be continuously sexually and socially potent as the following examples illustrate:

I was not a man (gentleman) with her tonight.
This is a man's (gentleman's) job.
Be a man (gentleman).

Whether males, therefore, feel competent or anxious, valuable or worthless in particular contexts is influenced by the demands placed on them by the expectations of the language.

Not only are men infrequently expected to be *gentlemen,* they are not often labeled *boys.* The term *boy* is reserved for young males, bell hops, car attendants, and as a put down to those males judged inferior. *Boy* connotes immaturity and powerlessness. Only occasionally do males "have a night out with the boys." They do not talk "boy talk" at the office. Rarely does our language legitimize carefreeness in males. Rather, they are expected, linguistically, to adopt the responsibilities of manhood.

On the other hand, women of all ages may be called *girls.* Grown females "play bridge with the girls," are hired as "girl Fridays," and indulge in "girl talk." Unlike men, although they are allowed to remain childlike, the implication is that adult women are basically immature and without power. Men can become men, linguistically, putting aside the immaturity of childhood; indeed, for them to retain the openness and gamefulness of boyhood is linguistically difficult.

Further, the presumed incompetence and immaturity of women is evidenced by the "linguistic" company she keeps. A brief perusal of categorical groupings of women include the following: (1) Harvard President Nathan Pusey lamented the effect the military draft would have upon graduate schools, commenting, "We shall be left with the blind, the lame, the women." (2) New York state worded its franchise law to include everyone but "women, minors, convicts, and idiots," (3) A student was criminally charged in Berkeley with using "indecent language within the presence and hearing of women and children . . ." (4) Spiro Agnew in a speech on Women's Liberation Day remarked that "it is difficult to tame oceans, fools, and women" (examples drawn from Key, 1975:82–84).

The use of these categorical designations is not accidental happenstance; ". . . rather these selectional groupings are powerful forces behind the actual expressions of language and are based on distinctions which are not regarded as trivial by the speakers of the language" (Key, 1975:82). A total language analysis of categorical groupings is not available; and yet, it seems likely that women tend to be included in groupings that designate incompleteness, ineptitude, and im-maturity. On the other hand, it is difficult for us to conceive of the word man in any categorical grouping other than one that extends beyond humanity such as "Man, apes, and angels" or "Man and Superman." That is, men do exist as an independ-ent category capable of autonomy; women are grouped with the stigmatized, the immature, and the foolish.

Fourth, in practice women are defined in terms of their sexual desirability (to men); men are defined in terms of their sexual prowess (over women). Most slang words in reference to women refer to their sexual desirability to men (e.g., dog, fox, broad, nice piece, cunt, chick, etc.). Slang about men refers to their sexual prowess over women (e.g., dude, stud, jock, hunk, etc.). The fewer examples given for men is not an oversight. In an analysis of sexual slang, for example, more than 1000 words and phrases that derogate women sexually were listed while there were "nowhere near this multitude for describing men" (Kramer, 1975:72). Farmer and Henley (cited in Schulz, 1975) list 500 synonyms for *prostitute,* for example, and only 65 for *whoremonger.* Shuster (1973) reports that the passive verb form is used in reference to women's sexual experiences (e.g., *to be laid, to be had, to be taken*) whereas the active tense is used in reference to the male's (e.g., *lay, take, have*). Being sexually attractive to males is culturally condoned for women and being sexually powerful is approved for males. In these regards, the slang of the street is certainly not counter-culture; rather it perpetuates and reinforces different expectations as sexual objects and performers.

Similarly, historically male-female equivalent words, e.g., *bachelor* and *spin-ster,* carry distinctly different sexual connotations. *Bachelor* is often preceded by *eligible;* spinster by *old.* Figuratively, a "real bachelor" implies sexual freedom; a "real spinster" implies frigidity. A *courier* is "an attendant at a court of a sover-eign"; a *courtesan* is "a prostitute or woman kept by a man of rank."

Further, we find sexual connotations associated with neutral words applied to women. A few examples should suffice. A male academician questioned the title of a new course, asserting it was "too suggestive." The title? "The Position of Women in the Social Order." A male *tramp* is simply a "hobo" but a female *tramp* is a slut; a male *pirate* robs other people's ships whereas a female *pirate* steals other women's men. And consider the difference in connotation of the following expressions: it's easy; he's easy; she's easy. In the first, we assume something is "easy to do"; in the second, we might assume a professor is an "easy grader" or a man is "easy-go-lucky." But when we read "she's easy," the connotation is "she's an easy lay."

In the world of slang, men are defined by their sexual prowess. In the world of slang and proper speech, women are defined as sexual objects. The rule in practice seems to be, If in doubt, assume *any* reference to a woman has a sexual connotation. For both genders, the constant bombardment of prescribed sexuality is bound to have real consequences.

Fifth, women are defined in terms of their relationships to men; men are defined in terms of their relationship to the world at large. A good example in our language usage are the words *master* and *mistress*. Originally, these words had the same meaning—"the power held by a person over servants." With the demise of the feudal system, however, these words took on different meanings. The masculine variant metaphorically refers to power over something, e.g., "He is the master of his trade"; the feminine variant metaphorically (although probably not in actuality) refers to power over a man sexually, e.g., "She is Tom's mistress." Although these words have retained the principal meaning of "power," "what has changed are the kinds of interpersonal relationships they are used to refer to," (Lakoff, 1975:29). Men are defined in terms of their power in the occupational world; women in terms of their sexual power over men.

The existence of two contractions for Mistress (*Miss* and *Mrs.*) and but one for Mr. underscores the cultural concern and linguistic practice: women are defined in relationship to men. The recent preference of many women to be called *Ms.* is, therefore, an attempt to provide an equivalency title for women, which is not dependent upon marital status. But even here, the title, *Ms.* connotes to many people something about a woman's relationship to a man: she is "probably divorced or hiding the fact she's not married or not getting along well in her marriage."[2]

Similarly, male-female equivalent social statuses are treated differently linguistically. For example, *widow* is well entrenched in legend and conversation; *widower* can hardly be uttered without difficulty. Although a possessive (a man's name) usually precedes *widow,* this is not the linguistic practice for *widower*. For men, perhaps, it is "until death do we part"; for women, the relationship both in common talk and formal etiquette remains "until death does *she* part" (Vanderbilt, 1972: Chapter 6). Even a divorced woman is defined in terms of her no-longer existing relationship to a man; and it apparently is assumed that the divorced state is not relevant enough to the man or to the society to require a label. A divorced woman is a *divorcee,* but what do you call divorced man?

Sixth, there is an historical pattern such that originally neutral words for

---

[2]After four attempts to convince a travel agent that I was not "Miss" or "Mrs." but "Ms.," she finally responded with, "Oh, I'm not married either—but it really doesn't bother *me.*" And a recent letter to "Dear Abby" stated that "Ms." meant "Marxian Sister."

women acquire obscene and/or debased connotations; and this pattern of deroga-tion does not hold for neutral words referring to men.

These processes of *pejoration* (the acquiring of an obscene or debased connotation) and *amelioration* (the reacquiring of a neutral or positive connotation) in the English language regarding terms for males and females have been studied extensively by Muriel Schulz (1975). It is to her work we now turn.

Leveling is the least derogative form of pejoration. Through leveling, titles that originally referred to an elite class of persons come to include a wider class of persons. Such democratic leveling is more common for female designates than for male. For example, contrast the following: *Lord-Lady* (*lady*); *Baronet-Dame* (*dame*); *Governor-Governess* (*governess*).

Most frequently what happens to words designating women as they become pejorated, however, is that they come to denote or connote sexual wantonness. For example, *Sir* and *Mister* remain titles of courtesy; however, at some time *Madam, Miss,* and *Mistress* respectively have become synonyms for *brothel-keeper, prostitute,* and *unmarried sexual partner of a male* (Schulz, 1975:66).

Names for domestic helpers, if they are females, are frequently derogated. For example, *hussy* originally meant "housewife"; it was pejorated into "a rustic woman," and eventually into meaning "a brazen, lewd woman or prostitute" (Schulz, 1975:66). *Laundress, needlewoman, spinster* ("tender of the spinning wheel"), and *nurse* all referred to domestic occupations within the home; and all at some point became slang expressions for prostitute or mistress.

Even kinships terms referring to women become denigrated. During the 17th century, *mother* was used to mean "a bawd"; more recently *mother (mothuh _____)* has become a common derogatory epithet (Cameron, 1974). Probably at some point in history every kinship term for females has been derogated (Schulz, 1975:66).

Terms of endearment for women, also seem to follow a downward path. Pet names such as *Tart, Dolly, Kitty, Polly, Mopsy, Biddy,* and *Jill* all eventually became sexually derogative (Schulz, 1975;67). *Whore* comes from the same Latin root as *care* and once meant "a lover of either sex."

Similarly, categorical designations or descriptions for young women and girls tend to become denigrated. *Nymph* used to mean "beautiful young female"; it has pejorated to refer to "a sexually loose woman." *Broad* originally meant "a young woman" and had no derogatory overtones; similarly *floozie* and *doll* were orig-inally descriptive words, later given sexual overtones.

Indeed, even the most neutral categorical designations—girl, female, woman, lady—at some point in their history have been used to connote sexual immorality. *Girl* originally meant "a child of either sex"; through the process of semantic degeneration it eventually meant "a prostitute." Although *girl* has lost this mean-ing, *girlie* still retains sexual connotations. *Woman* connoted "a mistress" in the early 19th century; *female* was a degrading epithet in the latter part of the 19th century; and when *lady* was introduced as a euphemism, it too became deprecato-ry. "Even so neutral a term as *person,* when it was used as substitute for *woman,* suffered [vulgarization]" (Mencken, 1963:350, quoted in Schulz, 1975:71).

Whether one looks at elite titles, occupational roles, kinship relationships, endearments, or age-sex categorical designations, the pattern is clear. Terms referring to females are pejorated—"become negative in the middle instances and abusive in the extremes" (Schulz, 1975:69). Such semantic derogation, however, is not evidenced for male referents. *Lord, Baronet, Father, Brother, Nephew, footman, bowman, boy, lad, fellow, gentleman, man, male,* etc., "have failed to undergo the derogation found in the history of their corresponding feminine designations" (Schulz, 1975:67). Interestingly, rather than derogating the male referent, a female referent frequently is used to debase a male. For example, a weak man is referred to as a *sissy* (diminutive of sister); and an army recruit during basic training is called a *pussy.* And when one is swearing at a male, he is referred to as a *bastard* or a *son-of-a-bitch*—both appellations that impugn the dignity of the man's mother.

In summary, in all these verbal practices, the conceptions and perceptions perpetuated are consistent with the gender stereotypes we encountered in Chapter One. Women are thought to be a part of man, incapable of leading autonomous, independent lives, relegated to roles that require few skills, characteristically incompetent and immature, sexual objects, best defined in terms of their relationships to men. On the other hand, males are visible, autonomous and independent, responsible for the protection and containment of women, expected to occupy positions based on their high achievement or physical power, assumed to be sexual potent, and defined primarily by their relationships to the world of work. For both genders, the use of the language perpetuates the stereotypes and limits the options available for self-definition.

Nonverbal Communication

As important as verbal communication is in the structuring of thought and relationships, there is some evidence to support the hypothesis that *nonverbal* communication is more salient for the transmission of attitudes and the maintenance of interpersonal relationships. One estimate is that the nonverbal cues are approximately four times as strong as verbal ones for the transmission of attitudes—both submissive and dominant (Argyle et al., 1970:222). Furthermore, studies of blind persons (Cull and Hardy, 1973b), suggest they tend more to associate different sexes with common words than do sighted persons. That is, important connotations of our language are transmitted nonverbally.

Although the study of gender differences in nonverbal communication is still relatively unchartered,[3] the existent data suggest that men and women

---

[3]The more nonverbal behavior is studied, the more the researchers realize both its complexity and its importance. Consequently, this section is to be understood primarily as suggestive of the kind of research that has been done and that needs to be done. For those interested in pursuing the topic further, I highly commend the following: Birdwhistel (1970), Hall (1959), Mehrabian (1972), Morris (1971), Scheflen (1972, 1974), Sommer (1969).

systematically communicate nonverbally (in interpersonal distances, gestures and postures, demeanors and etiquette) different self-images and different statuses. These nonverbal signs consistently communicate male dominance, independence, and activity, and female submissiveness, dependence, and passivity. The data to support this contention come from professional researchers in the field, the observations and norm-violation experiments of my students over the past six years,[4] and commentaries in student's journals kept for sex-roles classes.

Space

Social space is not empty or silent, nor is it distributed randomly. Rather, all indications from animal and human research suggest that there is a direct association between the amount of space surrounding a person and their dominance (Sommer, 1969). Professors stand behind lecterns on raised platforms, while students are arranged equidistantly side by side, row by row. The size of an executive's desk is directly proportionate to the position in the hierarchy of the organization. More space is given to the rich, the titled, the famous, and the powerful than to those who lack those attributes.[5]

This principle of the higher the status, the greater the space, when applied to males and females, suggests that even in the non-conscious use of interpersonal distance, females have lower status than males. In students' experiments over a period of four years, the norms regarding standing and sitting distances were studied. The general conclusions from their (800 plus) experiments are (1) that women have a greater tolerance for the invasion of their personal space, by women and men, than men do; (2) that when women get as close to males as they normally do to other women, the male subjects retreat; and (3) when men get as close to other men as they normally do to women, the male subjects "fight" (e.g., accuse the experimenter of being pushy, homosexual, etc.). In a more carefully controlled and measured study, Willis (1966) found that both males and females initiate conversation standing closer to women than to men (1966:222).

The final invasion of personal space is, of course, *touching*. Although touching may symbolize intimacy, it also symbolizes status (Goffman, 1967:75). In general, the principle seems to be that those with higher status touch those with lower status: the physician touches the orderly; the teacher, the pupil; the coach, the football player; the police officer, the accused; the priest, the supplicant. Women as a group—perhaps due to their roles as secretaries, mothers, nurses, etc., or perhaps due to their status as women—are probably touched by more people in more settings than are men.

---

[4]The students, by and large, were taught the techniques of observation while observing. They generally observed gender behavior in public places while in research groups of four to six members. The groups decided which aspect of gender behavior to observe and each member, while in the same setting as other group members, independently recorded their observations. Settings included bars, restaurants, transportation centers, stores, banks, sidewalks, public lobbies, sitting rooms, courts, etc.

[5]Time, too, is distributed unequally, and the rules governing its distribution are the same as those governing the distribution of space.

Students have noted that males initiate touching more often than women, and that, in public settings, the touching routine is fairly standardized. For example, in a movie theater or bar, the male's arm is over the female's shoulder; her response is to cuddle close, as if to have her own personal space wrapped up inside of his. Cuddling, a *submissive* response (Henley, 1973:17) was not observed in men in public settings. Further, more of the female's body is routinely touched in public than that of the male's. But perhaps the most subtle dominance differential was observed in couples walking side by side, hand in hand, apparent equals; invariably the male's hand would be clasped in front of the female's so that he was leading.

When men are "playing" with women, the activities are often thinly veiled aggressive invasions such as "swinging them (hard) at square dances, picking them up and spanking them, . . . throw(ing) them into the water . . ." (Henley, 1973:17). And some college women have reported having water bombs dropped on their heads "by dorm boys who decided to play Master/Slave."

In brief, women are accorded less personal space than men, are subject to more invasions of it by more persons, and are more likely to be the submissive recipients of the touch of intimacy and the powerless recipients of the touch of "playful" aggression. That is, in terms of one of the primary dimensions of interpersonal relationships—space—(Brown, 1965:78–82), women have lower status, less power.

Demeanor

Goffman describes demeanor as that which is conveyed through one's dress, bearing, and deportment (1967). Many differences in dress, bearing, and deportment of men and women are obvious. Male movements and gestures tend to be strong, outward, sustained, and large, whereas those of the female tend to be light, airy, jerky, small, and turned inward (see Chapter 4, pp. 65–66). Males tend to stand and walk with their hands in their pockets—a dominance gesture—whereas women hold their arms close to their bodies, frequently wrapping one or both of them around their midchest—a protective gesture. That is, the typical male and female movements are consistent with the images of masculinity and femininity, respectively.

Moreover, as Goffman postulates from observation in a hospital, "between social equals, symmetrical rules of demeanor seem often to be prescribed. Between unequals many variations can be found" (1967:78). The rules governing demeanor of males and females are not symmetrical. Although every element of demeanor is meaningful, we shall examine only a few of them. Based on research with both animals and humans, it is known that the stare is often an aggressive act (Ellsworth, Carlsmith, and Henson, 1972:310). "While looking directly at a man, a woman usually has her head slightly tilted, implying the beginning of a presenting gesture of enough submission to render the stare ambivalent if not actually submissive" (O'Connor, 1970:9). That is, even when being aggressive, the female presents herself submissively. And most likely, if she is confronted with a stare herself, she will avert her eyes, drop her eyelids, and perhaps smile—all appeasement postures or submissive gestures.

The act of frequently interrupting a speaker is not only an act of dominance, it is an act permitted to persons of higher status. Goffman, for example, reports that doctors could freely interrupt the speech of nurses, interns, etc., but not vice-versa (1967:78). Argyle (et al., 1966) suggests that interruption is used by males to dominate a discussion. Female students repeatedly report in their journals that their male friends interrupt them when they are speaking. In one young woman's words, "he assumes that *whatever* I'm doing is interruptible; that I will be ready to do what he wants to do when he wants to do it."

In one meticulous empirical study using transcripts of dyadic, cross-sex conversations in natural settings, Zimmerman and West found that "virtually all interruptions . . . are by the male speakers" (1975:115). Moreover, not only were there fewer interruptions in same-sex conversations, but these were evenly distributed between the speakers. Further, by examining each conversational pair, they suggest that "interruptions are idiosyncratic in same-sex conversations and systematic in cross-sex ones. In cross-sex conversations females appear to be "a class of speakers . . . whose rights to speak (are) causally infringed upon by males" (1976:117).

Interruptions are a way to control the topic of the conversation; another way is the delayed minimal response (a long pause followed by "um hm"). Such responses provide only minimal support for the speaker and suggest the listener is really not interested in listening. In same-sex conversations, lapses (long pauses) are fairly equally divided between the partners; in cross-sex conversations, females have more silences (Zimmerman and West, 1976:118). However, a substantial portion of the female's silences in cross-sex conversations comes after the male has interrupted her or given a delayed minimal response. The authors conclude, "Men deny equal status to women as conversational partners with respect to rights to the full utilization of their turns and support for the development of topics" (Zimmerman and West, 1975:125).

All small nonverbal communications add up to a larger bearing or "presentation of self" (Goffman, 1959), which is strongly related to perpetuating gender stereotypes. In American society, the person with higher status is not expected to reveal much about themselves to persons of lower status (Goffman, 1967:64). The professor, psychiatrist, and social worker can inquire about the personal lives of their students, patients, and welfare clients, respectively, but these privileges are not reciprocal. And availability of information about someone can give the knower power over that person.

In our culture, a well-demeaned young man acts "cool"—he does not reveal much about himself or his feelings and emotions (Henley, 1973:8). In contrast, the young woman is expected to be self-disclosing—both in her clothes and her expressiveness about herself. She is socialized to reveal a great many of her feelings and, therewith, to be vulnerable. Dress, bearing, and deportment of men and women are different. Women are socialized to be self-disclosing, to present a demeanor of dependence, frailty, passivity, and submission; men are expected to be nonrevealing, yet independent, strong, active, and dominant. The personal consequences are feelings of femininity *and* of vulnerability and powerlessness in women and feelings of masculinity *and* dominance and higher status in men.

Etiquette

In our everyday associations we abide by rules of conduct through which we convey an appropriate demeanor and appropriate *deference* or appreciation and confirmation of others (Goffman, 1967:56). Under our rules of gender etiquette, the male is obliged to open a door and the woman expects to receive this courtesy. The man lights the cigarette, hails the cab, picks up the restaurant tab, and helps the woman across the street (Walum, 1974b). These rules of conduct function simultaneously to support cultural values and reinforce self-images.

Masculinity is associated with activity, dominance, authority, strength, efficaciousness; femininity with passivity, protectibility, dependence, and weakness. This cultural stereotype of gender-associated traits pervades every rule of conduct governing the etiquette between the genders (Walum, 1974b). The male is in charge, in control of the doorknob (Walum, 1974a), the lighter, the lady's elbow. The female waits for the service to be performed—waits for a cigarette to be lit, a door opened, a taxi hailed, a bill discharged. And by so waiting, she is communicating nonverbally that she needs someone to help her through her daily round of activities. If men and women follow the etiquette, they *feel* "masculine" and "feminine." For in successfully performing their parts in the ritual dramas between the genders, they have *actualized* just those personality traits associated with masculinity and femininity (Walum, 1974a).

Etiquette does more than reaffirm gender identity; it reaffirms basic cultural values. It is not a cultural accident that the male's role activates those traits that the culture values most highly. In a very profound sense, these daily rituals between the sexes become the living testimony of a basic value of this culture—the superiority of men. Acting out in well-mannered ways, in effect, is taking an active part in maintaining cultural stereotypes. As Goffman succinctly states, "The gestures which we sometimes call empty are perhaps, in fact, the fullest things of all" (1967:91).

Women's Speech/Men's Speech

Our language reinforces the idea that women and men have different abilities, personalities, and goals in life. The long-term consequences of this learning for marriage, careers, and activities in the world will engage us in later chapters. But this taken-for-granted language has also had consequences for our everyday behavior, structuring the way we present ourselves. If the language socialization has been effective, we should find at the speech level, itself, different presentations of self by males and females. That is, men and women should "talk" differently, and those differences should be consistent with the presumptions the language reinforces.

Although ostensibly males and females share the same culturally prescribed neutral language, in actuality, girls speak in a distinctively feminine style of speech that is not condoned in boys. That speech style is apparently recognizable at an early age. In a series of carefully controlled studies of the voices of pre-puberty children, Sachs (et al., 1973 and Sachs, 1975) reports that judges can accurately describe the sex of young children by listening to their taped voices. Since there is no average difference in the voice mechanisms in children before puberty, the differences in speech cannot be attributed to anatomy. Sachs suggests that at least part of the reason that boys and girls sound different is that they have learned to use the voice and speech style that is viewed as appropriate for their sex (Sachs, 1975:168).

In learning to "talk like a lady," the girl finds herself when "grown to womanhood . . . accused of being unable to speak precisely or to express herself forcefully" (Lakoff, 1975:56). If she speaks as she has been taught, she will not be taken seriously; if she does not speak in that way, she is accused of being unfeminine. On the other hand, boys can speak one language and simultaneously confirm their masculinity and adulthood. Some theorists argue that boys unlearn their original speech style—an imitation of their mother's—and adopt the masculine mode to signal both their independence and their identification with the male sex role.

Considerable interest has been generated in discovering just what the differences are between men's speech and women's speech (Thorne and Henley, 1975). Although there seems to be little doubt that the speech of males and females is different, the cues that allow us to make the discernment have not been exhaustively studied. Much of the work that has been done is based upon observation, self-reporting (by linguists skilled in both English and the tools of its analysis), and an occasional study of natural or experimentally induced speech segments. The research thus far available, however, suggests that men's and women's speech differ in vocabulary, pronunciation, intonation (pitch, stress, and juncture), and sentence structure.

Apparently, the vocabulary of women differs from that of men. Several studies eliciting spontaneous speech from males and females have been done (Wood, 1966; Swacker, 1975). Wood (1966) reports an analysis of 90,000 words of elicited spontaneous speech in relationship to photographs of the same person with different facial expressions. Certain spatial and mathematical words, such as *centimeter, dots, fraction, shape, intersect, parallels, protruded, right-angular,* are part of the male's vocabulary. Although approximately one-third of the female's vocabulary is of this kind, the female list is characterized by connotative and interpretive words and phrases such as *cheese, death, family, confused, distasteful, skeptical, enjoying, might have just put, has been surprised.* Wood suggests that the male vocabulary tends to be more descriptive of the directly observable features, whereas female vocabulary lends itself to interpretative descriptions and greater imagery. Swacker (1975) also reports that males tend to use more numbers in their descriptions than females and the latter tend to precede numerals with approximations (e.g., *about six*).

Key claims that women are inclined to use intensifiers e.g., *so, such, quite, very,* etc. ("I had *such* pleasure" or "This is *so* exciting") (1975:75). Their expletives tend to be more constrained than males. Such expression as "My Goodness!" and "Oh, dear!" are clear indications that a woman is speaking. Even when women use the profanity of their society, they tend to use milder forms of expressions.[6] Wood (1966) reports more use of modifiers and Key suggests that certain adjectives such as *cute, divine, charming, lovely, sweet, greenish* are signals that a woman is talking.

In general, the vocabulary that characterizes women's talk is of two kinds. One set of words indicate a certain silliness, weakness, and inability to express strong aggressive feelings. When they use this specialized vocabulary they trivialize the ideas to which they apply. Consider, for example, the difference in impact between:

(1) Oh, my—such a lovely idea!

(2) Damn, yes—that's a tremendous idea!

The other set of words they use are concerned with human feelings and relationships. These words contribute to a different, albeit more pleasant, stereotype— namely, that women are sensitive, responsive, and concerned with others. In either case, however, in terms of the orientation of this culture, the specialized vocabulary "is not relevant to the world of power and influence" (Lakoff, 1975:12).

In terms of pronunciation, grammar, sentence-structuring, and intonation, there is some research to suggest that women's language differs from men's. There have been a number of studies cited by Kramer (1975) that report that females tend to enunciate more correctly than males (e.g., sing*ing*, not sing*in'*). Thompsen (1967), summarizing the research on public speaking, states that women speakers use more correct grammar and sentence structure than males. Trudgill (1972) proposes that males prove their social status through their achievements whereas females signal it linguistically. By using correct grammar and pronunciation, a woman can prove her social status.

The intonation patterns of male and female speakers also differ. Ruth Brend (1975) reports the difficulty she had teaching Russian male teachers of English the American English intonational patterns. Although they were mimicking *her* intonations correctly, she found herself dissatisfied with their pronunciations. This led her to an analysis of different intonational patterns in male and female speech in

---

[6]The fact that more women are using expletives normally reserved for male gatherings is interesting for several reasons. First, it is further evidence that the male language is, indeed, the dominant culturally approved one since it is almost invariably the case that the style of the superordinate group is emulated by the subordinate rather than the other way around. And secondly, the use of slang signals an interesting set of responses. Some men gravitate toward such women because they take it as a cue that the "woman is liberated"; and some women refuse to relate to woman's liberation because they view the language of liberation as vulgar.

American English. Brend found that certain intonational patterns "seem to be completely lacking from men's speech, while others are differently preferred by men and women" (1975:85).

Thinking of intonations in speech as tones on a four-note musical scale, the different intonation patterns of men and women can be seen. Men, for example, are more likely to use the "incomplete deliberative," intonating a small upstep from a low vocalization such as:

```
                 kn
        es,  es,    o
(1)  y    y    I    ow.
```

On the other hand, women tend to use the more polite, incomplete, longer up-sweep, such as:

```
        es,     es,       kn
        y       y         o
        y       y         o
(2)  y        y        I    ow.
```

Other patterns seem to be virtually absent from men's speech. These include the "surprise" pattern of high voice to low voice downglide, such as:

```
     O          th       aw
       o        a         w
         o      a         w
(3)       oh       t's       ful.
```

The hesitation pattern, such as:

```
                   stu
(4)   Well, I    died . . .
```

The "polite, cheerful" pattern, such as:

```
                        ing?
(5)   Are you com
```

In summary, Brend suggests that there are some clear differences in intonation patterns between males and females. Men tend to use only the three lowest notes on the intonation scale whereas females use four. Unlike women, "men avoid final patterns which do not terminate at the lowest level of pitch, and use a final short upstep only for special effects, incomplete sequence, and for certain interrogative sentences" (1975:86 all examples in the text are from Brend's work). That is, the female intonational patterns are more polite and less definite than the males.

Lakoff contends that women use certain sentence structures more frequently than men. For example, she argues that they tend towards highly particularized requests rather than direct assertions. (For example, "Will you please come here?" in contrast to "Come here.") Further, women are more inclined to use the "tag question formulation." A tag question is a semantical construction logically located somewhere between a statement and a question and is used when the speaker is stating a claim about which total confidence is lacking. For example, upon returning home, a mother might ask her son, "Mary is here, isn't she?" This question implies that she thinks Mary is present but is not certain and is seeking confirmation. Women are likely to employ this tag question formulation, however, when it is not contextually appropriate (Lakoff, 1975:15). Such statements as "I am tired, *huh?*" "I feel so depressed, *don't you s'ppose?*" and "I think the meat prices are absurd, *aren't they?*" are common speech examples of women employing the tag question. In each of these examples, the speaker is seeking validation inappropriately for only she can know her biological, psychological, and opinion states.

Closely related to the tag question is a particular intonation pattern that Lakoff claims is peculiarly female. This speech pattern has the rising inflection of a question but in form is intended to be an answer. The effect is to seek confirmation that the answer is correct from the questioner even though the person answering is the only one who knows the answer (Lakoff, 1975:17). For example,

Question: When will dinner be ready?
Answer: Oh ... around six o'clock?

It is as though the second speaker were saying, "Six o'clock, if that's O.K. with you" (Lakoff, 1975:17).

The use of intensifiers, meaningless adjectives, tag question formulations, and the intonated-question answer—all which characterize women's speech—all present the same message. The speaker appears to be someone who lacks confidence, is uncertain of her own feelings, seeks approval from others, cannot make up her mind, and lacks an opinion of her own. These, of course, are charges often leveled against women. Optimistically, this style may have nothing to do with her actual abilities to think coherently and decisively; pessimistically, it may cause her to see herself as an indecisive and uncertain person.

Women, then, are taught by the language they speak to appear weak, constrained, insecure, and dependent upon others. By using that language, women present themselves as persons not to be taken seriously, as persons whose opinions can be dismissed. Through the use of that feminine style of speech, they perpetuate the stereotypes and, perhaps, even come to think of themselves as persons who are indecisive, incompetent, and silly. If they alter their speech patterns they are charged with being unfeminine or given the supposedly supreme compliment "You think like a man."

On the other hand, men are ridiculed if they talk like women. Their language constraints are the opposite—restricting them to seriousness of purpose, hard-hittingness, and decisiveness, whether they feel that way or not. Linguistically, it is difficult for them to express feelings of self-doubt or uncertainty. Indeed, their language style makes it difficult to emotively express practically any feeling except anger. We might, therefore, hypothesize that the frequently noted lack of emotional expressivity in males (Deutscher, 1959; Sheehy, 1976) is linked to the speech style they are expected to adopt. While the emotional limitations of male speech does not in actuality turn off feelings, it does help men to repress their feelings and to see themselves as unemotional persons.

Further, differential speech patterns may have direct ramifications for the relationships between the genders in both formal and informal contexts. For example, it may be that, in order to be successful in a male-dominated career, a woman feels she has to adopt the male speech style, with the consequent feeling engendered in herself and her male colleagues that she is not sexually desireable. In intimate relationships, differential speech patterns may contribute to the problems men and women have communicating with each other. If one partner's speech style focuses on feelings about an issue, whereas the other's focuses on substantive concerns, there is little chance that either will feel satisfied by the exchange.

In summary, the male speech pattern expresses confidence; the female, hesitancy. Not only are these differences consistent with the stereotypes of masculine and feminine, but they also contribute to the perpetuation of those stereotypes and continued misunderstanding between the genders.

Black Language

Afro-Americans of various social classes and geographical locations share a distinctive language and speech style (Folb, 1972). Members of the black community learn to speak correctly a language that is structurally complex (Labov, 1972), grammatically ordered (Abrahams, 1972), action-oriented (Kochman, 1972), and capable of finely honed double-entendres (Labov, 1972).

"Talk" is an important element of the Afro-American culture and verbal encounters are both expected, and expected to be intense and entertaining (Abrahams, 1975), or meaningful. Further, skills with the black lexicon are increasingly understood as a necessity for personal and community survival. To speak excellent "soul" (Brown, 1972) is to achieve prestige and status, as well as to perpetuate the Afro-American subculture.

So complex and subtle is the language and so important is its mastery to self-pride and community identification, especially among black males, that a special vocabulary exists in the black culture to describe it. For example, distinctions are made between different *forms* of talk: rappin', signifying, and sounding (Kochman, 1972). *Rappin'* is a lively, highly personalized form through which the speaker dramatically presents real or fantasized exploits with the goal of impressing an audience. *Signifying,* on the other hand, is the use of language to goad, beg, or boast by indirection such as "loud-talking" (talking loud enough for the object of the goad to overhear), use of unexpected pronouns ("Who thinks his hair ain't nappy?") etc. (Mitchell-Kernan, 1972). And *sounding* is insulting an opponent or an opponent's family directly.

In addition to these forms of talk, a distinction is made between two *styles:* sweet talk and smart talk. Sweet talk is associated primarily with the home, children, and respectability; smart talk is associated primarily with the street, peers, and reputation (Abrahams, 1975).

As might be expected, the different forms and styles of talk are differentially used by males and females; but, as might not be expected, both genders know how and when to speak the language of the other. Although the particular words and connotations of words employed by males may be unfamiliar to the females, the style and forms of the smart talk are not.

With the exception of a few abbreviated years of adolescent freedom, girls and women are expected to affirm the values of a good home and to be respectable (Abrahams, 1975); and their language patterns are highly compatible with these cultural demands. Women are less abandoned in their talk, less public, less loud (Abrahams, 1975). The voice is modulated close to that of Standard English, and the style is sweet talk—so much so that some linguists consider it saccharine. A "respectable" woman "speaks little with the mouth . . ." (Abrahams, 1975); a "little momma" enunciates hypercorrectly (Abrahams, 1975), and her speech pace is slow (DeStefano, 1976).

Girls are lectured by both parents not to curse or indulge in any street talk. As one woman reported to me,

> . . . If I was even on the phone talking to a friend and my father overheard me say something like 'run that past me again' [say it again], he would click off the phone and lecture me about being a respectable lady.

In addition to the sweet talk style, women tend to use the indirect form of talk, namely *signifying.* The following remark is exemplary: "I saw a woman the other day in a pair of stretch pants, she must have weighed 300 pounds. If she knew how she looked she would burn those things," (Mitchell-Kernan, 1973:319). This comment was made in the presence of an extremely obese woman who frequently wore stretch pants. By indirection, the obese woman knows she's the object of the goad; the speaker has been signifying at her.

But in addition to sweet talk and signifying, a woman must be capable of street talk, rappin', and sounding, even if she doesn't know the language of the street. To earn respectability a woman must be able to control the talk in her presence. If her self-image is being threatened, she must be able to talk *smart* or *cold* (the silent treatment); she proves her respectability by contending with the street talk. Success in the confrontation earns her respectability.

For example, when this section on black language was in its second draft, I distributed copies of it for critical comments to a New Careers sociology class composed of lower-income black women. During the first hour of the class, although some of the women were "silent," most were vociferous in their disapproval of "this trash" they had been requested to read. They *rapped* about the vile language in it and *sounded* me for presuming they were so ill-respected that they would even read it. However, during the second hour when it was clearly established that their respectability was not in question, they offered many helpful ideas. At the close of the period, they began *signifying* at me and each other. When the entire class period was reviewed, most of the women agreed that they had fought in the classroom—*as they would anywhere*—to defend their sense of self-respect; and only when that was confirmed could the topic itself be considered seriously or playfully.

In contrast, men tend to reserve the sweet talk style for hustling women and "lames" (non-hip persons). The usual male language style is combative, aggressive, argumentative, and hostile (Abrahams, 1975). In addition, the personal style of the speaker is highly dramatized with more syllabic stress, tonal changes, and rhythmic variations than is found in Standard English or in black woman's speech (Abrahams, 1975).

Further, a male's *reputation* is a function of his ability to rap and sound. Good mastery not only indicates he has arrived with his peers, but that he has succeeded in freeing himself from his home. The sweet talk of home and childhood, during pre-adolescence, is replaced by the language of the street, the language upon which one's reputation is built. As H. Rap Brown comments:

> The street is where the young bloods [young males] get their education. . . . [W]e exercised our minds by playing the dozens . . . . The dozens is a mean game because what you try to do is totally destroy somebody else with words. . . . There'd be sometimes 40 or 50 dudes standing around, and the winner was determined by the way they responded to what was said. . . . The real aim of the dozens was to get a dude so mad that he'd cry or get mad enough to fight (Brown, 1972:205).

The *dozens,* therefore, is understood by the participants to be an aggressive, competitive, and destructive public sport.

The content of the soundings and raps tend to play on three themes. First, the lack of physical, mental, and sexual prowess of the opponent, of which these soundings by very young boys are examples: "At least, I don't wear bubblegum drawers" and "Nigger Bell, you smell like B.O. Plenty" (Labov, 1972). Second, the superior physical, mental, and sexual power of the speaker, as exemplified in the writings of H. Rap Brown (1972). And third, the peculiarities and shortcomings of the opponent's family, particularly the mother as these examples from young boys' speech illustrate: "Your mother so white she hafta use Mighty White." "Your mother so black she sweat chocolate." "They say your mother eat Gainesburgers." "They say your mother was a Gravy Train. At least my mother ain't a railroad—laid all over the country." (Examples drawn from Labov, 1972).

In summary, the black speech style, as we might expect, replicates the rather universal presumption of differences between males and females. Females tend to use the speech patterns of sweet talk and signifying; patterns which are *consistent* with the dominant culture's notions of feminity. If street talk is necessary, women are able to use it, but only to enhance their respectability. Males employ the street talk and direct forms of speech, sounding and rapping. Their wit, style, and aggression are the carriers of their reputation. Again, this male speech style is consistent with the dominant culture's notion of masculinity.

Although Afro-American lexicon is different from Standard English, gender-stereotypes similar to those discussed earlier are reinforced and socialized into young Afro-Americans through the content, style, and form of the black lexicon. Males are expected to achieve a reputation through their verbal abilities; women are expected to earn respectability.

If we assume that language structure is the basis of the culture, this analysis of black lexicon suggests that "black matriarchy" is a myth (convenient for the dominant group) (see Chapter 13). Black women and white women alike are subject to similar cultural restraints, and black men and white men alike are subject to similar cultural dictates to achieve.

Upon reflection, this should not surprise us. For the languages of Western society are patriarchal. Black English is no exception. Consequently, we can safely assume that the inculcation of cultural values, which will concern us in the forthcoming chapters, exists irrespective of race, creed, or color.

To summarize, language, both verbal and nonverbal, is subtle and pervasive, oozing into the interstices of everyday life, reflecting our thought, and structuring our interpersonal relationships. Our language reaffirms the cultural value of male superiority.

For those who are interested in altering cultural values as well as their self-images, the ideas expressed in this chapter have definite implications. Women, by becoming conscious of the role of nonverbal and verbal languages, might begin to communicate independence and autonomy. Men who are interested in getting out of their socially condoned power trip can monitor their own verbal and nonverbal languages, divesting them of their power messages. Such a restructuring at the everyday level has already begun, with the consequence of some confusion about how a person of the other sex *should* be treated (Walum, 1974a). As a purely valuative statement on my part, if each person is treated with a *humanitarian* etiquette rather than a gender-role etiquette, we might all lead better lives.

Language, then, is the beginning. We turn now to the shaping of the very young societal member in the context of that language toward prescribed destinies based on their biological sex, male or female.

3

Early Socialization: The Child from Birth to Five

The place is the Mercy Hospital maternity ward. Two babies, a male and a female, were born 12 hours earlier and are now resting in the nursery, wrapped in their respective blue and pink blankets. The time is two o'clock, and afternoon visiting hours have begun. The excited grandparents are peering into the glassed-in nursery. Let us eavesdrop on their conversations:

Grandma B: There he is—our first grandchild, and a boy!

Grandpa B: Hey, isn't he a hefty little fellow? Look at that fist he's making. He's going to be a regular little fighter, that guy is. [Grandpa B smiles and throws out a boxing jab to his grandson.] At-a-boy!

Grandma B: I think he looks like you. He has your strong chin. Oh. Look, he's starting to cry.

Grandpa B: Yeah—just listen to that set of lungs. He's going to be some boy.

Grandma B: Poor thing—he's still crying.

Grandpa B: It's O.K. It's good for him. He's exercising and it will develop his lungs.

Grandma B: Let's go congratulate the parents. I know they're thrilled about little Fred. They wanted a boy, *first*.

Grandpa B: Yeah and they were sure it would be a boy, too, what with all that kicking and thumping going on even before he got here.

And off they go to congratulate the happy parents. Let us listen to the other set of grandparents, though, while we're at the nursery.

Grandma G: There *she* is . . . the one with the pink bow taped to her head. Isn't she darling.

Grandpa G: Yeah—isn't she little. Look at how tiny her fingers are. Oh, look—she's *trying* to make a fist.

Grandma G: Isn't she sweet. . . . You know, I think she looks a little like me.

Grandpa G: Yeah, she sorta does. She has your chin.

Grandma G: Oh. Look, she's starting to cry.

Grandpa G: Maybe we'd better call the nurse to pick her up or change her or something.

Grandma G: Yes, let's. Poor little girl. [To the baby] There, there, we'll try to help you.

Grandpa G: Let's find the nurse and congratulate the parents. I don't like to see her cry.

Grandma G: Hmmm. I wonder when they will have their next one. I know Fred would like a son, but little Fredericka is well and healthy. After all, that's what really matters.

Grandpa G: They're young yet. They have time for more kids. I'm thankful too that she's healthy.

Grandma G: I don't think they were surprised when it was a girl, anyway . . . she was carrying so low.

Two simple conversations by two sets of grandparents. Although they may sound as though they are reading a soap-opera script, their lines have *not* been made up. Rather, they are a composite of actual conversation overheard and recorded in a maternity ward. Embedded in the thrill and excitement of a first grandchild are the various cultural beliefs and expectations for grandsons and granddaughters. It is not surprising that the grandparents of the girl infant begin to think, "well, at least she's healthy" and turn their attention to the idea of more grandchildren. Westoff et al., (1961) found that when the first child was a girl, conception of a second child occurred three months sooner, on the average, than when the first child was a boy. Nor is it surprising that the grandparents were slightly disappointed at not having a grandson. All studies indicate that most people prefer their first child to be a boy (Markle and Nam, 1971). Further, there is a preference for having more boys than girls in the family. Indeed, according to Etzioni (1968), if people could control the sex of their unborn children, the resulting sex ratio would be 133 males for every 100 females. The child, then, is born into a culture which has a preference for males.

Given that sexual identity has been determined and blue or pink blankets visually display what the diapers conceal; and given the cultural preference for boys, the task of gender-role socialization—of teaching the child to be a man or a woman—begins. The child must be taught to identify with the appropriate gender, and what the identification requires in terms of personality traits. In teaching the child, the parents and grandparents draw upon their culture's understandings of what is appropriate for males and what is appropriate for females. The conversations between the two sets of grandparents illustrate some of the cultural dictates concerning what the differences are between men and women, what they should be, and what differences are preferable.

Socialization of children begins in the first group with which they live—*the family of orientation* or a substitute for it. Such groups are examples of *primary groups* and are "characterized by intimate face-to-face association and cooperation" (Cooley,1909:23). The family of orientation is primary in three ways: (1) it is the first socializing experience; (2) it provides the most intense and complete experience of belonging; and (3) its greater longevity and stability teaches the social knowledge necessary to engage in associations outside the familial sphere.

Later, the child will experience other primary groups such as the play group, the friendship clique, etc. However, it is in this initial primary group that children learn to communicate. They acquire the language of the culture and with that acquisition how to think, what to think about, and how to relate to others is indelibly etched upon them. Most importantly, children learn about their fundamental social nature and the basic social ideals of their culture when they are profoundly psycho-biologically dependent upon others. Their needs can only be fulfilled through social interaction. Consequently, the kind of self that develops is a function of the kind of communication provided by the significant others, tending (or not tending) to their needs.

Within the context of a primary group, the child begins to learn the most central, basic, and gut-level feelings about the nature of gender differences, the importance of such differences, and gender expectations. These ideas and ideals are the most relevant to the child's subsequent gender behavior and the most difficult to contravene. So intense and striking, or subtle and pervasive are these primary experiences in childhood that to violate them as adults is difficult, uncomfortable, improbable, and in some cases, psychologically impossible. To choose to act in ways we learned were gender-inappropriate during our years of greatest vulnerability—childhood—is to potentially choose to lose the sense of self and belonging we knew as children. Or, so subtle and pervasive are these teachings (as we noted in Chapter 1) we don't even know we are acting a certain way until we violate it.

There are different explanatory models regarding how socialization works. Two of these—the *social-learning model* and the *cognitive-development model*—have been particularly concerned with the processes by which gender identity is acquired. Both of these models reject the notion that sexuality is biologically programmed. The social-learning model proposes that a child learns appropriate sex-typed behavior through rewards, punishments, and imitation of adult models. Accordingly, sex-typed behavior is learned in the same way as other behaviors.

Boys are encouraged to copy their fathers; girls, their mothers. Subsequently, children find that modeling their behavior on the same-sex parent is rewarding in and of itself. According to this perspective, teaching of appropriate sex-typed behavior and the imitation of it begin quite early in a child's life and is very difficult to alter. The child learns to conform to parental and cultural expectations. This viewpoint is widely held in sociology, anthropology, and psychology (Sears,1965; Bandura and Walters, 1963).

Unlike the social-learning model, the cognitive-development model is almost entirely the work of one scholar, Lawrence Kohlberg (1966). He maintains that a child's gender identity and sexuality are not directly taught by others; rather, "sexual ideas and sex role concepts result from the child's active structuring of his [sic] own experience" (Skolnick, 1973:171). The key experience is the child's categorization of himself or herself as a male or female. This categorization occurs at the same time language is being acquired, between the ages of eighteen months and three years. Once children have self-categorized themselves, they begin the process of categorizing the rest of the world on the same basis. At first the understanding is tentative. It is not until about ages four to six that children concep-tualize the idea of sex-constancy—that is, that their sex does not change like their hair style, age, etc. It is not until about age five or six that they recognize that same-sex persons of different *ages* are part of the same category. That is, the idea of "we male" or "we female" is a late cognitive development. In the development of gender identity and sex-typed behavior, children actively *use* the messages that the culture presents, such as different clothing, hair styles, and occupational roles for the sexes and cognitively rehearse being a fireman and a father, if a boy; a nurse and a mother, if a girl.

Because self-categorization occurs so early in life and forms the basis upon which children make sense of the world (categorizes and orders their experi-ences), it is nearly impossible to change one's belief about what gender one is after the age of three; and it does not matter if that belief is consistent with one's anatomy or not. If one has defined oneself as a male or a female, that categoriza-tion forms the crucial basis for the categorization of others and for self-socializa-tion. We turn now to the specific procedures through which infants and children are socialized into a gender.

Infant Socialization

Before the baby arrives, the probability of its sex has been speculated upon and the wishes of the parents and grandparents have been at least tentatively vocal-ized. The months of expectant waiting have been filled with reading baby manuals, outfitting a nursery, and deciding what to name the baby. If the prospective parents use a name glossary, they are instructed how to choose a name appropriate to the sex of the child:

> She's made of sunshine, sugar and spice
> She'll be pert and pretty and awfully nice

Someday she's bound to change her name
Now choose the one that will stay the same.

Or

The name that polls the winning vote
The famous name that makes up quotes
The name thousands on employ
May be the name you name your boy.
(*3500 Names for Baby,* Dell Publishing, 1969.)

Despite the awkward poetry, the message is clear: Boys' and girls' names are, and should be, different. Boys need important names; girls need pretty ones. Apart from the standard given names and the practice of naming an offspring after a significant relative, there does, in fact, seem to be some unconscious rules governing the name preferences in middle-class America. Male names tend to be short, hard-hitting, and explosive e.g., Bret, Lance, Mark, Craig, Bruce, etc. Even when the given name is multisyllabic (e.g., Benjamin, Joshua, William, Thomas), the nickname tends to imply hardness and energy (e.g., Ben, Josh, Bill, Tom, etc.). Female names, on the other hand, are longer, more melodic and softer (e.g., Deborah, Caroline, Jessica, Christina) and easily succumb to the diminutive *ie*-ending form (e.g., Debbie, Cary, Jessie, Christy). And although feminization of male names (e.g., Fredericka, Roberta, Alexandra) is not uncommon, the inverse rarely occurs.

But there is more to infant socialization than simply deciding on a given name. The child has to learn to live up to the gender identity and the gender expectations embedded in that name. Children learn what they are taught. And to the extent that male and female infants are treated differently—to the extent that the same behavior (such as the presentation of a fist) elicits a different response from the parents—these same infants are differentially taught or socialized. The discovery of such differential socialization requires intensive and extensive observations of the actual behavior of infants and their parents. Only through such observation might early gender differences, which are physiologically dependent, be separated from those which are sociologically dependent.

Physiologically, males at birth tend to be heavier (by 5 percent) and longer (by 2 percent). However, beyond that there appear to be few consistent physiological or behavioral differences between the infants during their early months. In a monumental review of the literature on differences between infants by sex, *The Psychology of Sex Differences* (1975), Maccoby and Jacklin conclude that,for most behaviors studied, the findings are either inconclusive or indicate thatthere are no significant differences that can be attributed to sex.

In terms of activity level, Korner (1969) reports that the spontaneous activity of the infant male and female are quantitatively the same, although they differ qualitatively. Boys, he reports, engage in more gross-body startle movements; girl's movements are predominately confined to the facial area—sucks, smiles, and rhythmic mouthing. Although the evidence is inconclusive, boys probably spend less time sleeping (Maccoby and Jacklin, 1974:171). However, as follow-up studies suggest, the activity level at one point in time does not consistently predict the activity level at another.

In terms of sensory perception, the research findings are also inconclusive. There is some evidence to suggest that females are more sensitive to smells and taste, but the research is too scanty to permit generalization. In relationship to sensitivity to touch, some research indicates no difference by sex for newborns; that which reports a difference suggests that newborn girls are more tactilely sensitive. Infant boys and girls are similar in their responses to auditory and visual stimuli, as well as in their receptivity to social (faces and voices) or nonsocial stimuli. From the research thus far there does not seem to be strong empirical evidence to argue that infant boys and girls are naturally different in regard to sensitivity.

Clearly, there is a great deal more to learn about what physiological differences, if any, there are between male and female infants. Once these are better understood, however, we still need to understand how they are related to subsequent social development. If further research, for example, continues to confirm the *similarity* between the physiological states of infants of different sexes, then we can be even more certain about the primary role of socialization for the development of masculine and feminine personalities.

Although most parents would probably claim that they do not alter their behavior to suit the sex of the child, there is research evidence to the contrary. In reviewing some of the literature, Lake (1976) reports that mothers described their newborn daughters as tiny, soft, delicate, fine-featured shortly after their first glimpse of them and described their sons as strong, alert, well-coordinated. In an exploratory study, five young mothers were presented Adam, a six-month-old dressed in blue overalls; a second group of mothers were given Beth, a six-month-old in a pink frilly dress. Compared to Adam, Beth was smiled at more, offered a doll to play with more often, and viewed as "sweet" with a "soft cry." However, Adam and Beth were in actuality the same six-month-old child.

Further, observational studies of infants and mothers have discovered some significant differences in the early socialization of males and females. Lewis (1972) has found that during the first six months of life, boys receive more physical contact (being touched, held, nursed) and *less* nonphysical contact (being looked at and talked to) than girls. This is true despite the fact that the *amount* of both verbal (Moss, 1967) and nonverbal activity of the three-month-old male and female was the same. That is, there was early differential reinforcement of males' *physical* activity and of females' *verbal* activity. However, after that initial six-month period, girls receive both more physical and nonphysical contact than boys.

The research evidence is quite consistent: parents "elicit 'gross motor behavior' more from their sons than from their daughters" (Maccoby and Jacklin, 1975:-307). In addition to Lewis's study, Yarrow (et al., 1971) reports that parents are more likely to play vigorously with their sons. Both fathers (Pederson and Robson,

1969) and mothers (Minton et al., 1971) have been found to be more apprehensive about physical danger to their daughters than to their sons and view the former as more fragile. "The form of the motor stimulation undoubtedly changes drastically with the age of the child, but the continuing theme appears to be that girls are treated as though they were more fragile than boys" (Maccoby and Jacklin, 1974:309). Further, more attention is paid to teaching daughters than sons to smile (Lake, 1975:24). Parents were observed giving seven-week-old infants a social and development test. Although the infant boys and girls performed similarly, their parents did not. More coaxing and terms of endearment were used to elicit a smile or a "coo" from the girls.

Lewis (1972) contends that the physically contiguous, face-to-face relationship between mother and child must be transformed into the visual-verbal relationship of adults. Consequently, mothers detach themselves from their children through such techniques as facing them away and drawing their attention to other objects and persons in the room. In this process of learning "independence" from the mother, boys are moved along much more quickly than girls. So by the time the infants are thirteen months old, boys venture further out into their environment, look at and talk to their mothers less frequently, and manipulate the environment more aggressively than girls.

There is no clear evidence to explain why boys and girls are differently socialized in these early months. The reasons may be based on the different physiological states or on different cultural expectations or on some admixture of both. For example, the males' developmental immaturity may lead to greater fretfulness and consequently the need to be held and fondled more; or, the greater cultural value placed on boys might increase the mother's desire to touch the male infant. Boys' greater gross activity, higher basal metabolism, and greater caloric intake may ready them earlier for independence or they may be sped on their way due to cultural expectations for dominance and mastery. Clearly, much more evidence is necessary to unravel the nature-nurture controversy embedded in the earliest socialization experiences.

We can only speculate at this point as to what consequences differential contact might have for subsequent personality development. To aid us in our speculation we need to consider what the kind of contact the infant receives signifies. Desmond Morris, an animal ethologist, who has turned his observational skills to the human animal, has recorded some typical maternal-infant contact behaviors (1971). These include a (womblike) embrace (providing as great a body surface contact as possible), rocking the child from side to side, fondling, kissing, cleaning, stroking, and significantly, rhythmic back-patting and cooing, humming, and talking. Back-patting, according to Morris, is an example of an evolutionary adaptation of an *intention movement,* signaling to the infant that the mother will cling tightly. Each pat on the back—and in particular, the usual pattern of *pat, pat, pat, stop, pat, pat, pat*—doubly soothes the infant, saying "Don't worry, I will cling to you like this if danger threatens" but also, "Don't worry, there is no danger or I would be clinging to you tighter than this" (1972:24). Similarly, cooing, crooning, and talking are mammalian messages to the young that all is well, that danger does not threaten.

If Morris is correct in his interpretation of the significance of touching and talking, we may find established, in the very earliest of infancy, the socialization basis for the masculine and feminine personality structures discussed in Chapter 1. To the extent that girl infants are talked to and touched more, perhaps a primary and visceral understanding that if danger threatens, they will (and should) be protected is established; boy infants, on the other hand, learn that if danger threatens, they must master it. Differences in subsequent ability to touch freely, to demonstrate physical closeness, etc., are also probably related to the way each sex is treated during infancy. However, until more substantial research on the quality, tone, types, duration, and occasions in which contacts occur is available, these crucial questions of parental behavior towards infants and their effects on adult personality must remain speculative.

Although we know very little about the actual day-to-day forms and styles of verbal and nonverbal communication between parents and infants, we do know something about the gender expectations, as demonstrated in the paraphernalia designed for infants. There are different styles and colors for male and female infants in such basics as cribs, potty seats, comforters, changing tables, diaper pins, and toys. But perhaps the clearest distinctions between the sexes is reflected in the most personal of possessions—namely, infant clothing.

In a trip through an infant section of any department store, gross imitations of the adult gender-linked styles are easily discernible. On the girls' racks are princess dresses, granny gowns, pink satin pantsuits, and bikinis; on the boys' racks are baseball uniforms, tweed suits with vests and decorative pocket watches, astronaut pajamas, and starched white dress shirts. All of these fancy clothes are available from size zero to three months onwards. Often, the differences in style are more subtle. For example, large manufacturers of infant ready-to-wear design male and female variants of the same basic romper. The male variant snaps from left to right, has a pointed collar and a football motif; the female snaps left to right, has a peter pan collar with lace trim and embroidered butterflies. (Only diapers and Christening dresses seem to be entirely immune to gender-typing.)

Although we have witnessed some relaxation of the infant dress codes, the differences still persist. Girls are more readily dressed in boy's play clothes than the reverse. And when the children are dressed up the distinctions are even clearer. The anxious mother dresses her infant son like a boy in the hope of avoiding the embarrassment of correcting the stranger who might otherwise croon "Whata sweet little girl." Further, the gender-linked clothing reminds the parents what sex their child is. After all, most of them have been referring to the unborn baby as "it" for the past nine months. When the infant girl is dressed in a frilly pink dress, she not only looks sweet and fragile, she is fragilely dressed and physically constrained. And when the boy infant sports his cowboy suit, he not only looks ready to be rough, he is able to be rough without undue impediment from his clothing.

Choosing different clothing styles not only signifies to others—including the parents and grandparents—what sex the child is and therefore how the child is to be treated, but also facilitates or hampers the activity of the child. The clothing itself reflects the cultural expectations regarding the appropriate behavior of each sex. Current trends toward unisex dressing, particularly in the realm of play and casual life, suggests that some of our expectations in those arenas have been altered. But even here we find that the adult mode parallels that of infancy. Females have a greater latitude in adopting men's clothing than vice versa, but the likelihood of dressing in clothes deemed female is greater, the more ceremonial (e.g., funeral, wedding, divorce) or important (first date, job interview, etc.) the occasion.

In brief, the earliest months of the child's life are not gender-role free. Differences in expectations, names, behaviorial responses, apparel, toys, furniture styles, and games treat the baby as belonging to either the male sex or the female sex. Indeed, as Stoller, the director of the U.C.L.A. Gender Identity Research Clinic, argues: in the *first two or three years of life,* core gender identity—the sense of maleness or femaleness—is established as a "result of the parents' conviction that their infant's assignment at birth to either the male or female sex is correct" (1967). Despite the potential existence of hormones, chromosomes, gonads, or internal reproductive organs to the contrary, if the parents define a child as belonging to a particular gender during its first few years of life, the child will identify with that gender.

Preschool Socialization

Although the studies of newborns are few, there is a vast literature on the older infant and preschool child, which Maccoby and Jacklin (1974) have also reviewed and summarized. What has psychology found out regarding the differences in personalities of young boys and girls? The two most frequently studied traits are aggression and dependency. *Aggression* is considered a complex "cluster of actions and motives" which share the "central theme . . . the intent of one individual to hurt another" (Maccoby and Jacklin, 1974:227). It may involve physically or verbally lashing out; or simply fantasizing hostile activity; and it may be done to gain control or simply to punish another person. Maccoby and Jacklin summarize their research: "The major fact . . . is that males are consistently found to be more aggressive than females. . . . The behavioral sex difference is found in a variety of cultures" (1974:228).

Their research, however, suggests that the differences in aggression between males and females increase as the children grow older; the younger the children, the greater the number of research studies reporting no difference between the sexes (see summary table in Maccoby and Jacklin, 1974:230–233). It is only after the 18th month that greater negative emotional outbursts following frustrations are found in boys (Maccoby and Jacklin, 1974:181). What appears to be happening as the children age is "not that boys are increasing in their emotional volatility . . . but that girls are decreasing in the frequency and intensity of their emotional reactions [to frustration] at a faster rate than boys" (Maccoby and Jacklin, 1974:-182). These differences in aggressive activity as the child ages seem to be related to the willingness of the child to act hostilely. For example, in studies of children in which models of aggressive behavior were presented (through films, tapes, etc.), boys were more likely to imitate the aggressive behavior than were the girls. However, when rewards were offered for imitating the aggressive behaviors, the differences between the sexes diminished (Maccoby and Jacklin, 1974:182).

The evidence still seems inconclusive as to whether greater aggression in the male is a biologically based trait or a learned one. Although Maccoby and Jacklin contend that "it has a biological foundation" (1974:242, for their arguments see 242–247), the extent to which biology is destiny for the male remains unresolved. For example, boys show the greater aggression when they are in active rough play with other boys and, as we have already noted, boys are played with more physically than are girls by their parents. Does the greater activity lead to greater aggression or does greater biologically based aggression lead to the greater roughhousing? And to what extent and through what mechanism does the society reward aggression in males? However it does so, we might pause for a moment to wonder why a society would choose to reinforce aggression.

Dependency may be defined as a complex behavior system that includes actions that a child performs in order to receive nurturance, help, or caretaking. Such actions as touching or clinging to someone and asking for help or protection or attention (directly or indirectly) are considered dependent behavior (Maccoby and Jacklin, 1975:191). However, despite the lumping of various activities under the rubric *dependency,* research indicates that they do not exist as a cluster. For example, seeking closeness and seeking attention appear to be quite different activities "which have distinct courses of development and are responsive to different antecedent conditions" (Maccoby and Jacklin, 1975:191).

The majority of the research concerning young children's dependency on their mothers as indicated by seeking closeness, touching, or resisting separation, reports no difference in the dependency actions of young (under age three) boys and girls (Maccoby and Jacklin, 1975:196). Further, seeking proximity to other adults and children is a behavior which both sexes perform equally often (Maccoby and Jacklin, 1975:200). In the early childhood years, both boys and girls will seek comfort or protection through dependency actions. "Clinging to parents or other caretakers or remaining near them under conditions of uncertainty or anxiety is characteristic of human children" (Maccoby and Jacklin, 1975:201).

For some other traits studied, Maccoby and Jacklin report that the findings suggest no differences in the early childhood years. These include such traits as *sociability, suggestibility, spatial-visual ability, mathematical ability.* For other traits, such as *fear, competitiveness, dominance, compliance, nurturance,* they report that the evidence is too inconclusive to reach any generalizations. Yet, for many of these traits, differences do appear in later childhood and in adulthood. And, for all of these traits discussed so far, there is a cultural belief that males and females are different. The question, therefore, becomes what consequences does the belief system have for the socialization of young children? Do parents treat their sons differently than their daughters?

At this point, the research strategies to help answer this question are just being mapped out. Thus far, persistent findings concerning the differential treatment of boys and girls are that boys receive more physical punishment, more negative feedback, and more positive feedback (praise and encouragement) than girls. That is, socialization pressures are applied more intensely to boys than to girls, and there is some evidence to suggest that the father is particularly instrumental in this regard.

More demands are made on boys at a younger age than on girls (Hartley, 1974:7). Parents reprimand boys more severely for acting in sex-inappropriate ways (such as acting like "sissies") than they do girls who, for example, act like "tomboys." Further, the demands to boys are defined primarily proscriptively (boys should *not*) rather than prescriptively (boys should). Consequently, young boys must either discover somewhat accidentally what they should do or receive repeated negative sanctions for straying into sex-inappropriate behavior. Hartley suggests these socialization practices—"the demand that the child do something which is not clearly defined to him, based on reasons he cannot possibly appreciate, and enforced with threats, punishments, and anger by those who are close to him" . . . induce sex-role anxiety in boys (1974:7). This anxiety expresses "itself in overstraining to be masculine, in virtual panic of being caught doing anything traditionally defined as feminine, and in hostility toward anything even hinting at femininity, including females themselves" (Hartley, 1974:8). Unfortunately, because this anxiety is produced when boys are young and vulnerable, the behaviors and attitudes—fear of and hostility toward the feminine—often persist into adult life.

Many parents insist that they treat their children the same—that they do not differentiate them by sex. In one study, parents report that they want both their sons and daughters to be equally neat, helpful around the house, able to control their anger, considerate, able to control their crying, competitive, and able to defend themselves (Maccoby and Jacklin, 1974:343–344). Similarly, in a class research project, where 50 college students interviewed their parents, parents claimed they did not treat their sons and daughters differently. However, for both of these studies, when parents were asked "In what ways do you think boys and girls are different?", their responses indicated that they felt boys were naturally more active, competitive, aggressive, noisy, and messy; and that girls were naturally more gentle, neat, quiet, helpful, courteous, etc. The students' own reports indicated greater awareness of differential treatment and expectations than their parents acknowledged; and the reconstructions of the students were consonant with parental definitions of the nature of boys and the nature of girls. Because the parents believed that boys and girls were naturally different, it is difficult to accept the claim that they treated them the same—despite their protestations to the contrary.

A particularly enlightening study of the differential socialization of boys and girls is found in the study of a set of twins (Money and Ehrhardt, 1975). The twins were both born male without any congenital malformation or sex-assignment ambiguity. At seven months, one of the twins lost his penis through a surgical error. (An overpowerful current of electricity during a routine electrocautery circumcision burned the entire tissue of the penis.) When the twin was seventeen months old, the decision was reached to rear the child as a girl. The parents "were given confidence that their child . . . [could] be expected to differentiate a female gender identity, in agreement with her sex of rearing" (Money and Ehrhardt, 1975:47). The first steps were changing the child's name, clothing, and hairstyle, followed by plastic surgery to construct female genitalia. The mother reported that she kept the girl in dresses and frilly blouses, that she emphasized neatness and encouraged her daughter to imitate her own domestic interests. By age five, the mother was happy to report that her daughter preferred dresses to slacks, was proud of her long hair, liked to be cleaned up and enjoyed imitating her mother's behaviors. In her own words during an interview, she said, "One thing that really amazes me is that she is so feminine. I've never seen a little girl so neat and tidy. . . . She is very proud of herself, when she puts on a new dress or I set her hair" (Money and Ehrhardt,, 1975:48). As might be expected, her son did not exhibit these traits. According to her report, he was active, messy, rejected housework, and liked to copy his father.

Money and Ehrhardt conclude that this case presents some of the cues to how parents treat boys and girls differently, and posit, "Most parents give them [cues] without conscious effort, routinely" (1975:50).

Consequently, the reports of parents that they treat children the same must be viewed skeptically. We find this skepticism an even more appropriate stance the older the child becomes. This is so because as the child matures, the parent increasingly depends on external agents for socializing the child. Chief among these agents in the preschoolers' world are books, toys, and television. Through them the infant's core gender-identity is translated into appropriate gender image, attitude, and behavior.

Artifacts for Children

Children's artifacts are a particularly cogent source for learning about cultural values. As Margaret Mead has commented, the ideas of the culture have to be presented to children in such simple terms that even a behavioral scientist can understand them. Something as important as the core values of a culture and the role expectations for genders cannot be left purely to the happenstance of parental socializing. Further, these values can be, must be, and are incorporated into material designed for the young. For example, McClelland (1961) found that by doing a content analysis of achievement motivation in children's readers, he was able to predict a nation's economic growth. That is, the values found in children's stories were a sensitive predictor of a society's actual (in practice) value system. Let us look closely, then, at the major socializing materials for young children— picture books, toys, and television.

Weitzman (et al., 1972) have analyzed gender roles in the Caldecott Medal Award books and in Little Golden Books, which have sold over 3,000,000 copies. The Caldecott Medal is awarded annually by the American Library Association for the best children's picture book of the year. Winning the medal assures the books virtual universal purchase by libraries, central positions in story hours, and wide circulation to homes and schools. Little Golden Books are priced inexpensively and are readily available. The researchers found three major significant differences in gender roles in these preschool books.

First, males are much more prevalent than females in stories and pictures. For example, in the Caldecott Medal books studied, the ratio of males depicted to females is 11:1 (261 males, 23 females). If animals with sexual identities are included, the ratio is 95:1—male animals to female animals. Only two books were about girls; one was a foreign princess and the other was named Sam. The child learns that women are invisible: the world of boys and men is the one worthy of story telling.

Secondly, the activities of the males and females differed. Males in the picture-book world are active; females are passive. Males engage in far-out adventures, riotous activities, and various pursuits requiring independence and competence. In contrast, most of the girls are passive and remain indoors. Even Sam, the female heroine of *Sam, Bangs and Moonshine* (1967, Caldecott Medal book), remains at home directing the activities of a younger boy in the fulfillment of her fantasies. The boy goes to sea, climbs trees, rides bicycles, while Sam awaits his return. Girls perform traditional feminine roles; no matter how young they are, they cook and clean for their fathers and brothers. Girls are rarely seen working or playing together. In brief, the activities of the boys are directly linked to preferable male values of activity, independence, and achievement, and the activities of girls are linked to passivity, service, and dependence.

Thirdly, the adult roles of men and women are differentially presented. The presentation of adults by sex teaches the children what they might expect for themselves when they grow up, and hence helps inculcate aspirations, goals, and self-images. The image of the adult women in the picture books is stereotyped and limited. She is passive and dependent, performing activities of service to men and children in the home. If she is not a wife and mother, she is an imaginary creature, such as a fairy godmother. Not one woman in all the books surveyed held a job or had a profession. Motherhood is presented as a full-time, life-long job. The adult male in these books, on the other hand, displays a wide range of roles: storekeepers, kings, story-tellers, monks, fighters, fishermen, policemen, fathers, preachers, judges, cooks, adventurers, etc. Fathers never help share in cooking, cleaning, shopping, or baby-sitting. They read newspapers and are waited on by their wives.

The prescription is clear. Girls can expect to grow up and become wives and

mothers and boys can grow up to do whatever they choose. The following excerpts from the twin Little Golden Books *What Boys Can Be* (Walley, n.d.) and
What Girls Can Be (Walley, n.d.) summarizes the often-repeated messages: A boy
can be a fireman, a baseball player, a bus driver, a policeman, a cowboy, a doctor,
a sailor, a pilot, a clown, a zoo-keeper, an actor, or at the culmination of his career,

> an astronaut who lives in a space station, and
> someday grows up to be President of the nation.

On the other hand, a girl can be a nurse, stewardess, ballerina, candy shop owner,
model, star, secretary, artist, teacher in a nursery school, singer, designer of
dresses, bride, or at the peak of her career,

> a housewife, someday when I am grown, and
> a mother, with some children of my own.

The ultimate goal for males is the presidency; for females, motherhood. Further,
female jobs tend to be located inside whereas male jobs are located outside.
Female occupations require either physical attractiveness or service orientation.
Male occupations cover a wider range of requisite qualities. And the prestigious,
powerful and well-paid occupations belong to the world of men. Men are doctors,
women are nurses; men are pilots, women are stewardesses.

One of the most important socializing agents for the preschooler is television
—the Saturday morning cartoons, the late-afternoon educational programs, and
commercials. The portrayal of gender differences in such programming is obvious.
For example, the widely heralded educational show, "Sesame Street," has been
designed to counter black matriarchy, the questionable idea that black women
dominate black society. Consequently, programming purposively teaches traditional white values regarding gender roles. The Moppets are introduced with such
patter as "You can tell I'm a girl; I have long eyelashes and curly hair." Problem-
solving of the what's-wrong-here variety includes episodes where men and women
change roles (e.g., women carry suitcases, while men are empty-handed). Boys
and men in action segments are active; women and girls watch. Susan, the her-
oine-wife, "does something nice for Gordon [the hero-husband] because she likes
to make him happy," but Gordon is not cast in the pleasing-people role. (Vogel et
al., 1970). Despite the criticism heaped on "Sesame Street" for its gender role
teachings, the stereotyping appears to be increasing. In 1970, the ratio of males
to females on the show was 2:1 (Vogel, 1970); in 1974, the ratio was 2.5:1 and
the segments which were male-dominated consisted of 75 percent of the viewing
time (Bernabei, 1974). Neither of the two women on the show are actively employed and all of the regular moppets have male voices and are either manifestly
male or likeable monsters. The latent teachings of "Sesame Street" are best
summarized by a five-year-old's response to her mother's query as to whether a
particular animal was a male: "Don't you know? It's always a boy unless it's a
mommy!" (Bernabei, 1974:9).

The cartoons repeat the theme. The heroes are males, the sidekicks are females. In the "Flintstones," the prototype aboriginal family, the men build, fight, fly to the moon, carouse, drive cars, and fish; the women cook, clean, stay at home, and tend babies. The commercials that accompany these programs add zip and zest to the selling not only of the commercial product, but the role-expectancies.

The themes of the children's books and the television are replayed subtly, but more persistently, when we enter the boy-toy and girl-toy worlds. A content analysis of the 195 pages of toys in the 1972 "Sears Christmas Wish Book" (a catalog) makes it obvious to both child and parents that toys are gender-linked. I viewed each half page of the toy section and cross-tabulated the kind of toy pictured by presence of a male child, female child, children of both sexes, or no children. Then I categorized the various toys into (1) preparatory for spousehood and parenthood (e.g., dolls and kitchen equipment), (2) preparatory for occupational roles (e.g., doctor's kits), (3) manipulatory toys (e.g., construction sets), and (4) cultural and educational (e.g., books, music, arts and crafts). The results are given in Table 3.1

TABLE 3.1 Percent* of Half Pages in 1972 "Sears Christmas Wish Book" Presenting Toys for Preschoolers

Sex	Play Context				
	Preparatory for spousehood and parenthood	Preparatory roles for occupational	Manipulatory	Cultural and Educational	Total number
Male	0 % (0)	25 % (3)	75 % (76)	9 % (5)	84
Mixed genders or no models	16 % (11)	67 % (8)	11 % (17)	89 (51)	87
Female	84 % (56)	8 % (1)	8 % (8)	2 % (1)	66
Total Number of ½ pages	67	12	101	57	237

*Percents rounded to nearest whole number.

Even the most cursory examination of the table suggests clear differences in the expectations, by gender, for young children. Girls are to play house. Boys are never depicted in the toy world by themselves engaging in fathering or cooking or cleaning. In fact, they are never shown in those capacities at all. Their pictorial representation in preparation for spousehood is being served tea or helping themselves to something from the toy refrigerator. More space is devoted to baby dolls, and the paraphernalia for them, than any other single category of toy. As Alice Rossi once remarked, a girl may spend more years playing with her dolls than a mother spends with her children (1964:105).

Few toys that are clearly related to subsequent gainful employment are available for either sex. With the exceptions of doctors and nurses kits (the former shown with a boy, the latter with a girl), heavy construction equipment, and science equipment, the catalog offers few job-specific toys. This probably reflects the fantasy that boys can be or do anything and that girls can be mothers.

Toys requiring manipulation (e.g., blocks, tinker toys, erector sets, construction trucks, wheeled vehicles) are almost entirely the province of boys. When girls are shown with such toys the actual toy has been feminized. For example, a boy is shown with a trail bike, "sleek, yet rugged . . . true dragster style"; the counterpart depicts a 'girl's petite bike with roomy basket . . . hot pink." When no children appear in the picture, the text usually clarifies that boys and girls are different. For example, a little tricycle is available "with decals to customize if for a girl or a boy." (The decals are rally flags and racing stripes for the boy and a butterfly and flowers for the girl.) Girls do not play with blocks, build "pirate ships for buccaneers" out of tinker toys, or "pour on the action" with the Tuff Boy construction fleet.

Only educational and cultural toys are least susceptible to gender-stereotyping. Both boys and girls may read, listen to music, work with craft sets, and play with educator-designed learning sets (e.g., computer spelling, adding, see-and-shake sets). But even here differences are noticeable. Girls' craft jewelry, perfume, and clothing; boys craft wooden objects (carpentry) and tumble rocks. Girls play pianos and (black) boys play the drums. Girls listen to records and boys operate the phonograph; girls read and boys use the teaching computer.

The adult-designed toy world—the most central and engrossing world of the young—is clearly two *separate* worlds. The young boy cannot with ease play with dolls, pretend to cook, or clean. Such tasks are deemed "feminine," and he is rebuffed from his initial interests in imitating a significant adult around him, the person in the kitchen. Indeed, so strong is the prohibition against boys playing with dolls, that nursery school teachers have been known to question parents if their sons spend "undue time" in the housekeeping area. They assume the boy is having a sexual identity crisis. Some child guidance specialists suggest that parents should let their boys, if they wish, engage in feminine activities, but add they should try to keep those activities within limits and within the closed walls of the house—much as you would the family skeleton. Bettelheim, a child psychiatrist, tells mothers that boys are "naturally more ready to fight" and if they inhibit these native tendencies towards greater aggression, the results will be "passivity and femininity in boys—and drug addiction and homosexuality" or "violence in the streets" (1967). Boys *are* to be boys. And that means they manipulate their environment. Their toys are designed to encourage this approach to life itself, to develop the necessary manipulative skills, and to prevent them from becoming femininized. A quiet, retiring "sissy" is regarded as a problem child. Even young children find boys engaging in girls' activities (e.g., dressing a doll or frosting a cake) something to laugh at (McGhee and Grodzitsky, 1973).

Although girls are geared to motherhood through the various agents of preschool socialization, they are allowed greater freedom than boys to veer from the approved play path. They are allowed *not* to play with dolls; and they are permitted to be tomboys. Girls may be cautioned and reprimanded for their unfeminine behavior, but they are not in these earliest years subject to the same condemnation that meets the boy who would rather dress a doll than hit a ball.

Perhaps the most chilling aspect of early socialization rests in the adult roles offered children. Neither gender is presented with realistic options; both are proferred limited and limiting choices. Girls are taught to restrain their aspirations, to look to motherhood as their sole and life-long destiny. They are taught that good looks might win them a glamorous job, but that without them their lives will be dedicated to the service of children and spouse. Because not all girls will marry or have children or even feel comfortable staying home, the expectations are false. Further, the development of alternative skills, images, and activities is truncated.

Boys are taught to aspire to positions of power, prestige, and wealth. They learn that their masculinity is intricately tied up with the performance of a powerful occupational role. Success as a male is dependent on success in an occupation. Because only a small percentage of the work force does achieve in actuality these positions of power and prestige, the young male is systematically prepared as a preschooler to doubt his masculinity as a youth. Other activities and emotional states (e.g., fathering, cooking, cleaning, crying) are not encouraged. He is either occupationally successful or he is not a man.

From birth to school age, then, children are treated differently depending upon their gender. By the time they start their formal education, they know what is expected of a member of their gender; but what they don't know is that they may not be able to fulfill—through no fault of their own—those expectations.

4
Education

Many of us still remember that special day in early September, when, dressed in scratchy clothes and new shoes and sounding like a one-person band with our crinkles and squeaks, we entered the world of the schoolhouse. Many of us had spent long hours role-playing or rehearsing pupil and teacher roles; most of us had been socialized by stories from our parents and siblings of the relevance and importance of the goods and evils to befall us in that new world. And probably nearly all of us saw the occasion as a momentous rite of passage: we were now "big" girls or boys. And so we entered with preconceived notions of what to expect and whether we should and would like it.

However, regardless of what parents tell children about school, they show by their own behavior that they took for granted the societal norm. *Children go to school.* Going to school means that parents are willing to let these other adults (perfect strangers all named Teacher) discipline, inspire, and evaluate—in short, socialize their children.

Subjective evaluations like "school must be important—even my parents act like it is" are reinforced by the objective reality. For the next 10 or 20 years, with the willing compliance of parents, a child's time is organized around schooling; the major portion of waking hours is spent in school and school-related activities. Days are now structured in order to attend school (e.g., the deferment of doctors' appointments to after-school, trips and outings relegated to the weekends and school vacations, etc.); the time to sleep and the time to rise are determined by "getting to school on time" and by "not being tired" once there. And rather than the laissez-faire play time enjoyed as preschoolers, children spend an hour or two in travel time, another five or six in the classroom, a few more doing homework, and, as they grew older, invest the last remaining wakeful hours in extra-curricular activities.

Any doubts that might be harbored concerning the parentally approved priority of school are often erased when the student complains about the teacher's

53

methods or assignments. Parents may be sympathetic with the grievances, but the usual message is, "The teacher is right: behave yourself!" That is, parents accept the schools as having a legitimate right to discipline, evaluate, and inspire. In short, the transfer of authority from the parents to the school is complied with willingly by the parents. Both the parents and the school take for granted that this transfer of authority will occur.

But in addition to the parental acceptance of the school as the legitimate educator, the school is formally charged through law to educate the young. The school is one of the few institutions recognized as a legitimate agent of socialization. In effect, the school not only stands in locos parentis ("in place of the parents"), but as importantly in locos societate ("in place of the society"). Children are required to go to school; and the school is held accountable for teaching what the society values.

But why should a society want a school system? Why is the task of socialization transferred at great public expense from the home to the school? The major reason is that compulsory public education contributes to the survival of complex industrialized societies. First, if any society is to survive, its value system must be transmitted to the next generation. In traditional societies, this transmission is accomplished through the socializing efforts of the entire society. Because what is to be learned remains fairly constant in such societies and because all adults in them are carriers of the general shared culture, there is little need for specialized institutions of education. However, in a complex and rapidly changing society, such as the United States since the late 1800s, the learning of the cultural values cannot be left to happenstance and the efforts of parents. Rather, such a complex society needs to ensure the survival of its culture by systematically teaching all of its future citizens how they should think, feel, and behave. In addition, a major requirement for the survival of industrialized societies is the creation of a particular kind of labor force. Indeed, by 1880 compulsory public education was universal in the industrialized world. The schools fulfill the labor force needs of a technological society not only by teaching basic literacy, but by preparing students to enter occupations upon which a technological economy depend. The public school system, therefore, is functionally integrative in a complex industrial society, because it transmits core cultural values and teaches the labor force skills required in expanding the technological base of the society.

Some of this approved and/or necessary learning is spelled out clearly in the formal curriculum. Students are expected to read (English), write (English), and do arithmetic (English system) as well as to master history, geography, civics, and possibly music, art, and physical education. But, in addition to this formal curriculum, an *informal* one exists *sub rosa.* The informal one teaches students about the value preferences of this culture regarding political, social, racial, economic, familial, gender, and other systems of thought, as well as teaches children what they might expect for themselves. Increasingly, sociologists and educationists have turned their attention to the content of this informal curriculum and its effect on the development of children (cf. Bruner, 1966). Indeed, much of the local-control and free-school movement of the last decade has been an attempt to provide children with an alternative informal curriculum.

Most children, however, go to public schools, where the informal curriculum—the means by which the cultural values are transmitted *sub rosa*—are rather standard across the nation. Because the school, as we have seen, is a very important agent of socialization and because the informal curriculum carries the same weight of legitimacy as the formal one, it behooves us to look at it rather closely. What are the schools teaching in their hidden curricula concerning gender roles? These shadowy teachings can be made visible through analyses of the school rules, classroom structures, curricular materials, extracurricular athletic activities, and counselling practices. To what extent are the schools socializing children into gender roles as a part of their latent curriculum?

Sex Segregation: Policies and Practices

Frazier and Sadlek (1973:76–77) discuss a school in California that discovered the ethnic origin of the student was an excellent predictor of future occupational choice. Anglo-American children entered professional and managerial occupations, whereas Chicano children became migrant workers. Because future careers were found so closely linked to ethnic origins, the "Program for Educational and Occupational Needs" (PEON) was instituted.

To prepare Anglo children for future professional careers, an academic curriculum was used; whereas Chicano children were prepared for jobs as crop-pickers through exercises in crouching, stooping, and stretching, and through docility games such as "Simon Says," "Follow the Leader," and "Mother May I?" Such programs as PEON are antithetical to our cultural values of equality of opportunity—and the authors are (thankfully) only putting us on. That is, they have imagined what a school system might look like if education for future employment was based on current occupations of persons by ethnicity. Although schools do not have PEON programs, they do routinely educate males and females for different careers. Through certain policies they structurally sanction lessened occupational opportunities for females.

Although most schools do not totally segregate the sexes in the primary grades, junior high schools routinely offer separate programs for boys and girls. Girls take home economics; boys take shop. It is assumed that only girls will need to learn to cook and sew and that only boys will need to use power equipment. Moreover, by the time high school begins, sex-segregated vocational training programs, and in some cases, sex-segregated schools, are normative (Frazier and Sadleck, 1973:132). Non-college-bound girls are routed into home economics, cosmetology, and secretarial programs. Their male counterparts are placed in an industrial arts program. The boys' program teaches skills that will command higher salaries in the skilled trades, whereas the girls' programs teach the less economically rewarding ones.[1] And thus, the official programs and practices in schools limit severely the kinds of occupations open to their graduates by virtue of their sex.

Only recently have these programs and policies been challenged in the courts and have some schools been willing to break down the traditionally sex-segregated educational offerings. Although the evidence is impressionistic, girls seem to be more easily enrolled in the regularly established boys courses (woodshop, auto mechanics, etc.) than vice versa. It appears that when boys are interested in the girls curriculum, new course offerings are added to the system. For example, in some schools, boys interested in cooking take "Bachelor Living"; and those interested in acquiring clerical skills are enrolled in a new "Office Management" program. That is, the school—like the parents—resists allowing boys to be associated with feminine activities. Upgrading the level of occupational attainment at the completion of the curriculum (e.g., office manager rather than file clerk) and viewing homemaking skills as relevant only to bachelor living defines those courses as permissibly masculine.

Another way in which sex stereotyping is perpetuated in the schools is through the office of the school's guidance counselor. Particularly by high school, problems of college choice, career, and course work press hard upon students who then may seek the help of the school counselor. The counselor may then administer to these students standardized tests whose purpose is to help students choose careers. Unfortunately, these tests are themselves sex-stereotyped in language and occupations suggested (Tittle et al., 1974), and their very administration reinforces cultural stereotypes. If women are indeed more sensitive to their environments and have a greater desire to please than men, the test situation itself is biased against women succeeding, because these characteristics are associated with low performance levels.

In addition, women are less likely to see themselves as capable of achieving career success. In an ingenious study, female students were given the Strong Vocational Test with the regular instructions and then again with role-playing instructions to imagine that men liked intelligent women and that women could manage careers and families simultaneously. Under those instructions, the career interest of women rose in six occupations: artist, psychologist, lawyer, physician, and life-insurance salesperson (Farmer and Bohn, 1970).

Nevertheless, the tests are administered and their results are accepted as credible evidence for career counseling. Of the two most commonly employed vocational counseling tests, the Strong Vocational Test (as of this writing) continues to label such occupations as biologist, social scientist, architect, investment manager, and school superintendent as male on the final profile. The other commonly employed test, the Kuder Occupational Interest Survey, directs women who score high in the health professions to careers as dieticians, nurses, dental hygie-

---

[1]One of the argument used against allowing women into an industrial arts program is "that the unions won't let them work anyway" (Federbush, 1973).

nists, and physical therapists; careers in medicine, pharmacy, and dentistry are proposed for men with similar scores. Further, only by leaving the sex item blank can women learn about their aptitudes for the most important and prestigious occupations, such as law, business, management, finance, government, and medicine. Similarly, men can learn about their potential for the less demanding and less prestigious professions normally assigned to women only by leaving the sex item blank. That is, the test is designed to perpetuate the inheritance of occupations by gender regardless of the abilities and motivations of its takers.

Moreover, frequently the counselor's role is defined as "the facilitator of adjustment" (Fields, n.d.). Consequently, not only do counselors prefer helping students with traditional aspirations (Frazier and Sadlek, 1973:138), but they may use their position to discourage deviant life choices. For example, women who select woodworking may be confronted with, "You're really only interested in being with the boys, aren't you?" (Federbush, 1973:14).

However, as some argue, if indeed children are to enlarge their horizons and successfully buck the conspiracy of their socialization, the counselor's role should be redefined as one of *advocate*. From this perspective, the counselor's task is to take an active and visible stance throughout the school, providing discussion groups, non-sex-stereotyped career role models, non-sexist library materials, teacher's workshops in non-sexist education, etc. Such a counseling role recognizes the relevance of changing the environment so that students have a greater number of life options, rather than adjusting them to socially prescribed career molds.

In addition, the pattern of staffing in the schools tends to segregate the positions open to the adults working within the schools according to sex. For example, custodians are male; lunchroom servers, female. But more invidious, perhaps, is the fact that although 88 percent of United States elementary school teachers are female, 88 percent of the elementary school principals are male. Only 6 percent of high school principals are female, and the disproportions have been increasing over the past 70 years (Frazier and Sadlek, 1973:97). In 1971, only 2 women were school superintendents in the United States (out of a possible 17,000 positions); and more than half of the school boards had no women members (Frazier and Sadlek, 1973:97).

This pyramidical staffing teaches the teacher and the female students to limit their aspirations: there is no room at the top for women. More subtly, children learn that although their teacher, usually female, is in charge of the room, the school is run by a male without whose strength she could not cope; the principal's office is where the incorrigibles are sent. This learning, which parallels what many children have already learned in their homes regarding the roles of their mothers and fathers, only perpetuates further the notion that women require the leadership of men and that men should be able to provide that help. This learning, along with others, is even more intensely taught everyday in the classroom itself.

The child spends approximately 1000 hours a year in a particular school environment, the classroom. Within that setting, incidental learnings about gender are a major part of the hidden curriculum. Boys and girls are routinely segregated in different lines, play areas, and classroom lists, pitted against each other in academic and deportment contests, rewarded and punished as groups, and assigned different classroom chores (boys carry books, girls grade papers). Comments from boys that "they don't want to read about any dumb girl" or their refusal to stand near one for fear of "getting girl germs" go unnoticed and uncorrected by teachers who would sincerely reprimand children for comparable racial or ethnic slurs.

Non-consciously, teachers transmit differential expectations for the scholarly behavior of boys and girls. For example, in a study of junior high school teachers, the following list of adjectives were offered to characterize the differences between good male and good female students (Kemer, 1965).[2]

Adjectives Describing Good Female Students		Adjectives Describing Good Male Students	
appreciative	sensitive	active	energetic
calm	dependable	adventurous	enterprising
conscientious	efficient	aggressive	frank
considerate	mature	assertive	independent
cooperative	obliging	curious	inventive
mannerly	thorough		
poised			

Expectations of teachers for children's performances do have real consequences. For example, Rosenthal and Jackson (1971) told teachers that certain randomly selected children were destined for rapid intellectual growth during the school year. However, these children had the same range of intelligence scores as another group. At the end of the term, the children labeled as high-growth potentials had significantly higher I.Q. standings than those of the other group. The raising of the intelligence level is attributed to the fact that the teachers expected these students to blossom and, therefore, treated them differently than the control group. Further evidence of the impact of teachers' expectations has been reported by Seaver (1975), who found that younger siblings' academic grades were a direct function of the teachers' expectations based on their prior experience with older siblings.

In similar ways, the expectations for children by gender become self-fulfilling prophecies; people come to see themselves as others see them. Both genders learn that boys and girls have different capabilities and talents, that they should be separated, and that war of the sexes is inevitable. In short, their school experience is "separate and unequal."

---

[2]I wonder if the same teachers would ever have been willing to characterize the differences between say "good Polish students" and "good Irish students."

Curriculum Materials

In teaching subject matter, teachers rely on specially designed curriculum materials (e.g., books, study problems, and visual aids). While these materials may or may not be successful in teaching the formal curriculum, they are successful reinforcers of the informal one. For example, Child (et al., 1960) commented that children rehearse symbolically the episodes stories describe. That is, the informal content of the materials provide models and morals valued by the culture, in which the children vicariously engage. To the extent that stereotyped images of genders are repetitively presented in these materials children are being informally socialized into prescribed gender behaviors.

The images of genders presented in elementary school readers have been particularly well researched and documented (cf., Child, Potter, and Levine, 1960; *Women on Words and Images,* 1972). Like the preschool books discussed in Chapter 3, the readers teach gender-stereotyping. One of the most carefully designed and executed of these studies is that of Jacklin (et al., 1972). The researchers systematically sampled stories in the first through third grades of the readers of four major publishers. They found that male adults and male children occurred far more frequently than females. The most common main character was a male child. In terms of the behavior of children and adults, very different images were presented. *Boys* were significantly more often displaying aggression, physical exertion, and problem-solving. *Girls* were significantly more often engaged in fantasy, following orders, and making statements (positive and negative) about themselves. *Men* were significantly more often engaged in constructive activities, physical exertion, and problem-solving, whereas *women* were engaged in conformity and verbal behavior other than statements about themselves. Little boys, then, can imagine that their early aggressive behavior will be transformed into the constructive behavior of their fathers; little girls can expect that their fantasy and self-involvement will give way to adult womanly interest in others and greater conformity.

Further, when comparing the readers from grade level to grade level, the authors find that the number of females decreases and the number of gender-stereotyped behaviors increases. That is, as the socialization process moves on through the grades, women become increasingly invisible, and the behaviors defined for boys and girls becomes increasingly stereotyped.

The classroom subject may change, but the informal curriculum of gender-stereotyping remains constant from kindergarten through graduate school. Even the texts for supposedly objective subjects like mathematics are blatant in their gender-stereotyping. For example, in a study of sixth grade texts from 1963–1974, Seeman (1974) found females were significantly under-represented and engaged in a significantly different array of behaviors than males. The behavior characteristic of females in the math books was sewing, housekeeping, teaching, food preparation, and, to a lesser but still significant degree, buying food and enjoying music, literature, and art. Male behaviors were characterized by leisure-time activities involving model toys and competitive sports, paper routes, yard work, farming, building, math, and science. Only in the most recent texts have there been any signs of change; in these girls now compete in sports, do math problems and travel, although still to a significantly lesser degree than males. Boys, however, are still unlikely to perform traditionally feminine activities like sewing and cleaning.

Perhaps the most telling research findings are those serendipitously uncovered by the American Heritage Publishing Company in preparing a new dictionary for children (1972). Five million words encountered by children in their schoolbooks were fed into the computer, which fed back citation slips with the word in its schoolbook context (Grahame, 1973). The study showed that the books eschew the universal *child* and carefully distinguish between *boy* and *girl.* And, as might be expected, males are more frequently cited than females. For example, when the overabundance of male pronouns (4:1) are analyzed in context, approximately 93 percent of them refer to actual male beings and not to the generic, indefinite *he.* "Moreover, no matter what the subject being taught, girls and women are always in a minority" (Grahame, 1973:12). Personality traits and role ascriptions also follow the expected stereotypic dimensions. Mothers are more common than fathers (although both are more likely to have sons than daughters); wives are more common than husbands. Further, "the computer citation slips contained the evidence that boys and girls were also being taught separate sets of values, different expectations, and divergent goals" (Grahame, 1973:13) along the stereotypic dimensions promulgated by the culture.

Throughout the curriculum materials in every subject, then, we find a consistent pattern—a pattern which differentially assigns students to lives based on their sex.

Sex segregation and sex-stereotyping in the school undoubtedly influence the life chances of children. However, because boys and girls are already well on their way toward gender-defined lives by the time they come to school, it will profit us to look at how the school is experienced by boys and girls. Not only are the objective outcomes of their education different, but so are their subjective experiences.

The Male School Experience

Although boys are developmentally approximately twelve months behind girls at age six and approximately eighteen months behind by age nine (Bentzen, 1966), both genders are expected to begin first grade during their sixth year and to progress uniformly from grade to grade. Consequently, in the beginning a boy is at a decisive disadvantage.

The boy is not ready to acquire the particular skills that are rewarded in the classroom, such as "coloring within the lines." Furthermore, the way he is supposed to behave is in direct contradiction to the behavior for which he had been previously rewarded. In school, he is to sit still, be quiet, keep his hands and belongings to himself, follow directions, and wait for the teacher to call upon him.

Consequently, the young boy is sent to a classroom for which he is developmentally and psychologically unprepared, which he comes to define as a "girl's world." (Kagan, 1964b). His school experience has no real importance to him and daily requires him to act in ways that are not encouraged at home. Little wonder that boys are more likely than girls to have learning and behavior problems at school (Bentzen, 1966).

Studies of reading, for example, indicate that boys are at least two to three times more likely to develop reading difficulties in the regular classroom (Frazier and Sadlek, 1973:93). However, in an experiment when children were removed from the classroom setting and taught by computers programmed to give positive reinforcement and to require all children to read the same amount daily, kindergarten boys performed better than kindergarten girls. But when they were returned to their regular classrooms, the boys were soon lagging behind the girls. Analysis of the interaction between the teacher and the children revealed that the boys were much more likely to receive negative comments (such as "Sit up!" "Don't play with your bookmark!") and were called upon less frequently to read than the girls (McNeil, 1964).

Observational studies in the classrooms repeatedly find the same pattern of teacher-pupil interaction. Boys are much more likely to receive negative comments, generally, and those comments are likely to be harsher than those addressed to girls guilty of the same offenses (Jackson and Lahadenne, 1971). Moreover, studies indicate that boys receive more attention of all kinds: negative comments, positive comments, instruction, and listening to (Frazier and Sadlek, 1973:91). That is, boys interact more, and more directly with the teacher than do girls. Some educators argue that this greater interaction encourages the boys to greater independence because they are interacting actively and directly with the teacher, who in turn is taking them, their questions, and their behavior more seriously than the girls' (Frazier and Sadlek, 1973:91).

Although this greater interaction may indeed lead to greater independence of thought and analytical ability, it certainly does not lead to greater success in terms of grades. Boys of the same intellectual ability as girls and who score as well on standardized achievement tests, nevertheless, receive lower grades on their report cards (Frazier and Sadlek, 1973:92).

School, therefore, is often an uncomfortable experience for the boy, and he may end up hating it, dropping out either in body or spirit. He has a constant struggle trying to make sense out of the contradiction between the two worlds of home and school. But despite his initial lack of success, as time goes on he is less likely to be an underachiever (Frazier and Sadlek, 1973:93). As he moves through high school, his academic achievement improves, and the occupational future looks increasingly bright.

But in addition to these classroom experiences, an important aspect of the male's school life is the emphasis placed on athletics. Young males, whether they choose to engage in competitive sports or not, are subject to the socializing impact of the societal norm: athletics are good for boys. By prepuberty, the male student is encouraged by the school (as well as parents and peers) to take up a sport, to join a team. If he does not, he is cajoled, shamed, and ridiculed; and if he does, he is also cajoled, shamed, and ridiculed.

Witness the chilly fall afternoon in which a Midwestern sixth-grade football team pretended not to be discomforted by the degradation ceremony in which they were the sacrificial lambs. Proclaiming to team and onlookers (of which I happened to be one), their coach shouted: "This isn't just football we're playing. . . . It's Life! Trample and be trampled! The one with the guts is the one who wins—out there in the field and in life. And you're cowards. I want to see you out there: Pop 'em! Hit 'em! This is life, and there's no place here for *losers.*"

Although young boys are told that their success as athletes is an indicator of their potential success in life, it is at adolescence that athletic achievement becomes firmly linked to prestige for males (Coleman, 1961; Eitzen, 1975). It is the single most important factor for a male adolescent's social standing in high school.

Not only does athletic participation provide the male with prestige, team membership offers a kind of initiation rite which helps ease the transition from boyhood to manhood (Fiske, 1972). In team sport, for example, boys learn to sacrifice self for the team effort, to develop confidence through public demonstration of their skills, to dedicate themselves to hard work and concentration, and to identify fully with other males through the joint display of aggression, physical prowess, and courage on the playing field (Fiske, 1972). In effect, team sports socialize the male for occupational roles in two important ways. First, they incorporate into their own personalities the traits necessary for success on the field— competitive spirit, achievement orientation, courage, aggressiveness, endurance, etc. Second, they learn to identify with the team—male bonding through aggressive activity towards other males (Felshin, 1974). Team sports, therefore, are seen as developing a boy's ability to cooperate with other males in a competitive framework.

By learning these skills, the adolescent male is helped in his transition to manhood and occupational success. To the extent he can compete successfully on the field—trample others before they trample him—and to the extent he can recognize his identification with the team, he is being prepared to be a "man." In short, athletics as taught and practiced in the school posits masculine stereotypes of aggression, competitiveness, strength, and male-bonding as ideal and natural for boys (Shaw, 1972), and relevant to their success.

Embedded in the athletics-is-good philosophy is the notion that there is but one singular, monolithic life toward which men are oriented. But many boys are not built either physically or psychologically to achieve athletically. And the accent on physical prowess during adolescence can be extremely disturbing to the non-jock. Although there are social class differences, "the primary resource the young male has is still his own body" (Gagnon, 1976:173). He measures himself by what he can do physically compared to others his age, and how he stacks up determines to a great extent his social acceptance to others and his own self-esteem. The nonathletic boy is not only less likely to be a leader (Coleman, 1961; Eitzen, 1975), but more likely to doubt his masculinity and perhaps harbor resentment towards women, as this brief excerpt from Julius Lester's autobiographical comments suggest: "While humiliating myself on the football and baseball fields, the girls stood on the sidelines laughing at me, because they didn't have to do anything except be girls" (1976:270). Undoubtedly thousands of boys have sat waiting (and still do) to be picked for a team questioning their masculinity and believing as Lester did, "As boys go, I'm ... [not] much" (1976:270).

Although the need for physical strength is decreasing in the technological world and although there is some indication that competitive sports are less valued presently in middle- and upper-class high schools (Gagnon, 1976), the emphasis on them is still visible in school-corridor trophy cases and conversations, daily announcements, and pep rallies. Athletics has traditionally provided a path for upward mobility for working class males, and it continues to do so. Therefore, despite some changes in adolescent society's concern with competitive sports, the institutional supports for competitive athletics have not particularly diminished. There are still few structural avenues open to the non-jock to learn sports skills for their own sake.

Not only are athletics associated with masculine traits, male competitive sports enjoy the greatest organizational and financial support within the school. More money, time allocation, and physical facilities are provided for these activities than for either female competitive events or either sex's acquisition of general athletic skills. Coaches' salaries, players' uniforms, and provision of facilities for the male athletic teams are considered "legitimate line items in a school's budget," as "an essential element in the comprehensive package offered by the school" (Saario, Tittle, and Jacklin, 1973:409). Schools communicate in many ways not only that girls' sports are not as important in the total educational experience as boys' sports, but that the athletic development of boys who are not interested in competitive sports is of little consequence.

In summary, then, boys tend to experience their early years of schooling as difficult. If they remain in school, however, their academic performance tends to improve and their career goals enlarge. Once in high school, the pressure to perform athletically provides the skillful athlete with prestige and the potential for upward mobility; for the boy uninterested in competitive sports, the challenge is how to earn the respect of self and others and accomplish the transition from boyhood to manhood.

The Female School Experience

The classroom world of neatness, docility, and passivity, which boys experience as frustrating, is simply an extension for girls of those virtues for which she has been previously rewarded. Unfortunately, these classroom virtues have little to do with the intellectual enterprise. Although the girl feels subjectively more at home there and is better able to meet the developmental and behavioral requirements of the teacher, the outcome in the long run is destructive. If the girl learns well the "stylized version of the feminine role" presented to her in the early grades, then the rewards "can be almost too successful in that in later years it is difficult to move girls beyond the orderly virtues learned in their first school encounters" (Bruner, 1966:123–124).

Rather than attempting academically difficult problems, many girls tend to avoid them, fearing failure and the subsequent loss of teacher approval. For example, in one study where failure was experimentally manipulated, girls and boys were asked to put together two seven-piece puzzles in one and one-half minutes. As soon as the subject had completed one puzzle and had two pieces joined on the other, time was called. When given the option to work on the puzzles again, girls were much more likely to choose the puzzle that they had already mastered, whereas boys more frequently chose the one they had not completed (Crandall and Robson, 1960). As Frazier and Sadlek comment, "For good grades and teachers' praise, the grade-school girl relinquishes the courage that it takes to grapple with difficult material. This naive young bargainer of seven or eight has made an exchange that will cost her dearly" (1973:96).

One of the costs is a declining I.Q.: children who show declining I.Q.s are passive, shy, and dependent (Maccoby, 1963). The school, through its reward system for docility, in effect robs the girl of her intellectual abilities. Another cost for the young girl is her perception of limited life options. For example, in a large survey of upper-elementary school children, practically all career choices made by girls were in one of four categories: teacher, nurse, secretary, mother (O'Hara, 1962). Boys' choices were dispersed and often fanciful.

When girls reach puberty, they are more likely to become underachievers (Maccoby, 1966). Even if they make good grades, they are less likely to see themselves as college material than are boys with similar grades, and are less likely to plan to go to college (Frazier and Sadlek, 1973:140).

If a girl becomes pregnant, she is likely to join ranks with the 200,000 other high school girls who annually drop out from school due to maternity. Only approximately one-third of the school districts have any kind of continuing education program for these women (Frazier and Sadlek, 1973:130).

The school athletic experiences of girls are different enough from the boys' to warrant discussion. The facilities, conditioning, coaching, and training of the female athletes has traditionally been inferior to that provided for the males. In effect, "learning that she should not be athletic is what makes the female inferior athletically—not the other way around" (Wilmore, 1974:40). In a series of experiments, Wilmore, a board member of the American College of Sports Medicine, concluded that for the three major components of athletics—strength, endurance, body composition (lean-fat ratio)—"there are few actual differences between the best female and male athletes when tested in the laboratory" (Wilmore, 1974:81).[3]

---

[3]Another aspect of Dr. Wilmore's research bears comment. When he and his colleagues trained nonathletic male and female college students through a ten-week weight-lifting program, the women

The female's lesser performance, however, can be attributed to "the degree to which the sport has been recognized or emphasized for women, and the time and effort given to coaching, facilities, and training techniques" (Wilmore, 1974:80). When facilities, training, conditioning, and coaching are equalized, the gap between male and female performances has been steadily closing. For example, several female Olympic swimmers in 1976 would have won silver and bronze medals if they had competed in the 1972 men's competition.

In addition to these rather clear and blatantly different treatments of male and female superior athletes, there are more subtle ways in which sports are culturally organized to exclude female participation—subtle ways in which the schools are, perhaps, unwitting dupes.

In order to succeed at a given sport, it is necessary to acquire a set of skills used in that sport. Most sports require skills based on certain body movements, "efforts in space" (Grunden, 1973a). That is, success in sport requires an ability to use the body in certain ways. For example, most sports that are available in this culture require direct, controlled, sudden, and strong motions emanating from a central body core. These movements allow the body to rise and advance in widening spheres and permit the player to move forward, upward, and laterally outward with speed and strength. Nearly all of our sports—hockey, football, bowling, tennis, basketball—require that repertoire of movement. Although the equipment, rules, and playing terrain differ, they all require similar body movements in the penetration of space.

These movements, the ones necessary for success in sports, are "not present in the daily movement vocabulary of most girls" (Grunden, 1973a:1). Girls, in learning to be women, learn how to move in a feminine way. This means they learn to move in a light, airy, and sustained manner. Movements are kept close to the body and, when projecting outward, they do so in a kind of "joint-by-joint" manner. (That is presumably what is described by the expression, "You throw like a girl.") The movement of the girl is not a sustained, strong one with the effort flowing from a center core throughout her body; rather there is either a jerkiness or a giving-into-gravity motion that signals femininity.

Consequently, when girls are exposed to sports, they are ill-prepared to be successful in them for two important reasons. First, they do not have the necessary movement vocabulary that sports require; and secondly, the acquisition of these movements requires that they move in ways culturally defined as masculine. To be successful at a sport means a woman is (movement-wise) defeminized.

The school sports program does not provide valid athletics for its women students, because it does not take into account the socialization of the female student. Such an athletic program would require teaching her "to explore movements that are concerned with aggression, the outside world . . . action and reach-

---

increased their upper body strength by 30 percent, *without* increasing their muscle bulk. Although they were still less strong than the newly trained men by body weight (7.6 percent), by *lean* body weight (weight without fat) they were actually 5.8 percent *stronger*. Incidentally, it is estimated that we only use 20 percent of our muscle power anyway.

ing out ... in order that she discover the range of movement and expression" (Grunden, 1973a:13). Only through such an expansion might girls learn to participate successfully in sports as they are now constituted. And only through such a program might the girls develop a movement vocabulary that can express confidence and strength in their daily lives and, consequently, allow them to act with greater freedom from gender-stereotyping.

In summary, although the girl experiences the early years of school as more comfortable than the boy, if she succumbs to the rewards, she is more likely to leave her school experience as docile, intellectually unmotivated, and with low self-esteem.

Some students go on to higher-education. What happens to them?

Higher Education

> "The admissions committee didn't do its job. There's not one good looking girl in the entering class."
> "Women are intrinsically inferior."
> "Somehow, I can never take women in this field seriously."
> "Any woman who has gone this far (in higher education) has to be a kook."
> "Why don't you find a rich husband and give all this up?"

These are but a sampling of the comments actually made to graduate and undergraduate women by their professors in universities across the nation (Harris, 1970:283).

In the classroom, a logic professor (illogically) distinguishes between "logic" and "female logic" (i.e., non-logic). A statistics professor anthropomorphizes the transformation of a double-peaked curve into a normal bell-shaped one as "a once busty woman who had breast cancer." Most of the students laugh. A woman professor draws all of her examples from her roles as wife and mother and her husband's role as college professor; her husband never mentions his familial relations. An English professor lectures on poetry and "pseudo-poetry," the latter written "for or by women." A male student's final rebuttal to a woman besting him in a seminar is, "Women just don't understand," and the male professor laughs. These are but a sampling of college classroom incidents reported by students in journals kept for a woman's studies course.

Professors' lowered expectations and open prejudice become self-fulfilling prophecies. If professors consider women innately inferior, less original, illogical sex objects who are better off married, might they not find the evidence to support their beliefs? Little wonder that, after four years of college, a woman's aspirations have decreased. Repeatedly, in studies of college women, "the encouragement or lack of such encouragement" is the catalytic agent toward achieving or not achieving ambitions (Almquist and Angrist, 1971). When these functions are combined with a high need for approval, the result may be the pursuit of a safe major. For example, one exceptionally talented senior woman explained her academic career as follows:

I came to college planning to get a Ph.D. in mathematics. However, I was disappointed when I didn't make the most advanced math class. I decided to major in astronomy. When I got a B in astronomy I decided it wasn't for me either. Meanwhile, I was getting A's in psychology, and a woman instructor encouraged me to major in it. Although I really didn't like it, I decided to become a social science major. I'll graduate with a 4-point in my major, but I wish I had stayed in mathematics.

This gifted undergraduate viewed her grades as indicators of approval to such an extent that they determined the course of her college career and her potential life options.

But in order to be exposed to these frustrations a woman must first be admitted to the university. And it is more difficult for a woman to enter college than a man. For example, it is estimated that women comprise 75 percent to 90 percent of the very qualified students who do not go to college. In a study of 240 colleges, women with the same qualifications as men were less likely to be accepted (Frazier and Sadlek, 1973:147). The reason? Universities adjust standards upward for females in order to achieve "sexual balance" (which usually means an over-representation of males). Higher standards for women are justified by the belief that women are poor risks, despite the fact that women earn higher grades than males and are more likely to complete their college careers (Harris, 1970).

If she is lucky enough to be admitted, she faces the next hurdle of financing that education. Women receive fewer fellowships and less financial aid than men and many of the best fellowships are "for males only" (Sandler, 1971). Although most upper-middle-class and upper-class families will assume the financial support of both daughter and sons through college, few consider the financing of a daughter through graduate or professional school as obligatory or desirable. Lower-class parents are likely to consider the education of their sons more necessary than that of their daughters. In fact, the greatest loss of intellectual potential is estimated to be from the lower-class daughters, who are not aspiring and do not receive financial aid. Part-time and returning students (due to age) are virtually eliminated from all federal fellowships; and these are most likely to be women. A married woman may be denied financial assistance because "her husband can support her," but the same reasoning is not applied to male students with working wives. Even the rules on many campuses that require women to live in supervised dormitories, rather than more cheaply in apartments, add an additional financial strain. Consequently, her education costs more (Roby, 1972).

If she begins to feel she doesn't belong, she is likely to have her fears confirmed, for there are very few role models with which to identify. Campuses are male-dominated by professors, administrators, and campus-elected leaders. Less than one-fourth of the university faculty in the nation is female, and they are concentrated in the lower rungs of instructors and assistant professors, and in such traditional female departments as home-economics and nursing (Roby, 1972).

In a recent survey, 100 percent of the presidents of coed universities, 97 percent of the graduate deans, 91 percent of the deans of students, 95 percent of the admissions directors, 96 percent of the registrars, and 100 percent of the development directors were male (Frazier and Sadlek, 1973:147). As Harris (1970:284) succinctly summarizes it, "The rule is a simple one: the higher, the fewer." No wonder female college students doubt that women are capable of superior academic achievement (Goldberg, 1968).

Women frequently find the barriers to their education at the undergraduate and especially the graduate levels nearly impenetrable. Added to those barriers are the social pressures upon her to find a husband—pressures which are especially heightened if she chooses to join a sorority. Although the evidence is unclear, at least some women "fear success," because every academic advancement is perceived of as endangering marital chances (Horner, 1972; Tresemer, 1973).

Although parental and peer pressures encourage women to marry, women, increasingly, have been resisting these pressures. For example, in a survey of graduating women that I conducted at Ohio State University, only 31 percent were planning on marrying within a year of graduation, 38 percent were planning life-long careers, 61 percent believed that women should be financially self-supporting whether married or not.

Unfortunately, despite the changing aspirations and expectations of women, as we shall see in later chapters, their chances for career success are not great.

Although men are probably more at home in college and although the demands of the academic program are more in keeping with the kinds of abilities they have already developed, they nevertheless face the increasingly mounting pressure of occupational preparation. If a man chooses to major in sociology, history, fine arts or English, the usual query is, "But what will you *do* with it?" Pursuing a course of study for the sheer intellectual pleasure is not acceptable, as a male he is expected to prepare himself for a career. If he plans on a postgraduate education, then he has to *make good* grades. As one male student explained when he asked to drop an elective, "I plan to go to dental school and I need a high grade-point average. I took this course out of interest, but I can't afford the C I'll probably earn in it. (Can I still sit in?)" In addition to the grade pressure, he knows he must make the right connections during this college period for jobs or graduate school, and he must make the important friendships that will aid and abet him in his career.

The pressure to perform academically in order to achieve occupational success are exacerbated by social pressures that he demonstrate his "cool" through success in dating, drinking, etc. The pressure mounts on him to finally shape up and take his reponsibilities seriously, but at the same time to be a "man." He can choose to lower his aspirations, and limit his extra-curricular life, but it may cost him social condemnation.

Children then are reared in a culture that assigns one set of traits to males and another set to females. The major agents of socialization—home, language, school, mass media—teach children what is expected for a member of their sex. The success of this socialization, however, depends in great measure on socially controlling the adults who socialize the young. In the following section, we will explore the nature of some of these social control mechanisms, which maintain the perspective of the culture in the actions and ideas of its adults.

Section Two
Maintaining the Culture: Ideational Elements

A child is born, taught a language, reared in a family and led through an educational system—along the way receiving the same messages which define for him or her how to act, how to feel, and what to believe. As we have seen, in order for a culture to be perpetuated the young must be socialized into the taken-for-granted attitudes, beliefs, and values of the culture. Such socialization is ensured because the child is psycho-biologically dependent upon the adult world. However, because human beings have volition, they can and do stray from prescribed paths and they can and do think heretical thoughts. Because indoctrination of the young is dependent on adults who are capable of deviant perspectives and behavior, in order for a culture to survive there must be strategies for enforcing the traditional among the adults. If the adults are not kept in line, the young will not be appropriately socialized.

It is authority structures that ensure the perpetuation of the culture among the adult population. Authority structures are of several kinds: scientific, legal, religious, economic, and political. In this section we will examine the first three—the scientific, legal and religious—with a particular emphasis on their ideational (ideas and values) components. In the last section, we will focus on politics and economics.

Religion carries with it *moral authority*, and frequently, threatens sanctions beyond the here-and-now on into eternity. Laws represent the formal codification of certain norms and mores and carry the *authority of the state;* to break the law is to risk social sanction, public punishment, and the loss of privileges. Science has the weight of empirical truth or pragmatic authority. To challenge scientific findings or to behave contrary to what has been declared to be normal, subjects one to ridicule or pity. These three authority structures—science, law, and religion—are effective methods of adult social-control. Disagreeing with them can result in ostracism (from Heaven or friends) or incarceration (in prisons or asylums).

As Marx argued, what is frequently proposed as moral/true/legal is often no more than an ideological rationalization for the interests of the dominant group. Further, what has been perpetrated as moral/true/legal in crucial areas of human concern rationalizes the theory of patriarchy. That is, many of the ideas posited as authoritative are simply "religionized/scientized/legalized" restatements of the cultural values we encountered in Chapter 1. These ideas, rather than representing absolute truth, are culturally relative and culturally dependent statements that in effect justify the existent social inequality between the sexes.

That this is so should not really surprise anyone; after all scholars, scientists, legislators, judges, and clerics are members of the society. As such, they do not act in value-free ways; rather, they bring their own socialization into their professional lives. Their values unwittingly impinge upon the kinds of questions they ask, the priorities given to research problems, the concensus they reach regarding reasonable proof—and in the most subtle and pervasive way of all—in their technical language.

In this section, we will look first at biological, psychological, and social-scientific knowledge systems, and then at religion and law. As we will see, science, religion, and law are not at odds with each other or with the culture as a whole in regard to gender-role reinforcement in adults. Rather, they stand as three boulders in a retaining wall: authoritative, powerful legitimators of culturally prescribed gender roles.

5

Biology and Society

One of the major strategies for maintaining cultural values is the repackaging of them as truths based on the research of scholars and scientists. As such, they are handed down matter-of-factly as wisdom from generation to generation, taught unquestioningly in the schools, and reiterated with conviction in the mass media. Doubting their veracity labels one "irrational," "ignorant," or "mentally ill."

If scientists and scholars remained sequestered in an ivory tower, their ideas would hardly concern us. However, their ideas do have direct consequences on our lives. Scientists and scholars provide definitions and descriptions of the world, establish the methodologies for apprehending it, and decide which areas of knowledge should be explored, thereby directly affecting the practices of journalists, doctors, social workers, and psychologists—all professional agents of social control and cultural maintenance. These knowledge systems and practices exercise control of the body, the mind, and structured social interactions.

Because the sciences of physics and chemistry have had such a remarkable impact on the material level of our existence, a kind of semi-sacred quality has been imputed to all of science. However, the findings of the biological, psychological, and social sciences do not have the same high level of reliability as the physical and chemical sciences. And further, for all sciences, that which is chosen to be studied or not studied is always influenced by the socio-historical context. Consequently, it behooves us to retain some degree of skepticism toward science and, on the subject of gender, to look for assumptions that may distort scientific findings.

In this chapter and the next, I plan to discuss some of the major systems of knowledge in terms of what they have assumed about the sexes, the consequences of these assumptions for the practice of medicine, therapy, and social justice, and to discuss some alternative views and practices.

Because most of our knowledge has been ideologically consistent with patriarchal values and has served to perpetuate that ideology in the world view of the adult, most of the alternative paradigms come primarily from feminist sources. I hope, however, to demonstrate that today's knowledge market is disabling for both sexes and that restructuring could lead to significant advantages for both.

Obviously, not all knowledge systems can be discussed in the confines of this book. Consequently, I have chosen certain aspects of the biological, psychological, and social sciences that meet four criteria: (1) the knowledge has a clear ideological bias, (2) the application of the knowledge has had consequences in the lives of laypeople, (3) alternative views have emerged, and (4) these alternative views have practical implications and applications. Whether the examples offered constitute a representative sample of knowledge systems is really not the question. For what I hope to show is how serious, extensive, and relevant the knowledge systems discussed have been in social control. We now turn to a discussion of the body, reproduction, and sexuality.

The Body

Our Bodies, Ourselves (Boston Women's Health Collective, 1972) is more than just a title of a feminist book; it is an elegant summary of a very important understanding. Our sense of our bodies—our knowledge about them, the pleasure we derive from them, and the joy or distress we experience when we contemplate them—is the basis upon which we build our self-image.

The cultural preference for males, as we have seen, has its tolling effects upon females. But more inclusively, the cultural definitions of attractiveness, the cultural inclination to limit and distort biological knowledge, and the cultural injunctions regarding sexuality and physical pleasure take their tolls on both males and females.

The perpetuation of ideal physical standards, which generally cannot be met, leads to self-doubt and self-denigration. The anguish of the young, middle-aged, and aging regarding how they look is endemic. Women are frequently concerned about their breasts—and for good reason—because they are often categorized and labeled on the basis of their cup sizes. Two comments, one from a small-breasted woman and the other from a large-breasted woman, are illustrative:

> ... Guys will get friendly with me and I'll really like them and then they'll say, Sorry, your lack of tits just turn me off. Here I am almost 30 and I still can't accept my flat chest. That's why I'm getting silicone transplants.
>
> ... When I was in junior high, I was always called a slut because I had big boobs. It was like I had no business looking like I did unless I put out; and they assumed I must put out because I looked that way.... I was a virgin till I was 22. And today, it happened again—these guys wouldn't let me pass into the restaurant just going on and on about me. I feel so dirty, so mortified and so guilty—like it is my fault. [The woman was crying in rage and guilt while retelling the episode.]

Although men are not as subject to the "sex object" assault as women are, they are subject to both the "sex object" refusal and the "social object" refusal.

Despite the changing values that permit young men to look "less manly," they are still subject *internally* (and, on occasion, externally) to doubts about their penis size or shape, doubts about their height or musculature, etc. That is, despite the freeing of the culture, persons still measure themselves and are measured by universal standards that usually cannot be met.

In the case of men, stereotypes about their behavior based on their body builds "is generalizeable across age, sex, and geographical location in the United States" (Lerner, 1969:366). Almost universally the male mesomorph—the one with a body build predominately of muscle and bone—is associated with socially desirable behavior, whereas his ectomorphic (thin and linear) and endomorphic (predominately fatty tissued) brothers are stereotypically associated with socially undesirable traits. (Lerner, 1969:363). The traits assigned each body type by college women is illustrative and is presented in Table 5.1. A review of Table 5.1 suggests that the male's body build is associated with behaviors and traits that go well beyond those one might reasonably expect to be body-related. Mesomorphs, for example, are not only seen as good athletes and soldiers, they are viewed as leaders, good friends, mentally healthy, and potentially the best fathers and doctors. In brief, a man's life chances are enhanced or limited based on the culture's interpretation of his body type.

Although children of different types are socialized differently and therefore

TABLE 5.1 Female Stereotypes of Male Behavior Based on Bodytype Frequency of Assignment of each Trait to each Bodytype*

Traits	Bodytypes		
The man who would:	Endo	Meso	Ecto
Assume leadership	8	77	5
Have many friends	30	55	5
Be the poorest athlete	75	0	15
Drink the most	68	11	11
Need friends the most	43	4	43
Eat the most	84	2	4
Be the most aggressive	18	63	9
Put his own interests before others	33	46	11
Endure pain the best	11	68	11
Make the poorest doctor	36	13	41
Make the best athlete	1	83	6
Make a poor father	33	16	41
Make the best soldier	0	87	4
Never have a nervous breakdown	22	61	7
Make the worst soldier	70	2	18
Be most wanted as a friend	6	77	7

Note: Endo = Endomorph; Meso = Mesomorph; Ecto = Ectomorph

*Adapted from Lerner, 1969:365. Reprinted with permission of the author and publisher. (Applying the Chi Square Test of Significance, Lerner found item 12 significant at .01; the rest of the items, at .001.)

develop differently (Lerner, 1969), the biological knowledge system has played a role in the perpetuation of the cultural standards upon which this differential socialization is based.

The role of the biological knowledge system in the perpetuation of these stereotypes begins with what appears to be simply an "objective" depiction of the physical characteristics of the "normal" male and the "normal" female (Hershberger, 1948:71) Accordingly, the "normal" male has broad squared shoulders, facial hair, bulging calves, blunt toes, small hips, heavy brow, and square jaw, whereas the "normal" female has sloping shoulders, bent arms, conical thighs, wide hips, small feet, demure nose, and slightly knocked knees. Accompanying the text are illustrations which clarify the descriptions.

These are presented as the typical, average, normal male and female; however, if we look around us, nobody really looks that way.[1] For what is being actually represented are the ideal offspring of the mating of statistical facts and cultural preferences. Unfortunately, these ideals, passing as normals, become the standards against which we measure our own physical deviances and "abnormalities." Not only do the billions of dollars spent on Mark Eden (breast-developers), Charles Atlas (muscle-builders), depilatories, hirsutes, silicone transplants, and cosmetics testify to the tyranny of the ideal, but more tellingly do the fractured self-images we carry with us when we judge ourselves as inadequate and imperfect.

Additionally, this knowledge system has distorted the facts concerning sexuality and sensuality, depriving many men and women of pleasure and causing them considerable confusion. By witholding information from the public—although perhaps unintentionally—medical and para-medical institutions prevent individuals from understanding their bodies, their feelings, and hence, themselves.

Reproduction

Although most children learn about human reproduction from older children, the knowledge system regarding human sexual behavior is officially written in the authoritative texts of biologists and sexologists. And although the sex tales handed

---

[1]The concept *normal* has two significant connotations in biology. It can be synonymous with *statistical average,* or *mean,* a statistic highly influenced by extreme scores. If all the characteristics of the human body are measured and separate averages computed for the male and females, a composite "average" male or female can be drawn. But no one individual male or female will look like that average. Further, the two sets of distribution of male and female scores will have considerable overlap. Put another way, for most characteristics, there will be greater differences *within* the sexes than *between* the sexes. Consequently, the depiction of normalcy is highly misleading.

A second meaning of the concept *normal* in biology is that a particular characteristic is widespread in the population and is important for species survival. In that it cannot be shown that most of the anatomical characteristics are relevant to the survival of the species biologically—and indeed it can be argued that the "normal" traits are a result of *selective-mating* due to *cultural* preferences—there is no reason to treat those characteristics as normal.

down by the already initiated, older and wiser child carry, a pecking-order authority, this authority is simple child's play compared to that which is given to the
scientist of human sexual and reproductive behavior. And just as the street knowledge is slanted and only partially true so is the knowledge propagated by the
scientist. As I hope to demonstrate, the conceptual language of reproductive
biology, as well as the questions it asks and the questions it does *not* ask are more
than just reminiscent of the cultural stereotypes associated with masculinity and
feminity: it is an exact replica.

The tone, orientation, and taken-for-granted assumptions of biology are well
illustrated in Herschberger's brilliant review of our society's male-oriented view
toward reproduction in contrast to a matriarchal society's viewpoint (1948). Selected examples from her work are presented in Table 5.2 on pp. 78–79.

In summary, in the usual, taken-for-granted account of impregnation, the male
sperm and organs are the central concerns. The sperm are manly little creatures
"single-minded . . . full of charm, resourcefulness, and energy" who decide to win
the egg, "the blushing bride" waiting receptively for the arrival of her suitors
(Herschberger, 1948:71). That is, the biological account of the sperm and egg is
strikingly similar to the social account of the mating process between men and
women. The egg is "feminine"—passive, receptive, helpless, waiting to be conquered—while the sperm is "masculine"—active, independent, daring, and selective.

Of course, the matriarchal accounting is also biased, aggrandizing the female
role and minimizing the male role in the reproductive process. And when reading
it, perhaps, we find ourselves laughing out loud. However, when we stop to consider how the socially accepted version of reproduction is received without even the
smile of irony, we can perhaps more fully recognize how totally ingrained the
ideological component of the biological knowledge system is in our own lives. This
masculine version of impregnation, however, is less ubiquitous than are the assumptions concerning "normal" sexuality, to which we now turn.

Sexuality

Persons are socialized sexually in the context of the culture in which they live.
Sexologists and biologists themselves are subject to a culture's predispositions.
Consequently, before addressing their work, we shall briefly review the process
of sexual socialization in this culture.

The process may begin as early as the crib, when anxious parents prevent
their infants from exploring their own genitals. Later, many children are specifically
told that their genitals must be always covered and never touched—for all practical purposes, viewed as nonexistent. Soon many children learn to associate the
words *dirty* and *bad* with their own genitals. Some would contend that this early
sex socialization "creates in the child, and subsequently in the adult, an elemental
negative attitude towards sexuality" (Johnson, 1968:63).

In regard to such practices as masturbation (and probably premarital inter-

TABLE 5.2   The "Facts of Life" as Usually Written Contrasted with a Matriarchal Cultural Perspective*

A Patriarchal Society Writes Biology	A Matriarchal Society Writes Biology
The simple and elementary fact behind human reproduction is that a fertile female egg awaits impregnation in the fallopian tube, and the active male sperm must find this egg and penetrate it.	The simple and elementary fact behind human reproduction is that the active female egg must obtain a male sperm before it can create life.
The female sex apparatus is a depression to receive the sex cells; the male organ is advanced in order to expel the cells.	The male sex apparatus is a tiny factory which continually manufactures sex cells for the female.
When the male becomes sexually excited by internal stimuli, his sexual mechanism is called into play. There is a spontaneous erection of the penis and the passageways from the testicles are thrown open.	When the female becomes sexually excited by internal stimuli, there is a spontaneous erection of the clitoris and a flow of blood into the fine sensitive tissues of the vagina. This causes a similar erection of the region and of the vulva, while the involuntary musculature of the vagina begins rhythmically to contract.
The sperm has a long way to travel through the vas deferens, through the penis, through the vagina and uterus, and finally into the tiny tube where the female egg is waiting.	The sperm is provided with a continuous enclosed passageway—thus making its conveyance as simple as possible. For the female, there is a remarkable gap—which the egg must traverse alone.
Nature has provided for this purpose an aggressive and active male cell. Each sperm is composed of rich and highly specialized material and is equipped with a fine wriggling tail which gives it the power of self-locomotion.	Because of the central importance in reproduction, the female egg has been provided with a size much greater than that of the male sperm. The female egg is actually visible to the naked eye and is the largest cell in the body. The male 'germ' cells are unbelievably small and must be magnified one hundred times to be visible at all.

course), it is as though our socialization procedures were masterminded by some evil experimental psychologist. Johnson suggests that if it were an experiment, the conditions of it would sound something like this:

> Arrange a most severe punishment for a certain behavior. But then, make the same behavior so rewarding that the experimental animal cannot quite resist it. Then, observe the avoidance, frustration, desperate action, and subsequent anguish of the animal as the punishment built into the experiment is administered (1968:69).

TABLE 5.2   The "Facts of Life" as Usually Written Contrasted with a Matriarchal Cultural Perspective (continued)

A Patriarchal Society Writes Biology	A Matriarchal Society Writes Biology
No less than 225,000,000 cells are emitted from the man's body with ejaculation.	The male sperm is produced in superfluously great numbers since the survival of any one sperm is improbable. The egg being more resilient, endowed with solidity, toughness, and endurance can be produced singly and yet effect reproduction.
When coitus and ejaculation take place, the male sperm, millions in number and each one swimming like a fish, begin their concentrated search for the egg.	At the height of orgasm, the uterus contracts, becomes erect, and prolongs its neck downwards dipping into the seminal fluid drawing up the semen to the vicinity of the egg.
The instant one of the sperm penetrates the receptive egg, the creation of a new human being has occurred.	Sometimes none of the sperm suits the egg. When an egg does select a male sperm, the sperm is required to shed its wisp-like tail. Nature seems to be insisting that the sperm sacrifice its independence for the larger destiny of the female egg. For the future, the new human being wholly depends upon the courage and acumen of the egg in establishing a placenta.
Many women say that they do not experience either pleasure or orgasm. . . . And from the point of view of function, it may be said that orgasm for women is a luxury. Whereas the satisfactory discharge of the male function of orgasm is indispensible for conception.	If a woman obtains orgasm before he obtains his, it is absolutely essential that she sees that he receives one. This is especially true if fertilization is desired . . . but, also, for the humanitarian reason in order to reduce the congestion of the penis.

*Adapted from Herschberger, 1948, with permission of the author.

That is, although children are sexual creatures (capable of deriving pleasure from their genitals), they are socialized to have negative feelings towards their own sexuality. Further, the cultural context in which this socialization occurs is one of intense preoccupation with sexuality—in the media, in advertising, and in adult conversations and humor. Children, therefore, are reared in the "context of a *sex-centric* society, which is at the same time profoundly *anti-sexual*" (Johnson, 1968:64). Such conditions are bound to create sexual problems.

Further, according to the traditional sexual code of our society there are four stages of sexual development. Before puberty, children are assumed to be *nonsexual*. During adolescence, the young are viewed as simply *asexual*—that is, capable of sexual experiences, but with that potential remaining dormant until marriage when they become *sexual*. In the later years of life, it is assumed that persons return to their original *nonsexual* stage.

This model of sexual development, of course, veers considerably from the actual behavior of persons. Pre-puberty children experience sexual arousal and often orgasm (although not ejaculation); adolescents frequently act on their sexual potential, and older persons can and often do remain sexually active (Johnson, 1968:60–84). Not only are guilt and anxiety consequences of this sexual code, but institutions are designed to enforce it, despite the actual needs of people. Examples are the routine prohibition against sexual liaisons in homes for the aged and sex education courses which stress the reproductive aspects of sexuality.

Although almost all manner of human biology has been subject to scientific study for generations, only recently has the human sexual response been taken into the laboratory. These studies—most notably, those of Masters and Johnson (1966)—have contravened many myths about sexuality we hold as a culture. Let us review some of the research findings that contradict the culture's teachings.

The society teaches that the male is more sexual than the female. Masters and Johnson find, however, that the female, if anything, is more sexual than the male in that her ability to experience multiple, intensive orgasms within a given time span is greater than the male's. Physiological measurements of the female indicate that each of her orgasms can be equally intense and as intense as the male's.

The culture has also misperceived the nature of orgasm. Members are taught that male and female orgasms are different; and that females have two kinds of orgasm, vaginal and clitoral. However, "Orgasm is orgasm" (Johnson, 1968:53). It consists of four stages—excitation, plateau, orgasm, and resolution. The orgasmic process is "not anatomically localized, but rather involves the whole body. . . . [T]he physiological events are the same" whether orgasms are produced by fantasy, masturbation, vibrator, or coitus (Johnson, 1968:50).[2]

Further, as has already been implied, the society teaches that masturbation is dangerous. Many children—probably boys especially—have been told that masturbation leads to pimples, loss of sight, hearing, hands, genitals, and sanity. Not only are these outcomes false, but Masters and Johnson suggest that masturbation is actually useful in helping people to overcome genital fears and in learning what sexually gratifies them.

There are several common folk beliefs about males' sexuality specifically. One is that penis size is related to sexual capacity; another that impotence is a sign that a man is not masculine. As for the first, there is no relationship between organ size, capability, or satisfaction to mate (Johnson, 1968:52). As for the other, impotence is usually the result of excessive fatigue, heavy drinking, and/or over-

---

[2]This is not to deny the importance of emotional relations; but in this chapter, the concern is not with loving but the physiology of sex.

anxiousness about sexual performance—all of which are characteristically associated with masculine activities.

Finally, there are two particularly disturbing misconceptions about intercourse —namely, that the man should be astride the supine woman and that simultaneous orgasm is the goal to achieve. As for the first, the female astride the male is more likely to lead to maximal female enjoyment; and as to the second, striving for synchronization may actually reduce a couple's pleasure.

Just what the consequences of the dissemination of these facts have been for sexual relationships is not totally clear. Some women argue that greater knowledge of their own sexuality frees them from dependence upon men for gratification. They see themselves in control of their own sexual needs. And some men report that women's greater knowledge and interest in receiving sexual gratification has threatened their own masculinity. Can they satisfy these "new women" capable of hours of orgasmic bliss? Should they try?

Some authors argue that the myth of the sexually passive woman (Koedt, 1976) will persist, despite the facts, because it is in the interest of men to keep women sexually dependent upon them. In other words, the quality of sexual life in general in our culture is a direct representation of the socially defined inequalities between the sexes. Given that our knowledge of sexual response has increased rapidly during the past decade, the question is to what extent have the professionals disseminated this knowledge, and to what extent have they retained the mythology of the culture.

Sex Manuals

In a careful analysis of the 18 best-selling marriage (sex) manuals since 1950, Gordon and Shankweiller found that "women have had their sexuality *defined* for them . . . but the constraints [for men] have been looser and fewer" (1971:459).

Although modern sex manuals do permit premarital sexual experiences and encourage pleasure and spontaneity, "sex is still assumed to take place within the social context of love and marriage" (1971:461), the latter according to Calderone "the most precious and deeply satisfying relationship we know" (1960:13). Consequently, extramarital relationships are rejected and "hedonism within the context of marriage is the new norm" (Gordon and Shankweiller, 1971:462).

According to Gordon and Shankweiller, the books of the late 1960s purport that men and women have equal sexual desire but that the nature of their sexualities are different. The manual writers, for example, assert "Men can enjoy sex—in an animal sort of way without love. Women can't, so remind her of your love often, in some way or another" (Hall, 1965:12). Such injunctions can result in self-fulfilling prophecies and filled the pages of student journals, as these two excerpts illustrate:

> Male Student: I try not to just lie to a girl, but the only way to get a good lay is to tell her you're falling in love with her. I sometimes feel rotten about it, but I also feel it's kind of true. I'm not telling her I *do* love her, and when I screw I kind of feel like I am *falling* in love.
> Female student: I've tried to go to bed with guys I've liked but haven't loved. It never

works out. I usually end up falling in love with them and he isn't feeling that way about me. . . . And then I hurt. I don't know if I make myself fall in love to justify going to bed with him or if going to bed with him makes me love him. I wish I could just enjoy the experience for its closeness and not get all hung up about it. I can't take the hurt.

Additional contributors to such self-fulfilling prophecies are the assumptions that a bride will be negative towards sex, will need the help of her more experienced husband, and is sexually, by nature, a late bloomer. Although women are urged to overcome their modesty, it is not for their own good, rather for the sexual pleasure of the man.

But, perhaps the most limiting of the manual writers' prescriptions are the continual references to the ideal of male leadership in sex. Males are told approximately 3.5 times more often than women what to do and how to do it (Brisset and Lewis, 1970:42). They are warned not to forget that they are men even when emotionally excited because "your sex life and your marriage will suffer if you allow [manly self-assertion] to be smothered and overrestrained by such qualities [as gentleness and consideration]" (Eichenlaub, 1968:82). In the long run, Eichenlaub argues, the most considerate thing for a husband to do for his wife's physical and emotional good marital adjustment is to become an assertive masculine figure (1968:82).

Neither sex, therefore, is being liberated from socio-sexual dogma; neither sex is encouraged to act beyond the domains of their socialization. Even the findings of Masters and Johnson have been ignored. Clitoral sex is suggested as a technique for gerontological sex (Gordon and Shankweiler, 1971:463), but the orgasmic potentialities of women and the implications thereof are virtually ignored. As Gordon and Shankweiller summarize their findings, "Women . . . have been offered a conception of their sexuality that has not allowed it to follow its underlying physiology" (1971:465).

In these manuals, men are encouraged to achieve sexually; inactivity and overemotionality are negatively sanctioned. Even in sex, the male is cautioned to keep his cool, to remain in control of the situation. Women are encouraged to provide pleasure for their husbands.

Most recently, a number of popular sex manuals have reached the mass market such as *More Joy* (Comfort, 1974). In these, greater freedom is allowed to both partners to explore their own and each other's sexuality. However, other aspects of female sexuality have been virtually ignored. It is to these experiences —childbirth and lacation (nursing)—that we now turn.

Childbirth and Lactation

The full range of a woman's sexual experience has been little discussed. As the work of Niles Newton (1973) has demonstrated (and as many women will attest) women are "trebly sensuous." Their sexuality includes three major functions: coitus, parturition (labor and birth), and lactation (nursing).

Because nursing is a voluntary act upon which the survival of the species has depended, it is logical for nature to have designed it to be pleasureable. Nursing mothers repeatedly report the sensual pleasure experienced in breast-feeding (Walum, 1972). And that pleasure is not just imagined, for certain physiological changes occur during nursing that are comparable to those that occur during orgasm—contraction of the uterus, the erection of the nipples, the stimulation of the breasts, vascular and skin changes, and a raised body temperature. In addition, nursing mothers report a greater interest in sex than nonnursing mothers (Newton, 1972).

Because childbirth has been advertised in our culture as a painful process that requires expert medical help, it can be shocking for some to discover that it is sexual. And, yet, Newton has demonstrated, by analyzing comments made by *undrugged* mothers and by studying the physiological changes that occur during parturition, that childbirth can be an orgasmic experience. Some women report the experience as the "most incredible orgasm ever." The similarities between intercourse and orgasm and the experience of undrugged childbirth are presented in Table 5.3.

This is not to argue that medical complications never occur in childbirth; nor do I suggest that obstetricians have no role to play. Obviously, the course of gestation and delivery is not perfectly predictable. Therefore, it is both fallacious and potentially dangerous (to the physical and psychological health of the mother) to establish natural childbirth as the goal to which all pregnant women must aspire. Rather, what is being argued here is that our taken-for-granted assumptions about childbirth limit the kinds of experiences women might have during the birth process.

Coitus, parturition, and breast-feeding all are sexual experiences based on neuro-hormonal reflexes; as such, they are affected by the environments in which they take place. If intercourse were on a schedule, limited to so many minutes, and occurring in a semi-public place with the participants partially clothed, it is unlikely that many people in our culture would find it sexually satisfying. Yet, what I've just described is the culturally prescribed way for engaging in nursing. Similarly, if intercourse were to take place in a brightly lit room with both parties drugged, their feet in stirrups, their hands strapped to a table, supervised by a sterile helper who manually or with forceps joins the members, few people would consider the experience as a "joy of ecstasy." And yet, this is our culturally preferred way of childbirth.

Consequently, even in the most basic of biological functions, the knowledge which is transmitted not only perpetuates dependence, helplessness, and frailty but, incredibly, robs the woman of experiencing the fullness of her sexuality. By the writ of authority, sexuality is reserved for her experiences with males; her other experiences as a sexual creature are not acknowledged.

Medical Practice

The writings of the biologist and sexologist, in turn, become content in the textbooks for the applied-biologist, the medical doctor and, in particular, the gynecolo-

TABLE 5.3 Some Similarities Between Sexual-Intercourse and Undrugged Childbirth*

Undrugged Childbirth	Intercourse and Orgasm
Breathing	
In early stage, breathing deepens. In later stage, deep breathing and breath holding.	During arousal, breathing becomes deeper and faster; during orgasm, breath–holding.
Vocalization	
Grunts, noises during later labor stage.	Gasping, sucking, grunting as orgasm approaches.
Facial Expression	
As birth approaches, face becomes strained, intense. (Some interpret it as "pained.")	As orgasm approaches, face becomes strained, eyes glassy (what Kinsey calls "tortured expression").
The Uterus	
Rhythmic contraction of upper segment.	Rhythmic contraction of upper segment.
The Cervix	
Mucous plug loosens.	Mucous plug loosens.
The Clitoris	
Becomes engorged from full dilation through birth.	During arousal and intercourse becomes engorged.
Abdominal Muscles	
Contract periodically during later stage.	Contract periodically.
Sensory Perception	
The vulva becomes naturally anesthetized; woman frequently can't feel baby's head emerge.	Body becomes increasingly insensitive to pain.
Become oblivious to surroundings; natural amnesia as delivery approaches.	Become oblivious to surroundings, loss of sensory perception, sometimes loss of consciousness as orgasm approaches.
After delivery, the woman becomes suddenly fully awake, energetic.	After orgasm, sudden return of sensory awareness.
Emotional Response	
After birth, "joyful ecstasy."	After orgasm, strong feeling of well-being.

*Table adapted from Niles Newton, 1973:24; used with permission of publisher.

gist. Incidentally, only 6.8 percent of gynecologists are female (*Time* magazine: March 29, 1972:89). Notably, there is no medical speciality for male sexual problems; these are handled under the rubric of urology.

With a title and degree, the gynecologist becomes enshrined as the officially legitimate specialist on women, their needs, personalities, and illnesses. Apart from learning what the culture teaches about women, the obstetrician-gynecologist learns from the official guidebook, the gynecology textbook. Scully and Bart report a content analysis of 27 such texts (which incidentally have changed little over the past 125 years, despite the work of Masters and Johnson). According to their analysis, "these texts continually define female sexuality as inferior to male sexuality, insist that 'aggressive' behavior in women is abnormal, and maintain that it is inherent in the female essence to submit to the male." (1972:10-11).

Traditionally, the medical profession has enjoyed a *legitimated* monopoly over the health of the population. Medical doctors have controlled entrance into their profession, resisted any external regulation, reserved the right to define and label diseases, the right to decide which clients and which problems are legitimate, and the right to determine which medical problems deserve research priority. In short, doctors have enjoyed a monopoly over knowledge, diagnosis, service, treatment, and research in health (Thorne, 1974). And this monopoly has been used to perpetuate cultural stereotypes. Not only are women defined as "constipated bipeds with backaches" and doctoring women considered "dirty work" (Bart, 1974), but common phenomena such as menstrual cramps, morning sickness, lactation difficulties are not considered important enough to deserve research priorities (Thorne, 1974).

Alternative Views and Practices

However, alternative models and practices have been developed and disseminated. Primary among these are the new theories concerning female sexuality and its implications, along with the institutionalization of para-medical social movements challenging the traditional monopoly of medicine.

Perhaps one of the most inventive of the new theories of female sexuality is that advanced by Sherfey (1966). She asks, "What does it mean in terms of the evolution of humankind and the structure of societies that women are capable of inordinate cyclic sexual capacity ... leading to the paradoxical state of sexual insatiation in the presence of the utmost sexual satiation" (1966:229). She hypothesizes that while the aggressive sexual behavior of early primates might have been an important factor in overcoming adaptive barriers leading to the evolution of humankind, it perhaps stood as a major impediment to the rise of civilization because "women's uncurtailed continuous hypersexuality would drastically interfere with maternal responsibilities and with the rise of settled agriculture economies" (1966:229). Consequently, social structures were invented to curtail the female's natural sexual insatiability. Two of the primary ones today—monogamy and deferred sexual activity—although directly contrary to the feminine biology, are functional for the survival of the family and hence of the society.

In effect, Sherfey is proposing that civilization is built upon the tethering of the female's sexual nature. To unleash this female sexuality, she suggests, will have consequences well beyond the bedroom, "the magnitude" of which "is difficult to contemplate" (1966:222).

Less abstract and radical in consequence is the resocialization language suggested by Shulman, who argues that although we have been taught that sex organs are used to create babies, "This is a lie. In our society, only occasionally are those organs used to make babies...." (1972:292).

Further, borrowing from her perceptive analysis, what a difference it would make in the expectations and attitudes of men and women if boys and girls were told something like the following about their sex organs:

> A boy has a penis; a girl has a clitoris. It feels good when the penis is touched, and it feels good when the clitoris is touched. The boy uses his penis for feeling good and making love, for reproduction and for urinating. The girl uses her clitoris for feeling good and making love, her vagina for reproduction, and her urethra for urination (1972:292).

In a more general context, men's and women's attitudes toward their sexual relationships are culturally learned; and their sexual responses are culturally conditioned. As Ford's and Beach's cross-cultural study of sexual behavior shows, there is a wide variety of sexual activities and symbols (1951). Because sexual response is culturally transmitted, it is capable of being more harmoniously tuned to physiology. But in order to effect a change in more than a few persons, it is necessary to alter radically the present cultural value structure.

In addition to alternative theories concerning sexuality, such social movements as La Leche League, Natural Childbirth, and self-help centers have offered alternatives to the traditional practice of medicine. Although these social movements differ ideologically on many points, they share in common the perspective that women have a right to experience their bodies and that these experiences constitute *bona fide* knowledge which can and should be discussed with others. Through these movements, women have shared "secrets" about their bodies, appropriated the medical knowledge concerning their reproductive biology, and distributed that knowledge along with their own personal experiences to other lay-people through books, pamphlets, courses, group meetings, and demonstrations, challenging the monopoly of the "M.D.-iety" (Thorne, 1974).

For example, La Leche League is an international organization that was founded in 1958 to improve mothering through breast-feeding; it has enrolled over one million women. Although ideologically traditional in most respects, the league has consistently challenged the authority of the doctor in the area of lactation, nutrition, and infant-mother relationships (Marshall and Knafl, 1973; Walum, 1973). Because breast-feeding is not common, the folk knowledge that was once routinely passed from mother to daughter has been lost. As the new knowledge giver, medical doctors know little or nothing about the practical aspects of breast-feeding or the psychological and biological benefits to mother and infant; they too readily assume that any difficulty with the infant can be traced to the mother's milk and order a bottled substitute (Walum, 1973). La Leche offers nursing mothers an alternative.[3]

More recently, there has been a growth in the self-help movement, a movement that has "seized the technology without the ideology" of medicine and placed it in the hands of laypeople (Bart, 1974). For example, within such centers women can learn to diagnose themselves as well as use the feminist doctors and paramedicals on the center's staff.[4] The oldest of these centers, The Feminist Women's Health Center of Los Angeles, accused and acquitted of "practicing medicine without a license," plans on opening a hospital shortly.

Although these self-help centers have been primarily developed for and by women, the model could be adopted for males as an alternative or adjunct to traditional medical practice. Although it is falsely argued that men do not need special treatment because nothing is hidden in the recesses of their bodies, consider for a moment the prostate: Where is it? How do you know if something is wrong?

Further, even traditional medicine is coming to realize that the more the patient knows about the cause, course, and symptoms of the disease as well as about the side effects of the medicine, the more quickly the patient recovers and the less severe the side effects. (*Columbus Dispatch* July 7, 1974). That is, by encouraging the patient to become a knowledgeable *advocate*, the practical outcomes for patient and practitioner improve.

In summary, satisfactory sexual lives of men and women depend upon knowledge of anatomy and physiology. Further, the application of the culture's ideology by medical personnel limits their ability to help their patients as well as their patients' ability to help themselves. Perhaps through the new self-help movements, a greater understanding of "our bodies, ourselves" will help us all reach—and enjoy—our potentials. Biosexual behavior takes place in the broader cultural context of social inequality between the sexes. We turn now to the role the psychological and social sciences play in the maintainence of this institutionalized sexism.

---

[3]For those interested, write La Leche League International, 9616 Minneapolis Ave., Franklin Park, Illinois 60131.

[4]*The Monthly Extract: An irregular periodical* (New Moon Publications, Box 3488, Ridgeway Station, Stanford, Connecticut, 06903) is the primary communications medium for the self-help clinics.

6
The Psychological and Social Sciences

Body imagery is socially learned, and cultural preferences regarding the body are buttressed by the science of biology. Similarly, personality traits and social roles are socially learned, and reinforced by psychology and social science. Although there are many forms of psychology, we will look at clinical psychology, and examine some underlying assumptions about mental health for men and women. Following that we will look closely at the discipline of sociology and briefly at history and research into the social behavior of animals. Major attention is directed towards sociology, because its consequences for adult socialization are particularly clear. Further, the social sciences tend to share common methodologies, theories, and assumptions. What is true of sociology is also, at least partially, true of the other social sciences.

Clinical Psychology and Psychiatry

From the 1950s onward, the moral and religious categories of good and evil have been increasingly replaced by the psychological categories of mentally healthy and mentally ill. Modern soothsayers are psychiatrists and clinical psychologists—missionaries of Scientific Doctrine from the Temples of Medicine and Academia. Yet with too few exceptions, the psychological theories espoused as scientific have not been tested in carefully designed experiments (Weisstein, 1971), nor are they formulated in a way that permits them to be nullified. That is, despite their tone of scientific respectability most psychological theories are not, in actuality, within the scientific tradition.

Further, there is no evidence to show that the practice of psychotherapy cures patients (Eyesenck, 1955; Barron and Leary, 1955; Cartwright and Vogel, 1960).

On the contrary, untreated "neurotics" have a higher remission rate than the treated ones.[1]

Nevertheless, despite the lack of reliable scientific evidence, the putative theories of clinical psychology are seriously discussed with little questioning in television, newspapers, magazines, child-guidance pamphlets, and classrooms. Wherever we turn, we find the theories presented as facts, reinforcing rigid rules for gender behavior.

Theories and Therapies

The theories and therapies designed to help people are legion; and it is certainly beyond the province of this book to explain and comment upon them all. Consequently, as a starter, I will let clinicians who have made major contributions to current psychological thought speak for themselves.

SIGMUND FREUD

Women refuse to accept the fact of being castrated and have the hope of someday obtaining a penis in spite of everything . . . I cannot escape the notion . . . that for women the level of what is ethically normal is different from that of man.

The work of civilization has become more and more men's business . . . What he [the male] employs for cultural purposes he withdraws to a great extent from women and his sexual life; his constant association with men and dependency on his relations with them even estrange him from his duties as husband and father (1930:73).

ESTHER HARDING

[Women's real goal is the] creation of the possibility of psychic and psychological relation to man . . . It is a significant turning point in [the successful women's] relation to a man, when she finds that she can no longer look him frankly in the eyes, for it means that her real feeling which may not be shown openly has begun to stir: . . . (1933, quoted in Chesler, 1972:78).

JUDITH BARDWICK

It is pathological when the male, having achieved an erection, is unable to achieve an orgasm . . . (1970:11).

The absence of a powerful sex motive in women is a logical extension of the anatomy of the female body (1970:12).

ERIK ERIKSON

[T]he identity formation of women differ[s] by dint of the fact their somatic design harbors an "inner space" destined to bear the offspring of chosen men and, with it, a biological, psychological, and ethical commitment to take care of human infancy. . . . (1968:266).

CARL JUNG

[Female] psychology is founded on the principle of Eros, the great binder and deliverer; while age-old wisdom has ascribed Logos [rationality] to man as his ruling principle (1928, quoted in Chesler, 1972:77).

---

[1]For example, Eyesenck (1955) found that neurotics treated by psychoanalysis had a 44 percent improvement rate; neurotics treated by psychotherapy had a 64 percent improvement rate, and those receiving no treatment had a 72 percent improvement rate.

JOSEPH RHEINGOLD
> [W]oman is nurturance ... anatomy decrees the life of a woman. ... When women grow up without the dread of their biological functions and without subversion by feminist doctrines—and therefore enter into motherhood with a sense of fulfillment and altruistic sentiment—we shall attain the goal of a good life and a secure world in which to live (1964:714).

BRUNO BETTLEHEIM
> Naturally, boys are more ready to fight ... [but] nature, physiology, and biology go just so far. They have to be encouraged to go in the right direction (1972).
> It's the mother who creates the predisposition for both boys and girls because natural-ly she is the one who takes care of the infant. But she should also have entirely different expectations about the future and personalities of the boys and girls (1972).

Notions about the natural differences between men and women as presented by these therapists and subsequently propagated are common place, repetitious, and tyrannical. Many of these clinical theories have been influenced by Freud's analyses of psycho-sexual development, which can be summarized simply: Geni-talia are destiny. Essentially, women are "breeders and bearers", occasionally generous of the spirit, but more likely "cranky children with uteruses, forever mourning the loss of male organs and male identity" (Chesler, 1972:79). The "masculinity complexes" and neuroses of women, are simply spiteful refusals to accept their naturally passive, morally defective natures. Successful manhood, on the other hand, requires overcoming the Oedipus complex (sexual attachment to the mother) and castration anxieties by sublimating the superior power of the (sadistic) phallus into the creation of civilization (Freud, 1930). Indeed, the theory of psycho-sexual development seems to be an intellectual reincarnation of what little boys supposedly believe about girls' "lost penises" and the consequent threat to their own (cf. Horney, 1967).

Clinical Ideology

Critiques of Freudian biological destiny theories are, at this point in history, almost as popular as the Freudian theories themselves (cf. Millet, 1970; Weisstein, 1970; Cooper, 1970; Szasz, 1970); and the numbers and kinds of therapies have multi-plied. Therefore, rather than looking only at the Freudian ones, I will discuss what appear to be central elements of a *clinical ideology*—a value system that unifies theoretically disparate clinicians and which (perhaps, unconsciously) guides their therapeutic practices. Like the hidden curriculum of the educational system, this clinical ideology carries with it presumptive truth; it is considered by practitioner and layperson, alike, to be scientifically correct. In this discussion, I draw heavily upon the work and analysis of Phyllis Chesler (1972).

One of the primary elements of clinical ideology is a belief in a double stan-dard for mental health. In a study of clinicians' judgments of mental health, Brover-man (et al., 1970) found that mentally healthy *men* and mentally healthy *adults* were attributed with the same set of socially desirable personality traits. Women, on the other hand, were deemed mentally healthy only if they did not have these (socially-desirable) traits. (See Chapter 1, pp. 8–10, for a more complete descrip-tion of the study.)

Secondly, clinicians treat procreation and child-rearing as exclusively female. Widely asserted in the theory and practice of therapy is the idea that women need to have children in order to be fulfilled and that once children are born, they need to be cared for by the mother. "The absoluteness of this conviction is only equaled by the conviction that mothers are generally 'unhappy' and are also the cause of the neurosis, psychosis, and criminality in their children" (Chesler, 1972:73). That is, women are simultaneously blessed and damned. Not to want to bear and nurture children is sick, but, if the offspring are disturbed, it is the woman's fault. Paternity and fathering, on the other hand, are apparently nonessential to men or children.

Even in our current climate of sexual liberalism, only certain forms of sexuality are legitimate. By many clinical standards, it is not mentally healthy for a woman to be promiscuous, to bear children out of wedlock, to be lesbian, or to be paradox-ically either seductive or sexless. Prostitutes are male-avengers, girls who experi-ence rape or incest bring it upon themselves through seductiveness, unwed mothers are immature, and promiscuous women are nymphomaniacs. Similarly, premature ejaculation, other forms of impotency,[2] homosexuality, Don Juanism (but not promiscuity) and sexual passivity in the male are suspect. In short, sexual behaviors that do not conform to those defined as normal by the paternalistic culture are seen as counter-productive to the happiness of the person and symptomatic of illness.

Not only is nonstereotyped sexual behavior considered aberrant in women, but in addition, women are judged mentally ill if they reject the stereotypes for their gender (Chesler, 1972:56). Such women are characteristically labeled schizo-phrenic, lesbian, promiscuous, or simply neurotic. Professionally employed women are neurotic because they behave in masculine ways such as swearing, drinking, acting competely, and "consorting with [their own] spouses who accept such behavior" (Rickles, 1971). Female schizophrenics are more dominant and aggressive than male schizophrenics or normal males and females (Cheek, 1964) and are more satisfied with their masculine strength than with their feminine parts (McClellend and Watt, 1968). Angrist (et al., 1968) compared normal housewives with those who had been hospitalized for schizophrenia. The ex-mental patients were more promiscuous, more aggressive, and less sociable than the normals. In brief, schizophrenic and angry women reject feminine role stereotypes.

Even behavior modification techniques (which are scientifically based) are used predominately to help individuals *adjust* to prescribed roles. An example from the files of one such therapist is illustrative:

> Mr. F. incessantly complained about his wife's lack of grace in handling the evening meal. . . . Mrs. F. grudgingly agreed that there was room for improvement and I

---

[2]*Potent* means "able to act." What a psychologically threatening—indeed, castrating—label is the word *impotent.* Note further that women can't be impotent, because it implies they can also be potent.

instructed her to start using a tablecloth nightly. . . . After one week . . . Mrs. F. had increased her performance to the complete satisfaction of her husband, who meanwhile had continued to give her positive support for her progress.

Mr. F. felt that his wife should do more sewing . . . and should iron his shirts. . . . Mrs. F. was fed up with the home they lived in, which was much too small. . . . I instructed Mrs. F. to begin to do more sewing and ironing and Mr. F. to reinforce this by starting to consider moving to a new home. . . . He was to make it clear to her that his interest in a new home was contingent upon her improvement as a homemaker (from the American Journal of Orthopsychiatry, quoted in Ms., April, 1974:97).

Not only is the woman to adjust to her prescribed domestic role, her behavior is the one considered in need of modification. That is, the question of whether the husband's requests are valid is not raised, and the idea that she make it clear to him that her improvement as a homemaker is contingent on his improvement as a home-finder is not even considered.

Although women are deemed ill if they reject their prescribed role, both men and women are judged mentally ill if they act out the female role (Chesler, 1972:-56). The female role, as we have seen, is not highly valued in this culture. If men act out that role by behaving in dependent, passive, sexually inactive, and timid ways or by choosing a male sexual partner, they are considered sick. If treated clinically, they are categorized as "schizophrenics" or "homosexuals." And, paradoxically, even if women fully act out their prescribed role, they are considered to exhibit character disorders, neuroses and psychoses. The major symptoms characteristically female are depression, frigidity, chronic fatigue, suicide attempts.

Depression is anger turned inwards,[3] the female role prohibits aggression toward others. It is safer and more feminine to be depressed than to be physically violent. Frigidity is the final feminine outcome of sexual repression. Chronic fatigue is a way of passively striking back, a technique employed by "slaves" (submissive women) against "masters" (domineering men) that allows them to "put their burdens down" and become even more helpless, frail, and dependent (Szasz, 1961). Female suicides are more frequently attempted than completed. Aggression—even in this most private and desperate act—is difficult for women to effectively express:

Like female tears, female suicide attempts constitute an essential act of resignation and helplessness. . . . Suicide attempts are the grand rites of "femininity"—i.e., ideally women are supposed to "lose" in order to "win." Women who *succeed* at suicide are tragically outwitting . . . their "feminine" role and at the only price possible, their death (Chesler, 1972:49).

For both men and women, then, acting out the devalued female role is to be mentally-ill.

The final element of clinical ideology that we will examine involves the differential evaluation of males and females as contributors to the society: Women are

---

[3]The anger is usually considered a result of loss. For a perceptive analysis of depression in middle-aged women as a result of "social role loss," see Bart (1975).

socially expendable; men are socially necessary. Practitioners tend to consider the dysfunctioning male as more of a loss to the society than the dysfunctioning female; an incapacitated female is a loss only to the family (Chesler, 1972:65). One of the outcomes of this differential evaluation is a greater denial of male dysfunctioning (Chesler, 1972:38–39). Seeking help is not masculine, and males are not encouraged to put themselves in the dependent child-parent relationship found in therapeutic practice. Therefore, men do not usually seek help until late in the disability.

Further, because interpersonal dependency is considered nonmasculine, many difficulties experienced tend to become submerged in drugs and alcohol. Ironically, the ultimate consequence is severe disability: between the years of 1964 and 1968, 75 percent of the hospitalized alcohol addicts and 64 percent of the hospitalized drug addicts were male (Chesler, 1972:42). Or, as an even more direct and insidious alternative to seeking help, males commit suicide; 70 percent of suicide victims are men. To the end of their "self-taken lives," they remain independent of others, as they act out their socially prescribed masculine roles.

Seeking help is consistent with the feminine role. As a result of such seeking and of the understanding that she is socially expendable, women are committed to mental hospitals (Chesler, 1972:38–39). While in the asylum, the patients are degraded and stripped of any sense of self (Goffman, 1961) and subject to "medication, surgery, shock, and insulin coma treatment, isolation, physical and sexual violence, medical neglect, and slave labor" (Chesler, 1972:34). And as Chesler laments, women feel at home in the asylum, where they can, at least, be wholly disenfranchised from their selves, totally dependent and cared-for.[4]

Lastly, what has been referred to as "the final solution to the women problem" (Roberts, 1972), psycho-surgery has reemerged simultaneously with the reemergence of a feminist movement. The procedure includes the destruction of healthy brain tissue in order to alter emotional and behavioral states. "The widest target group, according to all large-scale studies is women . . . 72 percent of the psychotics and 80 percent of the neurotics" (Roberts, 1972:14). Although some hospitals in Canada have discontinued performing lobotomies on men due to poor publicity, female lobotomies there continue. In an admonishing report to the U.S. Congress (Congressional Record, February 24, 1972), Dr. Peter Breggins explained that the remarkably large percentage of female lobotomies was justified on the grounds that creativity, which is utterly destroyed by the operation, is "an expendable quality in women" and that lobotomized women continue to make good housekeepers.[5]

In summary, then, clinical ideology reflects and reinforces the ideas about

---

[4]It is beyond the province of this book to discuss the degradation ceremonies of the asylum but, for the reader who is interested or who doubts the veracity of these paragraphs, see Chesler (1972), Goffman (1961), or Szasz (1970).

[5]*The Stepford Wives* (Levin, 1972) is a chilling novel on this theme.

gender. These ideas, sanctified by science and popularized by journalists, function as effective social-controls.

Clinical psychologists are not the only ones who have the patriarchal world views of the culture in which they were raised. Sociologists have also been similarly socialized.

Sociology

Until very recently, sociology has taken for granted many cultural assumptions about sex and gender that are reflected in its theories, paradigms, and research priorities. Although these assumptions have led to an increased understanding of certain areas of social life, they have blinded researchers to other aspects. The extent of the limitations of traditional sociology have been critically analyzed in a collection of articles entitled *Another Voice* (Millman and Kanter, 1975). In the introduction to the reader, Millman and Kanter summarize some of the major reasons why sociology has a limited understanding of the social worlds of men, of women, and of men and women. (See also Daniels, 1975; Lipmen-Blumen and Tickameyer, 1975.)

One important reason for sociology's limitations stems from its research priorities. Much of sociology focuses on the public, formal, and official aspects of social organization. The sociology of the interpersonal, private, and informal is rarely examined, and—until very recently—when it was studied, little interest was paid to the effect of sex status on the style and content of social interaction. On the face of it, however, many of the activities of women and men in this society take place in local, informal, and private settings. Consequently, not only do we have limited knowledge of the informal spheres of social life, but research priorities hinder sociology from coming to grips with the "interplay between the informal, interpersonal networks and the formal official social structures" (Carlson, 1972, quoted in Millman and Kanter).

Until recently, the culture's stereotypes of masculinity and femininity were inherent in most sociological theoretical models. Although sociologists have begun to question these models, the core ideas are still well entrenched in the substantive content areas of sociology (Kirschner, 1973). One of the building blocks is the notion of *instrumental* (task-oriented) and *expressive* (social and emotional) roles, which are assigned, respectively, to the male and to the female. It has been argued that this role division is necessary for human interaction and for the survival of the social system. Such ideas are more than merely descriptive; they quickly become prescriptive.

Embedded in the formulation is the belief in male superiority (Millet, 1969:-229). Not only are men assigned the more highly valued tasks, they are ascribed more desirable personality traits such as assertiveness, originality, and competitiveness which are associated with the performance of instrumental roles. Such ascription has consequences for the perpetuation of male dominance in the political and economic spheres (see Section III). Further, by assigning males the instrumental roles, they are encouraged to suppress their expressivity which, in turn, has consequences for the interaction between males and females.

Several further comments need to be made about this bias in sociology. Although the role analysis provides a prescription for appropriate behavior, it offers no empirical basis for determining how to categorize a particular behavior. On what grounds can the household activities of chauffering, check-writing, book-balancing, financial management, shopping, and housekeeping be classified as expressive, and the dining and wining of clients by male executives be considered instrumental? That is, the acts that men and women perform in daily life may be identical; the only grounds for differentiating them by gender is an ideological one.

Further, there is an assumption that if the males perform the instrumental tasks and the females the expressive ones, the division of labor between them will make them good (functionally interdependent) partners. This assumption finds its way into both the public and private spheres. At the office, a man needs a (female) secretary; a woman needs a (male) boss. At home a man needs a wife to tend to his physical and emotional needs; a woman needs a husband to financially support her. The ramifications are visible in political, economic and familial institutions (see Section III).

Implicit in the model is the view that the individual, alone, is not a complete(d) person. To become "whole" a person needs a member of the other sex. Such a formulation limits the areas of growth for an individual and prescribes that the social unit is (should be) the mixed-sex couple. In all probability it also limits the level and kinds of exchanges open to the male-female couple. By following the prescriptive norms, each party tends to see the other as filling or not filling the obligations as role performers ("He is a good provider," "She is a fine cook"); and further, they tend to see themselves in that fashion as well ("I am a good provider," "I am a fine cook"). Functional interdependency may lead to greater societal stability, but it does not enhance the possibility of intimacy. Further, in that the category "male" is viewed as superior to the category "female" it is unlikely that equalitarian relationships will exist (see Section III).

Nowhere is this normative bias more obvious and its effects most easily understood than in traditional marriage-and-family literature. For example, Ehrlich (1971) concludes, after a survey of six recent college-level texts, that the "female as viewed by the American male sociologist of the family belongs at home, ministering to her husband and children and foreswearing all other interests" (1971:-430). Although she does not detail the stereotyping of the male in these books, even a cursory overview of them suggests that genders are being cast into prescriptive roles. For example, Saxton writes, "The worst role failures are the husband-father's failing to provide income and material security and the wife-mother's failing to fulfill her nurturant and household duties" (1968:239). A major failure to fulfill one's role leads to "marital disruption" and "disturbed children" (Saxton, 1968:372).

Leslie clinches the presumed stresses caused by unconventional role alignments by stating:

The same husbands who rationally admire their wives accomplishments may [desire the apparently] ... comfortable marriage relationships that they think ... [are] enjoyed by men who have less talented wives. The phenomenon of the successful career woman cast aside by her husband for a less able but far more dependent woman is far from unknown (1967:575).

That is, both sexes are being set up in these texts to identify with particular role performances, to feel guilty if they violate them, and to demand of each other proper role behavior lest their marriage be disrupted and their children ruined.

More generally, as Ball (1972) argues, this literature reflects the Judeo-Christian ideals of what a family should be—rather than what it is. And, more insidiously, the concept assumes a prescriptive quality, so that any deviance from the ideal is seen as a social problem. For example, when a family is conceptualized as a living unit based upon a legitimate marriage, undertaken with the idea of permanence, reciprocal economic obligations, common residence, and the rights and duties of parenthood, such occurrences as homosexual unions, concensual unions, divorce, separation, and childless marriage are viewed as social problems (see Chapter 11).

However, as Ball suggests, we can refocus the lens and view the family *as sociologically defined* as a social problem. Then, we can reconceptualize it through an empirical assessment of the kinds of units that people *do* create to ensure adult sexual gratification and the perpetuation of the species, and explore the kinds of problems these arrangements generate as well as various possible resolutions. The researcher, thereby, is directed to the kinds of negotiations and accommodations that participants engage in to reduce the potential strains and enhance the pleasures of living together.

As discussed in Chaper 1, gender is both prescribed and chosen. But what is true for gender, is also true for any status—wife, student, teacher, father. Holding a given status *prescribes* certain options; but, the degree of psychological investment, acceptance, or rejection of those options is a matter of *choice*. Consequently, in terms of living together, apart from economic survival, the major problems for individuals—and hence the problems that a humanistic sociology should be concerned with—is the *gap between the prescribed and the chosen*.

Conflicts are attempts to close those gaps. In this context, then, neither the Men's nor the Women's Liberation Movement can be viewed as social problems leading to the demise of the family. Rather, they can be seen as attempts to *redefine* the prescribed so that the subjective experience might be different. The social problem, in *subjective* terms is how to move the prescribed closer to the chosen.

History

Historiographers, who are concerned with the methods of historical accounting and the interpretations given to facts, have long recognized that history as a discipline has an inherent problem—namely, historians rewrite history, not only as new data is discovered, but as new world views emerge. That is, history is *interpretative*, and those interpretations are grounded in a particular world view. Hence, the same events will be explained as the act of the gods, or of a God, or results of political, economic, demographic, or social conditions, depending on when the historian lived and wrote.

However, in one world view, the historians have been rather consistent—namely, the interpretation of history from a patriarchal point of view. "History has been the record of those who control other people's lives" (Rosen, 1971:541)—the history of military, economic, and political leaders and not the history of ordinary people's lives. Consequently, women, children, and everyday life are almost invisible in historical writing.

The writing of prehistory has had, further, a particularly patriarchal bias. Archeologists, social historians, and others have attempted to reconstruct humanity's beginnings. This history declares that cave*man* invented civilization, enslaved women, protected the family, devised the fine arts, and created religion.

However, as the work of Elizabeth Gould Davis indicates, the evidence from prehistorical times can be interpreted quite differently. In an inventive analysis of archeological finds and mythologies, Davis argues that women were "the first sex" existing prior to and independent of males, who were "mutants, freaks, produced by some damage to the genes" (1972:35). Men were the weaker sex, subservient to women, entrusted with the unimportant task of hunting, while women created and nurtured civilization—agriculture, milling, weaving, potting, cooking, animal domestication, and decorative arts, including cave painting. Women, not men, Gould argues were the stimulus for the arts of industrialization and the providers for the household; early civilizations were matriarchal, advanced, and peaceful. In the beginning, and in "the natural order of things" women are superior.

Although her analysis may be somewhat distorted, so is the more conventional male-oriented view of our primitive beginnings. The crucial point is the fact that the tales told as truth evade crucial facts which have consequences for both men and women.

The invisibility of women in the archives of history insures their invisibility as historical personages in novels, Sunday supplements, television shows, and obituaries. The visibility of men in history, however, enlarges the *reference group* against which men compare themselves. With any sense of history, the average-to-talented male mathematician, businessman, or politician comes to recognize how minor a person he is compared to all the great men in history. Because males are socialized to achieve success in the world at large and because history provides them models of the greats, their accomplishments, in effect, are devalued. Just as only few males will make it to positions of power and prestige in the occupational world, even fewer will be of historical consequence, as the discipline of history is now construed. For men, then, the field of history provides but another pressure for accelerated performance, and other ideals that cannot be met.

Social Behavior of Animals

From approximately the 1960s onwards, there has been an interest in the study of primates in order to unravel the mysteries of humankind. One of the primary conclusions of these studies has been that the stability of the primate culture depends upon the dominance of the male and the nurturance of children by the female. These conclusions have been quickly applied to the human species by such authors as Tiger and Fox (1971). They argue that there is a primate species differentiation between males and females, which psycho-biologically directs males into dominance-striving and females into child-bearing and rearing. "Females are more interested in infants than in hierarchies, are unable to organize themselves or their activities without male stabilization, and engage in dominance interactions that tend to be inconsequential squabbles" (Lancaster, 1973:5). Males who compete successfully win a high position in the hierarchy and a disproportionate share of the females.

This type of conclusion drawn from primate studies, however, is judged by one ethologist as "simply a scientific statement of folk beliefs about men and women" (Lancaster, 1973:5). Further, these conclusions have been reached on the basis of sampling bias and insufficient observation (Lancaster, 1973:5).

Adult male primates, although large in size, are small in number in any given animal troop. Because most observational studies, like most historical studies, have focused on the behavior of the *male* rather than on the females and offspring, they have incorrectly concluded that the social behavior of the male is equivalent to the social organization of the group. Secondly, such studies require at least one year of careful observation, which early primate studies truncated.

However, in the late 1960s, observational studies of long duration suggested a different major element of social organization in primate societies: the mother-infant bond. As these long-term field and captive studies suggest, "It is the matrifocal core that provides a primate group with stability and continuity" (Lancaster, 1973:6). Although adult males travel at the head of the society, *decisions* regarding the route the troop will take comes from the center of the group where other males walk with adult females and young infants. Further, a monkey's place in the group dominance hierarchy is "based on its mother's identity and its birth order among siblings" (Lancaster, 1973:7). And finally, females also form coalitions against aggressive males. In fact, the male role is so small in importance to the family and society that the troop needs only one male to play it. Because the male will venture off and leave the troop, the stable members, the females, familiar with the dangers and resources of the environment, are probably the functional leaders of the primate society.

Not only have long-term studies discovered the leadership role of the female in the troop, but very recently researchers have observed fathering behavior. In a series of studies with captive primates, it was found that not only will males nurture the young, but they frequently develop stronger attachments to the children than do the mothers; and interestingly, the fathering role is reportedly thera-peutic for those monkeys who had been raised by chicken-wire mother surrogates.

In short, the kinds of questions asked in animal research have determined the kinds of answers found. Although the way we choose to study animals tells us a great deal about our own human social organization, it is doubtful that the social structure of primates will in and of itself tell us anything about the "proper nature" of human social behavior.

Alternative View: The Idea of Androgyny

Perhaps while reading parts of this book, you have wanted to shout, "But, that's not true of me!" Recently, the social and psychological sciences have also come to that realization: not all males are masculine, not all females feminine, nor is the occasional gender-reversed person deviant (Bem, 1972). They have come to this viewpoint by readdressing some of the most basic assumptions of their disciplines and by testing them empirically.

One of the most powerful concepts to have recently emerged is that of *androgyny* (from the Greek meaning male and female). The idea of androgyny is that persons can be *both* masculine and feminine, both aggressive and gentle, active and passive, instrumental and expressive, depending on the requirements of the situation.

The notion of androgyny conflicts with several popular beliefs. First, it denies that masculinity and femininity are two ends of the same continuum. Rather, it suggests that they are separate dimensions, each potentially available to men and women. Second, it questions the concept of traits, implying instead that individuals, by and large, are not consistent types but respond appropriately to the varying demands of situations. And third, it directly challenges a latent assumption in most social and psychological research: sex-typing is good for the individual and for the society.

So much of social-psychological and psychological research has been con-cerned with the acquisition of gender, that the researchers have not asked whether maintaining sex-typed differences actually enhances social, psychological, intel-lectual, or behavioral attributes. In reviewing the scant literature relevant to that question, Bem concludes that not only does sex-typing not enhance the develop-ment of people, but that "a high level of sex-appropriate behavior may even be harmful" (1972:5).

Cross-sex typing is strongly correlated, for example, with higher intelligence scores, greater spatial ability, and higher creativity in both boys and girls (Maccoby and Jacklin: 1974). That is, girls with more masculine components and boys with more feminine components tend to do better on intellectual activities.

In terms of mental health, high femininity in girls and women is associated with high anxiety, low social acceptance, and poor social adjustment (Bem, 1972:6). In the only large-scale mental health study of masculinity, Mussen (1961) found that high masculinity in late-adolescent boys was associated with better social and psychological adjustment than low masculinity. However, in the follow-up study 20 years later, the high masculine group showed less self-acceptance, more need for abasement, less self-assurance, and less likelihood of being leaders than the low masculine group. These results have been corroborated by Harford (et al., 1967), who reports positive correlations in adult males between high masculinity and anxiety, guilt, and neuroses; low masculinity he found associated with emotional stability, sensitivity, warmth, and brightness. Although other studies of masculinity and mental health have produced contradictory findings, there is enough research evidence to question whether masculinity is unequivocally good.

If sex-typing is dangerous to one's mental health and intellectual development, is it also detrimental to one's behavior? According to both Kagan (1964) and Kohlberg (1968) (also see Chapter 3), individuals who are highly sex-typed are more motivated to exhibit behavior that they view as consistent with their image of masculinity or femininity. In effect, they are carrying around an evaluative standard of masculinity and femininity by which they judge themselves and by which they assume others are judging them. Presumably, behavior that contradicts this self-image (e.g., a man crying, a woman asserting power over a man) is constantly monitored and repressed. Such individuals are likely to exhibit a kind of traitlike consistency as a defense mechanism. Research studies in this area, however, suggest that people who are defensively motivated to present a particular image tend to respond to somewhat similar situations as if they were exactly the same (e.g., responding to all red-haired men in the same way as one did to his or her redheaded father.) Consequently, they succeed less well at many tasks that require sensitivity to the actual situation and that require behavior inconsistent with the traits the person associates with his or her self image (Mischel, 1968).

Pulling these various threads together, we are confronted with a number of research questions. Do androgynous individuals actually exist? Are masculinity and femininity at opposite ends of a single dimension? Or do they belong in separate dimensions? If so, how are they related to each other? And finally, are androgynous people better off than those who are highly sex-typed?

Spence, Helmreich, and Stapp (1975) have found some intriguing answers to these questions through the development and administration of an androgyny scale. First, androgynous people do exist—approximately one-third of their college sample (n=530) were androgynous. Second, rather than finding that masculinity and femininity were opposites, they found they consisted of separate dimensions; and rather than being negatively associated with each other, they were *positively* correlated. Third, they explored whether androgyny was related to self-esteem. Defining androgyny as *high* scores on both masculinity and femininity, Spence reports that androgynous students had the highest self-esteem. Persons who were *low* on both masculinity and femininity had the lowest self-esteem, and persons high on one dimension but low on the other scored in between. (High masculines/low feminines had higher self-esteem, however, than low masculines/high feminines.) These results held for persons of both sexes.

The conclusion is that "androgyny . . . may lead to the most socially desirable consequences," because such individuals possess the "strengths of both components (masculinity and femininity), influencing attitudinal and behavioral outcomes for the individual" (Spence et al., 1975:35). Hence, at least in terms of positive attitudes toward oneself, androgynous people seem to be better off than nonandrogynous ones.

However, the next question is whether androgynous persons are less behaviorally restricted than highly sex-typed people? To explore this issue, it is necessary to review the work of Sandra Bem and her associates. Although Bem's androgyny scale is constructed differently than Spence's, they are similar in item choice. In one experiment sex-typed males and females and androgynous males and females were given the opportunity to perform a common sex-typed activity (e.g., nailing a board, ironing a cloth napkin) or a neutral one (e.g., playing with a yo-yo). Masculine men and feminine women were significantly more likely to choose the stereotypical activity for their sex than the androgynous students. Further, the highly sex-typed students reported greater nervousness and anxiety when required to perform the cross-sex activity than did the androgynous persons (Bem, 1967). Further, Bem and her associates have been exploring the broader dimensions of masculine independence and feminine nurturance in a series of laboratory experiments. In the four experiments thus far reported, they have found that androgynous persons of both sexes exhibit masculine independence when under pressure to conform (Bem, 1975) and feminine nurturance when allowed to interact with a kitten (Bem, 1975), a human baby (Bem et al., 1976), or provide sympathy to an adult in distress (Bem et al., 1976). Masculine males were low in nurturant behavior and feminine males low in independence. Similarly, feminine women were low in independence, and in two of the experiments masculine women were low in nurturance. That is, feminine individuals of both sexes were behaviorally limited in independence activities, masculine individuals of both sexes were behaviorally limited in nurturant activities, and androgynous individuals successful in both areas. Sex-typing, then, would appear to have negative consequences for both males and females by restricting their competence in performing various tasks.

Clearly, the research on androgyny is just in its beginning stages. There is so much more for us to know. However, I think we will soon lay to rest the question "Are there androgynous people?" The statistical and experimental findings already have successfully challenged the notion of opposite genders. And, many of us have recognized in ourselves and our friends the androgynous spirit.

Rather, the next set of research priorities needs to be directed toward discovering the correlates of androgyny, the conditions under which it is nourished, and the conditions under which it is preferable to sex-typing. Assuming that the research will continue to support the value of the androgyny for both the individual and for the society, the task will be the discovery and implementation of policies and practices that will support its development. One of the major tasks, therefore, will be the job of legitimatizing androgyny through the resocialization of agents of social control.

If successful, we will no longer be living in the rather dull world of sex-typing, nor will we be living in the even duller world of "unigender." Rather, because a greater number of possible skills would be encouraged in both boys and girls, men and women, we will create a world that is richer for its diversity.[6]

---

[6]Many males and females have commented recently that women have become much more interesting than men. I would hypothesize that the women referred to have moved towards androgyny, and that more women have moved in that direction than men.

7
The Law

A paradox is the law, simultaneously freeing and constraining. Without rules of order and mechanisms for their enforcement, anarchy would result. The most powerful would be safe, but everyone else would be subject to terror. And yet with laws, individual autonomy is less. Most scholars would agree, therefore, that some laws are necessary to preserve a semblance of social order. And hence the paradox: only through constraints can there be freedom.

The task of preserving social order belongs to the state. And as such, the state has the right to determine the nature of the constraints, that is, to legislate. Further, the state is expected to enforce those laws—to arrest, prosecute, judge, and punish offenders. As such, it has a legitimate right to violence. Consequently, it is a powerful agent of adult social control.

The power of the legal system as a social control mechanism, however, does not primarily rest in its ability to deter crime or to reduce recidivism. Indeed, in some studies, crime rates were found to vary directly with the severity and frequency of punishment (Wilson, 1966:567). Rather, the power and importance of the legal system is its impact on the law-abiding—the offended rather than the offender. As Durkheim argued a century ago, the function of punishment is to reconfirm the culture's values, to kindle in the law-abiding a renewed commitment to conduct consistent with the value system. "Punishment is only the symbol—a language through which either the general social conscience or that of the authorities expresses the feeling inspired by the deviant behavior" (Wilson, 1966:568).

As for what laws are righteous, there is an unquestionable association among legal statements, a society's norms, and the interests of the powerful. Laws stand as the formalized and enforceable symbolic representations of the culture's preferences, ideological stances, mores, and norms. As such, they justify inequality and protect the powerful. And although it is probably true for all areas of law, perhaps, nowhere are the norms and laws more "intimate and reciprocally influential" than in the area of male and female relationships (Kanowitz, 1966:4). The presumptions about the differences between the sexes taken for granted in the culture are formalized as the rationales for *legal discrimination* between them. As Kanowitz argues, laws that pertain directly to the sexes "inevitably produce far-reaching effects ... upon male-female relationships beyond the limited confines of legislative chambers and courtrooms" (1966:4). The irrelevant differences emphasized in the law influence the content and tone of the social and power relationships between the sexes, as well as their legal relationships.

Although there is a mirroring of social norms and legal norms, in a changing society this reflection is far from perfect. Old laws remain on the books, unenforced and perhaps unenforceable—such as those specifying the positions of married partners during intercourse. And new laws that are inconsistent with the culture's norms are sometimes introduced. However, because a major function of the law is to bind together the law-abiding, a change in the law can have a substantial impact on changing the norms.

Obviously, there is no way to legislate prejudice, only the overt acts of discrimination. But if a lesson can be drawn from the effects of the changed legal system regarding racial integration in the school, we might expect that public sentiment favoring sex equality will increase *subsequent* to the changed policy; and in those areas of the country already oriented toward such policies, the official policy in and of itself will speed the process of social acceptance. As Hyman and Sheatsley summarize this process in regard to racial integration (based on a statistical trend analysis) "apparently, the pattern is that, as official action works to bury what is already regarded as a lost cause, public acceptance of integration increases because opinions are readjusted to the inevitable reality" (1970:413–414).

Although the focus of this chapter is on the legal system, it will be profitable for us to consider briefly the question of crime itself from a gender-role perspective. Criminologists have considered two general forms of criminal behavior: so-called normal crime, such as homicide, burglary, and assault, and white-collar crime. The latter refers to purposeful nonviolent illegal behavior to obtain financial or other advantage such as tax evasion, price-fixing, and consumer fraud. Both forms of crime are more likely to be committed by males than by females. For example, in 1972, 85 percent of all arrests were males.

One theory used to explain the overrepresentation of males on police dockets is the theory of differential opportunity. The theory proposes that in order to commit a certain offense, an individual must have the opportunity to do so. That opportunity results from one's social and occupational roles (e.g., executive vs. housewife, soldier vs. nurse, factory worker vs. cashier). The roles one is likely to fulfill both within and outside the criminal world are a function of sex stereotypings. Shoplifting, petty theft, and forgery, for example, are crimes associated with females; murder, assault, safe-cracking, loan sharking, etc., are associated with males. There is probably "no more macho group than the traditional 'family' units of organized crime" (Adler, 1975:12). A Mafia woman is a property of her father to be exchanged in furthering underworld alliances, a showcase for her husband's status, or a supportive mistress—but she is not a "hit woman" or a "Godmother."

Watergate is an excellent modern example of how the combination of different opportunity and sex-typing works. In Watergate we find a great range of criminal behavior, including the wedding of normal with white-collar crime. The only suspected female participant was Rosemary Woods, the president's private secretary. The burglary, phone-tapping, money washing, executive organization and cover-up all were accomplished by males. The kind of normal criminal activity required is that which is sex-typed male; and in that powerful positions within the government are also sex-typed male, no women took part at the executive crime level. The argument here, of course, is not that men are less moral than women, but that they have access to different positions which give them a greater opportunity to engage in all manner of crime.

Currently, however, the rate of female crime of all kinds is going through a dramatic upswing. "By every indicator available, female criminals appear to be surpassing males in the rate of increase for almost every major crime" (Adler, 1975:15). Although males commit a greater absolute number of offenses, the female rates of crime are growing at a rate 6 to 7 times that of males (Adler, 1975:15). For example, in 1950, 1 out of every 10.6 arrests was a woman; in 1972, 1 out of every 6.5 arrests was female. In 1953, about 8.5 percent of property offense arrests were women; in 1972, women constituted more than 21 percent of those arrests. The explanation offered is that as women adopt a more liberated definition of self and enter new occupational roles, they have a greater opportunity and desire to engage in traditionally male crimes. The high rate of growth of property, financial, and white-collar offenses among women support this view (Simon, 1975:40). According to Adler (1975) women are no longer reluctant to move up in the criminal hierarchy.

In what follows, the focus will not be on the differential criminal activity of males and females. Rather, the concern is in the areas of the law in which legal inequality based on sex continues to exist. We will examine the assumptions that justify these laws and discuss some of the newer legislation designed to alleviate sex discrimination.

Domestic Law

Domestic law is based upon the premise that women and men fulfill different functions in the home and that, therefore, different laws are applicable. The outcome is that both men and women are discriminated against in ways consistent with the culture's presuppositions about men and women.

Discrimination against men begins with a wedding license. In some states, women can marry at an earlier age. The reasoning behind such laws is that men are financially responsible for their families and need extra time to get established. In some states, only men are required to submit an affidavit proving them free of any contagious venereal disease. The legislators apparently believe that single women, as opposed to single men, *should* be virgins. As Kanowitz explains it, requiring women to submit proof of virginity allows for the "possibility that they have engaged in pre-marital sex relations. But, as all know, only 'good' girls or 'pure' girls are the ones who marry" (1969:14).

Once wedded, the law requires that the husband support his wife and family—the specification of what constitutes such support, however, is usually not spelled out until a marriage is dissolving (Kanowitz, 1969). In some states, wives have the duty of secondary support *if* their husbands become incapacitated, but the rationale for these laws is not to alter sex-stereotyping, rather to keep people off welfare (Kanowitz, 1969). If divorce occurs, in most states men are responsible for their own and their soon-to-be-ex-wives' legal fees and temporary alimony. Permanent alimony can be awarded only if a state statute specifically prescribes it. Very few states *permit* alimony to be awarded to the male. Custody of the children is almost invariably awarded to the mother on the grounds of "the best interest of the child." Unless the mother can be shown to be morally unfit, it is taken for granted that the mother is better for the children than the father. An unwed father is in an even worse legal position, in that if the mother chooses to have the child adopted, he can rarely prevent it. And although custody is awarded to the mother, child support legally continues to rest with the father. However it should be noted that in the only study thus far done on court-ordered child support, Eckhardt (1968) found that one year after divorce, 42 percent of the fathers paid nothing; five years later, 67 percent had defaulted; and ten years later, 87 percent were not in compliance with the court order. The women involved still had minor children. (As we will see later in Section III, custody is a greater financial liability than asset.)

Discrimination against women also begins with a wedding license. In some states, she is required to take her husband's name, to accept his choice of domicile, to lose her credit and her right to lease or own separate property, to service him sexually (a husband cannot be accused of rape), to do her duties of cleaning house and caring for children. In some states, men can be granted divorces based on their wives "gross neglect of duty"—dirty houses, unkempt children, and refusal to have intercourse. Under "common law," the man and women become one—that one being the man, the woman losing her rights to enter into legal contracts and for personal inheritance.

In addition, the physical abuse of wives by husbands is covered under "domestic disturbance." In some states, the first beating is legal; in others, based on the ancient "rule of thumb"—the right of a husband to strike his wife with a stick not thicker than his thumb—the severity of the beating is the criterion (Gringold, 1976). But, in all states wife beating is not processed as a criminal assault. Wives report that calling the police only serves to escalate the husband's violence, because the husband normally is not arrested but left at home with his wife (Gringold, 1976). Given the mortification and shame that women feel if their husbands abuse them, the extent of physical violence against wives must be enormous. Further, abusive husbands span the entire social class system, wife-beating is not a peculiarity of the working class. For example, in the second wealthiest county in this country, 600 cases of wife-assault were brought to police attention during 1975 (Weekend, ABC Television, March 6, 1976).

The law, therefore, continues to assume that a woman belongs to a man after marriage. It also assumes that he will provide for her economically, as evidenced in the income tax laws. They were originally premised on the notion that when a man married he took on the burden of an economically dependent wife. To aid him, his income tax was reduced. However, a working wife was taxed at a greater rate than a single woman (Lloyd, 1975:19). Although the Revenue Act of 1971 has made a step forward by allowing child-care tax deductions for working women, the law still remains sexist. Women can deduct as *bona fide* expenses the hiring of substitute mothers and housekeepers. This is so because women can deduct their expenses for hiring individuals to do jobs that the women would (should?) normally be doing if she were not working (e.g., childcare, housekeeping). She cannot deduct expenses for lawn work, maintenance, etc., nor can the male deduct child-care as *bona fide* expenses enabling him to work. Domestic law therefore codifies the stereotypes and discriminates against both husbands and wives.

Employment and Employment Benefits

Of all the tenets of the Women's Liberation Movement, the one that has the most public approval is the idea of "equal pay for equal work" (Walum and Milder, 1974). This idea has been expanded to include equal opportunity generally in employment. These demands have not really altered the economic power structure in this country, but they have become a law of the land.

In 1964, an omnibus Civil Rights Act was passed. One of its provisions was designed specifically to prevent discrimination in employment based on sex—and that included discrimination against either men or women. The key provision of the most important statute, Title VII, states:

> It shall be an unlawful employment practice for an employer (1) to fail or refuse to hire or discharge any individual, or otherwise to discriminate against any individual with respect to his compensation, terms, conditions, or privileges of employment, because of such individual's race, color, religion, sex, or national origin (42.U.C.S.A. 1974 2000 [e]–2[a]).

Under this law, litigation concerning discriminatory practices in hiring, promotion, and salaries have been heard by the court. Only those occupations for which it can be shown that sex is a *bona fide* qualification of employment are excluded from the act. However, it is worthy of note that sex is the only classification upon which discrimination in employment can be legally defended. Laws are upheld and made that would be unconstitutional if they pertained to color, religion, race, or national origin (Di Iorio, 1976). If the complaints were processed solely on the basis of biological sex differences, the only excludable occupations would be wet-nurse, semen donor, etc.

Although an outcome of the legislation has been an invalidation of many restrictive state labor laws and employment practices, it is unwise to be overly optimistic. For example, although grooming requirements that require men but not women to have short hair have been held unlawful discriminatory practices, when litigated, requiring women to wear revealing costumes as a condition of their employment, but not men, has been upheld. "Customer preference" has been ruled invalid, and Pan American Airways was ordered to hire and train men as flight attendants despite claims that clients preferred women. Similarly, in that ruling ease of administering a training program for one sex was held invalid grounds for discrimination. And in the first major sex discrimination litigation brought by the Equal Employment Opportunity Commission (EEOC), the Federal Communication Commission (FCC) denied a rate increase to American Telephone and Telegraph Company—the single largest commercial employer of women in the United States —on the grounds that "the corporation's discriminatory employment practices were not in the public interest" (Freeman, 1976:189). After a year of testimony and hearings, a final settlement of backpay of $38 million was awarded. However, when that amount is contrasted with the 3.5 billion due to women at the Bell monolith since unequal pay became illegal, the gains are still minor. Indeed, the adjudication of this case illustrates rather clearly how the law in practice protects the interests of the powerful.

Protective labor-legislation, which has excluded women from the better-paying jobs has also been struck down. For example, in 1969, a Circuit Court of Appeals ruled that under Title VII weight-lifting restrictions on women, and the exclusion of women from night work was illegal.

And, in the first case concerning sex discrimination heard by the Supreme Court in 1971, the role of mother was ruled extraneous to the right to work. In *Phillips vs. Martin Marietta Corporation* the Supreme Court ruled that the corporation did not have a right to refuse to hire women with preschool children, because its hiring policy for men did not include such restrictions.

Differential employee benefits have effectively operated to discriminate against men and women simultaneously. As these cases regarding differences in work week, overtime pay, retirement, and fringe benefits go through the court they are (usually) held unlawful under Title VII. For example, a policy specifying the number of hours a woman can work discriminates against her by limiting her overtime; but, it also puts the male at a disadvantage, making it difficult for him to refuse extra hours without jeopardizing his job. Similarly, a policy requiring that women be paid more for overtime disadvantages the male; however, the effect of the policy can limit the woman's potential earnings—because she costs more, she is not hired. In these cases, the court has ruled the policies unlawful.

Health plans that cover only the wives of male employees but not the husbands of female employees have been held unlawful. Similarly, plans that allow widows to automatically collect death benefits, but that require widowers to demonstrate incapacity for self-support have been struck down. And under Title VII earlier mandatory retirement age for women as well as pension plans that provide the same benefits for women with fewer years of service than men, have been held unlawful. Each of these differential benefit systems discriminate against both sexes. Women are discriminated against, because in most instances they receive fewer fringe benefits from their employment; men are discriminated against, because they do not receive the same survivor and health benefits from their wives' work.

As is probably obvious, the old laws and policies are based on stereotypical assumptions about men as breadwinners and women as dependents. But, it is nevertheless striking how immersed these cultural stereotypes are in minute interstices of employment practices. To the extent that these policies remain unchallenged, employment discrimination will affect both males and females.

Education

Although any random 37 words will *not* change the world (Weber, 1974), the 37 words contained in Title IX of the Education Amendments Act of 1972 might have an impact on the educational institutions of this country. The provision reads:

> No person in the United States shall, on the basis of sex, be excluded from participation in, be denied the benefits of, or be subjected to discrimination under any educational program or activity receiving federal financial assistance.

The Department of Health, Education, and Welfare, the agency charged with interpreting and enforcing the provision, has written guidelines such that *all* programs (with some major exceptions regarding athletics) whether they receive direct aid or not within *any* educational institution that does receive federal aid must meet the standards of Title IX. Because nearly all educational institutions in this nation—from preschools to post-graduate training centers—receive federal assistance, virtually all educational institutions will be subject to prosecution under Title IX. And the ultimate weapon, the withholding of funds, has been specifically approved. If the regulations are enforced, the outcome will probably be some fundamental changes in the schools. For example, sex-segregated classrooms, admission quotas, differential admissions standards, dress codes, and propriety rules applying to only one sex, and discriminatory promotion and tenure policies all will be illegal. Probably, textbooks and standard curricula will have to be revised as well as workshops provided (in-service training) for teachers on nonsexist education.

However, it is a big "if," for when we look at the results of the contract review compliance legislation of 1965, the "affirmative action" legislation, optimism vanishes. In the case of universities, thus far, all that has been required is "affirmative motion, not action." According to Freeman in an interview with Rose Brock (a compliance review officer for sex discrimination in higher education), although the investigations may be thorough, the demand for implementation is not enforced. "HEW [Department of Health, Education, and Welfare] . . . allows schools lots of time to comply. . . . At best, two dozen schools have had contracts slowed down and none have had them terminated" (Freeman, 1975:199).

At this writing (despite reorganization of the compliance authority and major class action compliance suits brought against the nation's major universities, all medical and law schools, the entire state of New York's university system), the Civil Rights Commission reports that the Office of Federal Contract Compliance has still not adequately provided mechanisms for fulfilling compliance regulation and is thus itself instrumental in maintaining sex-discrimination in employment. Further, the widespread notion that there has been "reverse discrimination" (the preferential hiring of women and minorities over white males), is not born out in the facts. For example, there have been practically no changes in the academic world in terms of pay, employment, or promotion resulting from Affirmative Action (Huber, 1976).

Consequently, because discriminatory policies in education have continued for the past 10 years *after* legislation, it is doubtful that they will suddenly cease.

Criminal Law

According to the ideology underlying the law, men and women are different in terms of their sexuality and their propensity to violence. These beliefs about differences have consequences for the structure of criminal law.

Early beliefs and theories imputed the kind of criminal behavior engaged in as explainable by inherent differences in the physiology and psychology of males and females (Klein, 1973:4). More recently, these differences have been explained along the instrumental-expressive dichotomy (see Chapter 6). Males who are maladjusted or blocked in their instrumental roles resort to criminal behavior; females who are maladjusted or blocked in their expressive roles, turn to crime, delinquency, and prostitution (Heidensohn, 1968:166–167). These theorists argue that, because women are not required to perform instrumentally, they act through men inciting them to crime or using their sex to engage in crimes against morality.

For some of these theorists, the kinds of crime committed are explainable by the biology of sexual intercourse. Pollak, for example, argues that "Man must achieve an erection in order to perform the sex act and will not be able to hide his failure. . . ." Whereas women can make a pretense of orgasm, and "neither her pretense or lack of orgasm prevents her from participation" (1950:10). Therefore, man's crimes are overt, manifest, obvious; women's crimes are hidden, secret, deceitful. Indeed, Pollak argues further that because "our sex mores" require women to "conceal their menstrual periods every four weeks," they are conditioned to hold a "different attitude towards veracity than men" (1950:11).

Pollack's viewpoint would have us conclude that male crimes such as bribery, embezzlement, kickbacks, price-setting, and fraud are not hidden, secret, or deceitful. Obviously, such a conclusion is as unwarranted as the assumption upon which it is based—namely, that one's sexual apparatus determines the kind of crime one will commit.

Although most modern sociologists and criminologists no longer adhere to the physiological explanations of crime, it is still primarily these ideas that form our legislation, as well as form the basis for policy decisions. For example, as late as 1967, Reckless and Kay, both distinguished criminologists, reported to the President's Commission of Law Enforcement and the Administration of Justice:

> A large part of the infrequent officially acted upon involvement of women in crime can be traced to the masking effect of women's roles, effective practice on the part of women of deceit and indirection, their instigation of men to commit their crimes (the Lady Macbeth factor), and the unwillingness on the part of the public and law enforcement officials to hold women accountable for their deeds (the chivalry factor) (1967:-13).

In these few sentences, the criminologists—without empirical evidence—have reported to the president that women have a lesser moral character inherited from their Mother Eve whose lifestyle they emulate by seducing (lesser) men to misconducts and (better) men to protect them from punishment. Not only are they impugning women, they are implying that men are suckers—fools led around by their penises.

These ideas intrude upon the sensibilities of governmental commissions and invade the processing of the offender. As Cicourel and Kitsuse (1963) have demonstrated, the social organization of justice is such that the probation officers, social workers, counselors, police officers and other specialists process cases based on normative assumptions about female and male crime and delinquency. The ideas become self-fulfilling prophecies.

Despite the ideals of chivalry presented as fact by the criminologists, in actuality "female adolescents are sanctioned more severely than their male counterparts" (Chesney-Lind, 1973:2). Females, while awaiting the disposition of their cases, are more likely to be sent to a detention home and to be retained there longer before a court hearing (Chesney-Lind, 1973:57). And while girls constituted only one-sixth of the cases, they constituted one-half of the cases sent to institutions. "Three times as many girls as boys were recommended for institutionalization" (Cohn, 1970:193), and female "sexual delinquents were never recommended to probation" (Cohn, 1970:199). That is, at every stage in the processing of female delinquents, the court rendered more severe and radical punishment than it did for male violators (Chesney-Lind, 1973).

Why is the chivalry notion not upheld empirically? One of the major reasons, of course, is that such notions have never extended to the black, the third world, or poor women—the ones most likely to be sent before the judge. But perhaps, an even more significant reason is that this chivalry is intended to protect only "good" women. By the standards of criminological ideology, women accused of transgressing their sexual or social roles are suspect of not being "good" women. And, the female offender is processed in such a way as to establish that her "crimes" were *sexual* offenses. According to official statistics, approximately 75 percent of female delinquency are offenses that are "sexual or create danger of sexual infractions" (Block and Geiss, 1970:429), such as running away, curfew violations, incorrigibility, and sex delinquency. But according to self-reports, "running away, incorrigibility . . . and fornication account for only eight percent of the girls' delinquent acts and not much less of the boys, six percent" (Gold, 1970:64).

How does it happen, then, that the official statistics vary so considerably from the self-reports? To answer this, we need look at how females and males are processed. One of the elements of processing females that is practically routine is the court order for a gynecological examination. Doctors report on the health forms the condition of the hymen—intact, ruptured, admits intercourse. Although the state of the hymen is irrelevant to the health of the accused, not to mention her role in a burglary, this information is given to the probation officer, who in turn uses that information to broaden an original offense such as "car theft" into a sexual one such as "potential runaway" (Chesney-Lind, 1973). Further, while held in the detention home, intensive investigation for their "own protection" usually reveals other offenses (Chesney-Lind, 1973).

That is, offenses that girls commit are categorized as sexual offenses. *Incorrigibility* is assumed to mean something different in a boy than in a girl; and second, offences that are not originally under the rubric are sexualized through finding physical evidence of a ruptured hyman and/or psychological evidence of sexual intent. In effect, the processing of male and female youthful offenders is based more upon ideological assumption than upon the actual crimes committed.

Crimes of Violence

Apart from forcible rape, which we shall discuss later, crimes of violence such as murder, manslaughter, and assault are presumed under the law to be committable by members of either gender. Yet, the processing of men and women in such cases differ. For example, although Nagel and Weitzman (1962) found that men were more likely to be awarded counsel and a jury trial than women—a due process consideration—they found two other patterns of treatment that discriminate against men. The first, the "disadvantages" pattern, results in greater harshness to the black and the indigent. The second, the "paternalistic" involves greater leniency to women and children. Similar to the assumption that female juveniles' offenses are sexual (and therefore deserving of harsher penalty than boys receive), male acts of violence—and especially black males' violence—are perceived as somehow more violent and dangerous than females' and, therefore, requiring greater punishment. Men, as a class, then, are likely to receive harsher sentences and more convictions for their violence than are women.

The presumption that male violence is worse than female violence is further underscored by the 1970 State Supreme Court decision regarding a male escapee from a maximum security prison (Supreme Judicial Court, Maine, 1970). The prisoner sought relief on that grounds that, in Maine, a female prisoner escapee serving the same sentence for the same offense would be subject to a much shorter maximum sentence. The court ruled, however, that it was reasonable for the laws to discriminate against men in this kind of case, because a male escapee created a greater threat to the public and prison guards than did a female. Although this may be true in general, the prisoner in question is being held accountable for the typical male rather than being considered on his individual merit. In effect, then, male defendents and male prisoners in cases of violent crime are processed and punished for belonging to the suspect category—male.

Prostitution

The traditional double standard of morality is well represented in the laws governing prostitution and in their administration. Recently, for example, California women appealed convictions for prostitution on the grounds of "sexual discrimination." The men involved were not criminally charged or sentenced (Kanowitz: 1969:15).

Prostitution is variously defined in the states such as "the practice of the female offering her body to an indiscriminate sexual intercourse with men for compensation" or "common lewdness of a women for gain" (Kanowitz:1969:16). Obviously, the law makes guilty only one partner—the female—and, further, is written in such a way as to exclude the possibility of a male being a prostitute (Kanowitz: 1969:16).

Although in some states it is legally possible to punish men for patronizing prostitutes, in most states no such direct provisions are provided. (Kanowitz: 1969:16). Where indirect provisions are given, such as fornication, lewdness, solicitation, or associating with a prostitute, the interpretations of the laws are usually such as to exonerate the male. Thus, various courts have ruled that visiting a house of prostitution does not constitute "open and gross lewdness," that occasional intercourse outside of marriage is not "adultery or fornication" (providing there is no pretense of living with the woman), and that, if a male solicits a prostitute to achieve personal gratification, he is not convictable for "solicitation" (Kanowitz, 1969:16–17).

Most importantly, of course, is the fact that the decisions regarding the processing of the crime are made by police officers and prosecuting attorneys. Consequently, although males could be charged with a direct or indirect crime involving their visiting a prostitute, this rarely occurs. Male "customers are arrested as an inducement of their cooperation in convicting the women" (Kanowitz, 1969:17).

The sex bias in the processing of prostitution is only too obvious. In effect, only women are held criminally accountable. As Flexner argued in 1914, to undo this inequity, "the stigma and consequence of the crime—must—be either removed from the woman or affixed to the man" (quoted in Kanowitz: 1969:18).

Some states have recently revised their criminal statutes to define prostitution as commitable by either males or females. However, as a counter even to that trend, prostitutes, led by Margo St. John (President of COYOTE, for "Cut Out Your Old Tired Ethics") have organized to challenge any criminal legislation concerning prostitution. They are not interested in "affixing the stigma" to the male, but in removing the stigma *entirely* by decriminalizing prostitution *entirely*—viewing it as a professional service (sex therapy) voluntarily sought and rendered.

Statutory Rape, Seduction, and Enticement

Historically, common law has been concerned with the protection of innocent— that is, virginal—women from the sexual advances of older men. No parallel concern with protecting the innocent male from the mature female existed— presumably because females were considered incapable of sexual aggression. The existence of these protective laws was based on the presumption that families were unable to adequately shield their young women from the temptations and abuses of the adult male and on the grounds that the state had an interest in such protection. In a society that valued a girls' virginity as a "sexual treasure" not to be unwisely disposed of (62 Yale Law Journal, 55 quoted in Lopez, 1974:1) and that was concerned with the legitimate inheritance of property from father to sons, such laws were seen as necessary to protect "the society, the family, and the infant" (judicial decision quoted in Kanowitz, 1969:25).

The modern legislation regarding statutory rape, enticement, and seduction has arisen from these concerns. In all three offenses, the victim (by law) is almost invariably female, the offender, male (Kanowitz, 1969:18–19). And in all three offenses, the double standard of morality is apparent.

In most states, statutory rape specifies sexual intercourse with a female under the age of consent (Kanowitz, 1969:21). The seriousness of the crime is deter- mined by the age of the female, her previous chasteness, and/or the age differen- tial between the male and the female. Only a few states have statutes that permit as a crime the statutory rape of a young male by an adult female. That is, the laws are written specifically to protect underage females, not males, and to specifically deny to females the right to consent to sexual intercourse. Such intercourse is legally defined as rape, while a male's ability to consent to an adult female is not questioned. Only underage females are protected by the legislation and only underage males are deemed capable of a voluntary, consensual union. The argu- ment presumes that if a female were capable of making a right decision, she would refuse sexual intercourse; because she did not, *ergo,* she was not capable of making the right decision.

The double standard is further evidenced in seduction laws. The crime is usually defined as the male's use of a false promise of marriage to trick the female into engaging in sexual intercourse (Kanowitz, 1969:21). In some states, promises of gifts constitute subtle deception (Kanowitz, 1969:21). A victim of deception (in most states) can be of any age—as long as she is of "previous chaste character." Further, in contrast to the statutory rape laws, if the offender actually marries the victim, the charges must be dropped in most states. Further, the property value of the woman's sexual treasure is clearly spelled out in some states where "a civil remedy for *damages* [emphasis added] (i.e., financial settlement) for seduction is often provided for the victim or her parent" (Kanowitz, 1969:2). Apparently, the promise of marriage to a chaste male by a female would not occur, and would not be a deceptive practice if it did. And civil redress for the loss of a male's virginity is by legal standards preposterous.

The third crime, enticement, is usually defined as the persuasion by a male of an underage female to leave her father's home to enter upon a clandestine marriage without consent of her parent or guardian (Kanowitz, 1969:21). It is presumably unheard of for an overage female to entice an underage male into an elopement. Despite the societal notion that marriage is fitting for a woman, the notion of parental approval and protection of the innocent female is more salient.

In the prosecution of these crimes, then, it is the innocent woman who is to be protected. Granted that the young may need special protective legislation, does it not then follow that the *same* protections should be extended to males and females alike? That is, if it is true that sexual abuses are destructive to young girls, are they not also destructive to young boys? And, further, if adult females are considered innocent until devirginized and, therefore, in need of protection, does it not follow that males should be equally protected—or, that protection is unnecessary for adults of either sex?

In brief, these examples of criminal law treat as objective fact ideological preferences for the sexual attitudes and behavior of males and females; as such, they help perpetuate a double standard of morality. In those states where criminal laws have been revised to meet the standards of State Equal Rights legislation, the legal perpetuation of the double standard has been eased. The question, of course, still remains as to whether the laws will be enforced.

Forcible Rape

Legal thinking transforms the innocent girl incapable of consenting to intercourse into a woman at age 16 (or 18, depending on the state) capable of—indeed desirous of—sexually seducing and tricking men. This ideological belief in woman as sexual seducer is perhaps most evident in the legal processing of the victims of rape.

Although the mass media have depicted the police as insensitive and threatening to the rape victim, in the one social scientific study in which rape victims were interviewed while being processed through the judicial system, the women did not see the police as the culprits (Holmstrom and Burgess, 1974). Rather, they saw themselves as victimized first by the rape, and secondly by the court. "Going to court for the women is as much a crisis as the rape itself" (Holmstrom and Burgess, 1974:8).

Some of the feelings of being a victim of the court system arise from the interminable delays arranged by defense lawyers. Twelve to eighteen months can easily elapse between the rape and the final verdict, during which time the women report feeling their lives have been suspended. Secondly, women report feeling victimized by the public setting of the court, a setting in which they must face the accused, and speak in a microphone before thrill-seeking strangers who vicariously "witness the rape." The women relive the event at each stage of the court processing—the hearing, the Grand Jury, and the trial at the Superior Court. Thirdly, women report feeling as though they are treated as the offender. Although the male is on trial, the rape laws of most states are structured to protect the accused. In many states, a man cannot be convicted solely on the testimony of the alleged victim; corroborative evidence is required. This includes (1) proof of penetration, (2) proof of the identity of the assailant, and (3) proof that the act occurred without consent.

Penetration is not always possible to prove, because women frequently wait before going to the police; and proof of identity of the assailant is also sometimes problematic due to the settings in which some rape occurs such as parks, alleys, dark streets, and rooms. But, proof of nonconsent is the one kind of corroborative evidence that especially marks the sex bias of the legal processing of rape. A woman can be seen as instigating the crime—and, therefore, guilty of seduction— by such activities as going to a bar alone, walking on the streets at nights, and hitchhiking. It is the only crime where the victim is held responsible. For example, if a women went to the bank and carried money out in her purse, she would not be accused of precipitating a robbery. But a women who walks alone at night or hitchhikes has to prove in court that she was not out looking for sex. Further, if her previous history has included extramarital relationships (or in some cases even "familiarity with alcohol"—that is, working as a cocktail waitress), there is *prima facie* evidence that she is of low moral character. Ironically, although a man's previous convictions for rape or assault cannot be used as evidence against him in a new case, a defense attorney can pry into the private life of the female victim and use this information to undermine her moral credibility. In fact, the defense attorney's questioning can be so vicious that according to Holmstrom and Burgess (1974) women feel those attorneys are like the rapists—twisted, degraded, offensive. Rarely will a judge interfere with the defense attorney's line of questioning as either irrelevant or badgering to the witness.

Rape, according to Griffin, is the "All-American Crime' (1971). Not only is rape the most frequently committed violent crime (Griffin, 1971:2), but rape is held to be natural and not raping, learned (Griffin, 1971:3). This belief is held despite the fact that in other countries, such as Canada and Norway, rape is virtually nonexistent. And this belief is held despite the fact that most rapes are not spontaneous, but *preplanned* (Amir, 1971). A companion myth, that all women secretly want to be raped, completes the basis for the legal reasoning: women precipitate the inevitable. Further, given that in our culture normal heterosexuality involves a dominant male and a submissive female, the courts have difficulty distinguishing rape from mutual consent. "Rape is simply at one end of the continuum of male-aggressive, female-passive patterns, and an arbitrary line has been drawn to mark it off from the rest of such relationships" (Medea and Thompson, 1974:11–12, quoted in Hudnell and Dunham, 1974:1).

Although there is no statistical evidence, it is quite probable that males and females have different conceptions of what constitutes rape. For example, in one case a polygraph (lie-detector test) was administered to both the accused and the accuser. The results showed *both* were telling the truth. That is, the female defined her refusal as a *bona fide* "no"; the male perceived her "no" as "c'mon, yes" (Hudnell and Dunham, 1974). As long as women are trained to act coy and expect to be chased, subdued, and seduced and as long as males are taught to view these female behaviors as enticements—as part of the normal romantic foreplay—it will be difficult for the law to sharply demarcate rape from normal heterosexual intercourse.

In addition, "Male sexuality and violence in our culture seem to be inseparable" (Griffin, 1971:3). In a society "where James Bond alternately whips out his revolver and his cock" (Griffin, 1971:3), rape represents an archetypical model of eroticism—the blending of sex and violence in one act. Despite the myths to the contrary, "the typical rapist might be the boy next door. Especially if the boy next door happens to be about 19 years of age and the neighborhood you live in happens to fit the socioeconomic description of lower class or bears the appellation 'ghetto' " (Brownmiller, 1975:174). Statistically, the male convicted of forcible rape has the same attitudes towards sexuality as the "normal, well-adjusted male," differing "only in having a greater tendency to *express* [emphasis mine] violence and rage" (Amir, 1971, referred to in Griffin, 1971:538). As a final example of the attraction to rape taught to males in this society, Hudnell and Dunham (1974) report the following episode from a documentary movie (*Rape: Law, Justice and Public Opinion*):

> [A defense lawyer] ... related the story of a local prosecutor who belonged to a businessmen's luncheon group in which it was customary for the members to give gifts to each other. The prosecutor decided his gift would be indictment forms with the members' names filled in as defendants for the crime of rape. This would ... signify the masculinity and prowess of these men (1974:16).

When these ideas of eroticism are located within the more general legal and social ideology which views women as "sexual objects," the rationale for the processing of rape in the courts becomes clear. Illustrative is an explanatory opinion of rape laws, which appeared in the Yale Law Review. The authors stressed that the rape laws both foster and bolster "a masculine pride in the exclusive possession of a sexual object." Consequently, by establishing a consent standard in the law, men are assured that the women they do possess are personal prizes. Further, sole ownership of the sexual object enhances their status. If other males forcibly rape his possession, they are threatening *him*. Accordingly, "The law of rape provides an orderly outlet for ... [male] vengeance" against other men (quoted in Griffin, 1971:6).

Rape, therefore, historically, is not seen so much as crime a man perpetuates against a woman as one that a man perpetuates against another *man*. Rape laws were not written to protect the rights of females over their own bodies; rather their purpose was to protect the rights of men as owners of females (Griffin, 1971:6).

Without restructuring societal attitudes toward sexuality and "possessor-possessed" relationships between men and women, the administration of justice in the case of rape will only continue to reflect this ideological bias, which victimizes the victim. And the impact of this ideology continues to affect not only the law-breaking but the *law-abiding*. Women continue to structure their employment opportunities and social activities around their fears of rape. They remain prisoners by night, at home "where they belong." The threat of rape and the knowledge of how it will be processed in the court are effective deterrents to female freedom of movement. The law continues to hold in line the law-abiding—and, in this case, the line is drawn at the front door.

What is to be done? Obviously rape will not cease until the views held toward women are altered and until men are no longer socialized to revere violence. But, in the meantime, there are possible changes that would contribute to greater justice and equity. In some states, some legal changes have already occurred. For example, in Ohio, the new revised criminal code defines rape as,

> sexual conduct (i.e., vaginal and anal intercourse, fellatio and cunnilingus) between persons, regardless of sex, when the offender uses force or threat of force or when s/he administers any drug or intoxicant to the other person for the purpose of impairing the person's judgment in order to prevent resistance, or when the other person is less than thirteen (13) years old (Hudnell and Dunham, 1974:7).

The new rape law, which exists in only a few states, has moved away from the archaic concept of viewing woman's virginity as the property of her father and her sexuality a property of her husband and has placed it in the context of modern criminal violence (Brownmiller, 1975:377). Viewed as such, "the crime retains its unique dimensions, falling midway between robbery and assault. It is in one act both a blow to the body and a blow to the mind and a 'taking' of sex through the use of threat or force" (Brownmiller, 1975:377).

Secondly, the revised rape law has become less sex-activity specific (intercourse) and become more gender free. It recognizes that "acts of sex forced on unwilling victims," whether male or female, "deserve to be treated in concept as equally grave offenses in the eyes of the law" (Brownmiller, 1975:378). Sexual assault does not occur only genitally, nor is it solely a male-on-female offense. "As men may invade women through other orifices, so, too, do they invade other men" (Brownmiller, 1975:378). Is the assault to the dignity of the male any less than that of the female? Is forced oral or rectal penetration any less a violation "of the personal, private inner space, a lesser injury to mind, spirit and sense of self?" (Brownmiller, 1975:383).

Thus far, only a few states have adopted new laws concerning rape. And although these new laws rectify much of the abusiveness of the old ones, not until the socialization of males and females and our socialization towards sexuality is radically altered will the crime of rape disappear.

Abortion

Until the 1960s, the word and practice—abortion—lay sealed in silence. Although there are few accurate statistics, there were probably more than one million illegal abortions annually in the United States. Most of these were performed on married women in the upper socioeconomic classes who wanted no more children. Legal abortions were permitted in most states only to "save the life of the mother" or in some states if the pregnancy "endangered the health of the mother." In court cases, 10-year-old victims of rape, menopausal mothers, mentally ill girls, and intellectually slow girls were denied the right to a legal abortion.

Then, after many years of controversy on complex moral, religious, and legal issues, the Supreme Court in January of 1973 ruled on abortion. Its seven-to-two ruling stated that during the first trimester of pregnancy the decision to abort was a matter between the woman and her physician—in which the state could not intervene. During the second trimester, when abortion is more dangerous to the woman, however, the court ruled that the state has a legitimate interest in the woman's health; thus, the state can legislate statutes concerning where abortions may be performed. The court also reasoned that when the fetus was viable, the state could prohibit abortion during the third trimester unless the life or health of the mother was threatened.

The *right* to abortion still rests with the woman and her physician. Yet, the goal of the pro-abortionists to gain the absolute right to abortion for all women was not accepted by the court. Rather, the grounds upon which the ruling was based was the Fourteenth Amendment's concept of "personal liberty and the right to privacy."

As a consequence of the ruling, therefore, abortions are legally available to women, although the state has some leeway to legislate pregnancies during their last six months. Predictably, however, because abortions are expensive, they are more obtainable by women in the upper socioeconomic classes.

In 1976, the court ruled that neither the father of the fetus nor the parents of an underage girl have the right to prevent an abortion if she chooses one. Both of these rulings are effectively further removing the "property value" that was attached to women and children. Only the state is seen as having a vested interest in the issue. The continued extension of "personal liberty and the right to privacy" extended to minors and married women may have additional ramifications.

Very deep emotional and moral concerns have been generated by the abortion ruling. Judging from the continued growth of the anti-abortion groups and the anti-abortion stance of many political leaders, the controversies and legal issues surrounding it are far from over.

Anti-abortionists ask, "How can abortion be justified?" And many pro-abortionists have attempted to answer that query. The moral, ethical, theological, and medical responses to this question go well beyond the province of this book. However, we might profitably ask, as Hardin did (1975), a different question: "How can compulsory pregnancy be justified?" This question places the issue squarely within the context of sex roles. What are the rights of males over the bodies of females? What are the interests of the state?

If men have the right to enforce pregnancy in their wives, Hardin argues, then "such compulsion is akin to rape" (1975:246). Further, it is a form of indentured servitude, because if "pregnancy is continued to term it results in parenthood, which is also a kind of servitude, to be continued for the best years of a woman's life" (1975:248). It is the female whose body is being used for the prenatal period; and the mother who will be held principally responsible for the upbringing of the child. One wonders, if males were the child-bearers but still had their positions of greater power, if abortion would not have been routinely allowed decades ago.

In addition, it can be argued that the state has a vested interest in the preservation of the lives of its female citizens. "Making abortions illegal will not prevent them" (Branscom, 1976). Women will return to the pre-legal forms of abortion—self-inducement and the dangerous knife of the unskilled abortionist. Consequently, it can be argued that the state has an interest in providing abortions in order to preserve the lives of women.

Further, Hardin argues that the society has another vested interest in allowing women to abort. A study of Swedish children born to mothers who were refused abortions found that these children received less education, needed more therapy, were arrested more frequently and bore children sooner (if females) than their matched controls. The result was a vicious cycle of unwanted children producing more unwanted children. Hardin asks, "How then does society gain by increasing the number of unwanted children?" (1975:248). Clearly, voluntary parenthood is in the interest of the society; not compulsory pregnancy.

Equal Rights Amendment

The Federal Equal Rights Amendment states that equal rights under the law shall not be denied or abridged by the United States or any state on account of sex. Such an amendment proposing equal rights for males and females was first introduced by the National Women's Party (NWP) in 1923. However, judicial and legislative opinion held that "sex-based classification has always been made and—unless prohibited in express terms in the constitution—is a natural and proper one to make" (judicial decision, Salt Lake City vs. Wilson, 46, Utah, quoted in Freeman, 1975:210). The resolution was introduced in each succeeding congress, but it was not until after the emergence of the women's movement that the idea was taken seriously. Finally, on March 22, 1972, the amendment passed both houses. As of this writing, 34 states have ratified the federal ERA. Four more states must do so before 1979 if the constitution is to be amended. Its fate still remains uncertain.

Of all the arguments against ERA, the argument that says that what is needed is not a constitutional amendment but a state-by-state law revision in such areas as divorce, family law, employment, and criminal code seems particularly misplaced. As Rosemary Gunin, New York State Assemblywomen commented, "We have just passed a bill requiring both parties in a divorce action to file financial statements. . . . That little piecemeal item took us five years" (quoted in Lear, 1976:115). Given all the piecemeal items in our 50 states, we can see that full legal equality between the sexes would take an interminably long time and be extremely expensive.

Although ratification of the ERA will not change sex discrimination overnight, its existence will be not only a symbolic statement of the mutual dignity of both sexes, but it will provide the courts with a principle through which the legacy of sex discrimination can be removed. Without such a general principle, the court has no clear basis for processing sex discrimination cases; hence, they are judged one way sometimes, another way other times.

It is ironic and sad that more women oppose the ERA than do men (Lear, 1976). Part of this opposition stems from the fear its opponents have generated in women regarding the consequences of ratification: unisex bathrooms, mandatory employment for mothers, no alimony, etc. In a very successful anti-ERA campaign, upper-class women (e.g., Phyllis Shafley and Annette Stern) with funds from conservative organizations, such as the John Birch Society and the Knights of Columbus, have managed to convince vast numbers of women that the only supporters of the ERA are "radical feminists" who wish to improve their own lot at the expense of the housewife and low-paid female worker. Despite the fact that Betty Ford, Liz Carpenter (Democratic National Committeewoman), Elly Peterson (former Republican National Committeewoman), the Coalition of Labor Union Women, and the League of Women voters are active leaders in a national coalition to ratify the ERA and despite the fact that feminists have in actuality been struggling to unite all women, the idea has stuck. Women who favor "equal pay for equal work," oppose the ERA. It is as though they are saying they do not want to be associated with "women's libbers." They are saying "I am affirming the worth of my life: I am not one of you" (Lear, 1976).

In summary, the domestic, criminal, educational, and economic legislation has a tradition of affirming gender stereotypes. Only in the past few years have we seen any substantial alteration in the legal code. But those legal gains have not been systematically practiced by the agencies charged with their enforcement, and powerful interest groups have arisen to turn back the legal clock.

8

Religion

Although the separation of church and state is an historical principle, from a sociological perspective such a separation is not evidenced. Institutionally, churches[1] are active in education, child welfare, prison reform, care of the aged, social services, mass media, unemployment, political action, as well as capitalist ventures such as real estate holdings (Wilson, 1971). That is, the church as an institution plays an active and integrative role in the larger society, rationalizing activities and providing a sense of consistency to the whole. In addition, it receives certain benefits from the state (e.g., tax-exempt status on its financial and real estate holdings). Because the church invests its energies, money, and time, it has a stake in preserving the *status quo* (Wilson, 1971). And because the status quo favors the interests of the more powerful, religion helps perpetuate social inequality. This is not to deny that the church can and does play a role in social change; rather, it is to recognize that one of its primary functions is to maintain the existing order and its own place within it.

Further, not only is there institutional overlap, there is an ideological consistency. Indeed, the legal system uses the doctrines of religion to rationalize legislation and adjudication. Religion, in effect, provides the final moral authority—the divine sanction—for the human values that are enacted into law. The deployment of the divine sanction effectively ensures compliance not only with the legal system but with society's norms.

Although the source of the truth is different, the Judeo-Christian tradition—from Genesis to the 1970s—parallels rather closely the teachings of the academician and the counsel of the therapist. To disagree with a scientist risks being labeled ignorant; to disagree with a therapist risks being labeled crazy. But to

---

[1] I am using the term *church* as it is used in sociology to refer to beliefs and rituals about the sacred, which bind people together in a moral community.

disagree with the teachings of the church or its interpretation by a "man of God" risks much more, because religion plays, in the lives of many people, a particular kind of role that science and therapy do not.

In the first place, the doctrines of a religion are usually learned at a young age. As we have seen, socialization of the young is etched deeply. The messages of the religion are carved into vivid scenes by the child's literal interpretations of Heaven and Hell, God and Satan, Good and Evil. The childhood literalness may be finally rejected by the adult, but the feelings and imagery initially associated with those learnings tend to linger. Questioning the moral authority of the church or its spokesperson, therefore, raises the deep-seated childhood images and fears of the transcendental, as well as whatever concerns about the transcendental the adult carries.

Secondly, religion, unlike science and therapy, fulfills certain psychological functions for the individual. It can answer the unanswerable, rationalize the unreasonable, predict the unpredictable. Chaos, cruelty, disaster, inequity, pain, and suffering—can be explained to the individual on the basis of "God's will" or "purposes of a grander nature." To question the moral authority of the church about its prescriptions for gender performance means to risk losing the reassurance and support that religion can provide at those times of uncertainty, struggle, and suffering.

Third and perhaps most important, in terms of its impact on adult social control, religion is more than just a set of beliefs about the sacred. Religion takes place in the context of a community of believers—friends and relatives who share common lives which extend beyond the stained glass windows. To challenge the doctrine of the church means, then, to risk the ostracism, rejection, and censure of one's community.

The impact of early socialization combined with the risks involved in questioning religious teachings—risks at the psychological, interpersonal, and transcendental levels—function to present the adult with an external control system that is enduring, deep, and forceful. Unlike any other social control system, religion has all bases covered—the here-and-now and the forever-after. Its hold on its parishioners, combined with its own institutional stake in the perpetuation of the status-quo, makes it a formidable social force.

Biblical Heritage

There can be little doubt that the parables, stories, teachings, and gospels of the Judeo-Christian tradition that our culture has chosen to emphasize are those that perpetuate gender-role stereotyping. A few samples from that heritage will illustrate the perspective:

Leviticus 12:2, 5

> If a woman conceives and bears a male child, then she shall be unclean for seven days. . . . But if she bears a female child, then she shall be unclean for two weeks.

Job 4:4
>How can he be clean that was born of a woman?

Daily Orthodox Jewish Prayer (for men)
>I thank Thee, O Lord, that thou has not made me a woman.

St. Paul
>Let the Woman learn in silence with all subjection. . . . I suffer not a women to usurp authority over men, but to be in silence.

Ephesians 5:23–24
>Wives, submit yourselves unto your husbands . . . for the husband is the head of the wife, even as Christ is the head of the church.

The church's position, consistent with that of the culture, is particularly evident in the choice of which version of the creation of humankind to emphasize and in its interpretation of it. There exist in Genesis two versions of the story. The one that has been virtually ignored is the following:

>And God said, Let us make Mankind in our image, after our likeness; and let them have dominion . . . God created man ('ādām) in his own image. In the image of God he created him. Male (zākār) and female (n^egābāh) he created them (Genesis 1:18, 20, 26–27).

This version is particularly interesting for it implies that God is either simultaneously male and female, or neither, and states clearly that both male and female were created simultaneously. Several interpretations are possible. For example, the passage can be understood to mean that originally mankind ('ādām) contained both sexes within one form and that the taking of the rib, served to separate the entity into two distinct sexes. Or, it can be interpreted that each sex contains within itself the elements of both sexes.

The creation story that is usually taught, however, is the following:

>And the Lord God formed man ('ādām) of the dust of the ground;
>and breathed into his nostrils the breath of life;
>And man became a living soul.
>And the Lord God said, It is not good that the man should
>be alone: I will make him an helpmeet fit for him.
>And the Lord God caused a deep sleep to fall upon the man
>and he slept; and he took one of his ribs and closed up
>the flesh instead thereof.
>And the rib which the Lord God had taken from man, made he
>woman and brought her unto the man.
>And Adam said, This is now bone of my bones, and flesh of my
>flesh; she shall be called Woman, because she was taken out
>of Man (Genesis 2:7, 18, 21–23).

The most popular interpretation of this story is that woman was made after man, designed to serve man, as man serves God. However, in Hebrew the word *helpmeet* (^cezer) carries no status connotations; and *fit for* means "opposite" or "corresponding to." Therefore, another interpretation of the story is that man and woman share an essential unity, a basic sameness of bone and flesh—the two of them, *one* separate order of creation (Bird, 1974).

In the Christian tradition, two major images of women are emphasized: Eve, the first "sinner" and responsible for the loss of paradise; and Mary, "the unattainable ideal combining virginity and motherhood," the epitome of "perfect obedience" (Hole and Levine, 1971:380). Christianity's accent on only the Eve-Mary images in the Bible means women in general are viewed as "symbolic representations of male ideas about sex": the sexual evilness of the temptress, the sexual purity of the virgin, the sexual procreativity of the mother (Hole and Levine, 1971:-381). For males, the role models in Christianity are more diverse. Two of these— God the Father, and God the virginal Son—are exceptionally powerful symbols. Analagous to what happens to men in the secular world, they are offered models that are virtually impossible to attain. Even the disciples and the angels, including the fallen Lucifer, are exceptional. Whether saints or demons, they are interpreted as epitomizing the highest forms of achievement or power. And the lesser models as well—kings, leaders, warriors—are fulfilling the traditional male roles.

However, there are many passages within the Bible that offer alternative images of masculinity and femininity, as the following examples illustrate:

Judges 5:24, 26
> She put her hand to the tent peg
>   and her right hand to the workman's mallet'
> she struck Sisera a blow,
>   she crunched his head,
>   she shattered and pierced his temple.

I Kings 10:1–2
> Now when the Queen of Sheba heard of the fame of Solomon concerning the name of the Lord, she came to test him with hard questions. She came to Jerusalem with a very great retinue, with camels bearing spices and very much gold, and precious stones . . .

Jeremiah 31:22
> The Lord has created a new thing on earth:
>   a woman protects [encompasses] a man.

Proverbs 31:10
> A good wife . . .
> She considers a field and buys it;
>   with the fruit of her hands she plants a vineyard.
> She girds her loins with strength
>   and makes her arms strong.
> She perceives that her merchandise is profitable.

Hosea 4:14
> I will not punish your daughters
>   when they play the harlot,
> nor your brides when they commit adultery;
> for the men themselves go aside with harlots,
>   and sacrifice with cult prostitutes.

Proverbs 3:30
> Strive not with a man without cause, if he have done
> thee no harm.

Proverbs 3:31
> Envy thou not the oppressor, and
> choose none of his ways.

Proverbs 6:3
> Do this now, my son, and deliver thyself, when thou are come into the hand of thy
> friend; go, humble thyself, and make sure the friend.

These passages reflect nonstereotyped ideas about the roles and personalities of men and women. That is, there are Biblical women who are strong, wise, warriors, and respected leaders. Men are urged in some proverbs to humble themselves, to forego competitiveness, and to not follow in the footsteps of those whose success depends on the oppression of others. The New Testament presents many nonmachismo messages: Jesus and his disciples are men of emotion—they cry, fear, and agonize; they are able to be weak (Luke 22:54 ff., John 20:24 ff., II Corinthians 4:5 ff.), to be controlled by others (John 2, Luke 22–23, 24:13 ff.), and to demonstrate compassion (John 8, Mark 6:34 ff.) and humility (John 13, Luke 6:17 ff.).[2]

Further, not only are alternative images presented, alternative ways for the sexes to relate to one another are revealed in the accounts of Jesus's life. The amount and kinds of associations that Jesus had with women goes way beyond those permissable in his culture. Included among his close friends, traveling companions, and disciples were Mary Magdalene, Joanna, and Susanna. Such inclusion "must have seemed highly unconventional in [that] traditional society" (Reuther, 1975:64). Further, Jesus violated Judaic law by touching bleeding [menstruating] women (Mark 5:25–34, Matthew 9:20–22), by speaking alone with a woman not his wife (John 4:27), and by allowing the women to witness and testify to the resurrection (John 20:1ff., Luke 24:10, 22–25). Because Jewish law did not accept women as responsible witnesses, "to make women the first witnesses of the resurrection was to make them the original source of the credibility of the Christian faith" (Reuther, 1975:65).

Granted that the culture decides how to interpret the Bible, which passages to teach to children, which Saints to revere for what, it can, nevertheless, be said that on the whole there are more elements in the religious heritage favoring different role performances and expectations for men and women than there are favoring a gender free society. At one level, this is perfectly understandable because the events and individuals described in the Bible lived in patriarchal societies themselves and were imbued with a set of beliefs about the natural order to things. They taught that which they had learned.

---

[2]For this section, I am indebted to John Seidler for his theological and sociological insights.

In reviewing these teachings, then, we find that women are defined primarily in terms of their sexuality—virgins, wives, mothers; men in a wider diversity of roles. For example, in the Catholic tradition, each day of the year is dedicated to one or more saints. Sixty women are so honored—all of them virgins or martyrs. In contrast, 396 men are so honored—bishops, abbots, popes, martyrs, doctors, apostles, etc. (St. Joseph's Daily Missal, 1957). Virginity or death are the role-model options for would-be sainted women; achievement or death, for men. Further, like the stories in the children's readers, an analysis of Jesus's parables reveals that 26 of them are about males; 7 about females (Ryan and Schirtzinger, 1974).

Indeed, some argue, that the Bible itself was written exclusively for men. Examples of this come from the Ten Commandments (eg., Thou shall not covet thy neighbor's wife). Another example can be found in the pact made with God by the Israelites during the exodus: The covenant with God required circumcision; only men, therefore, could have this special relationship with God and take part in the sacred public rituals.

Despite major religious upheavals during the mid-20th century, such as the "Death of God" movement and the disenchantment of the clergy with organized religion, the doctrine of male dominance/female submissiveness has been left virtually intact. In the writings and sermons of the modern clergy, the sex stereo-types persist. Women are still admonished to embrace the "eternally feminine" roles of wife and mother. Further, they are instructed that "True emancipation will not involve false liberty or unnatural equality with their husband (Pope Pius XII quoted in Daly, 1970:126). Seeking a different kind of liberation and failing to fulfill their duties may create in women the feeling of having failed in their duties to God. And in a parallel fashion, if men see themselves as responsible for the leadership of their families and if they also fail, they, too, may view themselves as less worthy in the eyes of God.

Church Structure

Religious ideology has consequences for the social organization of religious insti-tutions. That which is taught from the Judeo-Christian heritage is reflected in the heirarchal structuring of the church and the expected performances of males and females within it.

In various surveys reported over the past 20 years, one finding is repeatedly verified: women have a greater religious orientation than men. That is, more women than men attend church, are active in the church social life, and express a greater need for a religious dimension in their lives (Wilson, 1971).

There are several possible explanations for this phenomenon. Generally, oppressed groups in any society are more likely to be oriented towards the "other world" than are the dominant group. Whether one explains this, as Karl Marx (1964), did—as a method by which the dominant group provides the masses with an opiate—or whether one views religion as providing the oppressed with much-needed relief, it is understandable that more women than men are attracted to religious institutions.

Yinger (1957) suggests that because women have fewer options open to them outside the home, they are less likely to become secularized. Moreover, because women are expected to uphold traditional values, the church provides a setting where they can do so and at the same time engage in extra-familial, but "safe," social interaction.

Diamond (1976) hypothesizes that a part of the appeal in Christianity is linked to women's sexual attraction to both the Biblical superheroes (as illustrated in the song "I don't know how to love him" from *Jesus Christ Superstar*) and to the clergy themselves. Although totally unresearched, the deflection of a woman's extra-marital or pre-marital sexual interests into safe fantasies about religious personages may contribute to her greater time and emotional investments in the church.

In addition, the values of the church are consistent with the values espoused by the family, such as the ultimate authority of the father (God the Father), sacrificial love, the acceptance of another's burden, the power of love. Because it is especially the woman who is expected to carry these virtues into the home, the church provides a divine rationale for her own role in the family. Coupled with the value consistency is the important part the church plays in the life stages of many families—marriage, birth, death. These rites of passage are frequently solemnized or celebrated in religious ceremonies. In that religious tradition encourages women to bring into the home the teachings of the church, an interesting question is, what positions do women hold within the formal church structure? The Roman Catholic Church does not ordain women priests; consequently, women cannot be bishops, cardinals, or popes. The role of the Catholic nun is defined primarily as a service role—to the priest, to the young, to the sick. That is, she is expected to fulfill the traditional woman's role. Laywomen service the domestic needs of the church, but the sacraments—the communion between God and parishioner—must be mediated through a male.

Reformed Judaism (as of this writing) has ordained two women rabbis. Orthodox and Conservative Judaism prohibit females in that role. The Episcopalian Church permits women to go through the seminary, but still hedges on their ordination. Neither the Reform or Missouri-Synod Lutheran churches ordain women. Although the rest of the large Prostestant denominations do ordain women, approximately only 2 percent of this ministry are women, and these are clustered in religious education positions (Reuther, 1975:73). As one female ex-Methodist minister explained, "Although the Methodist church has ordained women for many years, they do not guarantee them congregations. The assumption is that a woman minister is really interested in church education and is sent to teach the children" (Browning, 1974). In 1970, the liberal Unitarian-Universalist Church passed a sweeping resolution to use women at all levels of the church, including the ministry. As of this writing, approximately 1.4 percent of that ministry are women (884 males, 10 females).

Also, fewer women than men hold other positions within the church. A 1969 survey of church boards and agencies of 65 denominations concluded "that the status of women employed by the church is no better, and perhaps worse, than that of their secular counterparts. . . . [And] as the salary rose, the percentage of women dropped markedly" (Hole and Levine, 1971: 389).

The lack of women in high positions in the church is frequently justified on the basis of the religious credo itself. In the more traditional Jewish congregations, the exclusion is based on the interpretation of Talmudic Law. And some Christians argue that, because Eve was created out of Adam, she was secondary, and women should remain so. Others argue that, because Jesus was incarnated as a male and selected only males as disciples (and ordered Peter to so build the church), that women should be excluded from the ministry. Because many important positions in the church are expected to be fulfilled by clergy, women are excluded from those, too.

The church, then, tends to be a social organization controlled by men to service women. Ironically, one of the outcomes is that the church takes on "feminine" characteristics, and the male clergy are not expected to be "masculine." For example, clergy are expected to excel in the traits usually assigned to women— sympathy, humility, obedience, sensitivity to others, and, in some religions, chastity. And Seidler (1976) goes further in pointing out, "Childlikeness [is] expected of clergy by laity who don't want or expect clergy to really know the ways of the world, from handling money to knowing how to fix a car." And, even further, some male church members may view the clergy as men unable to succeed in the nonreligious occupational world.

Organized religion, therefore, systematically excludes women from positions of sacramental authority and at the same time tends to devalue those roles (in the eyes of the society), by associating them with feminine skills. Whether based on scripture, tradition, or modern prejudice, the outcome is the perpetuation of the current system and the devitalization of the church itself. Both males and females are effectively held in line, socially controlled by the imagery presented to them, and "projected into the realm of beliefs, which in turn justify the social [structure of the church]. The belief system becomes hardened and objectified seeming to have an unchangeable, independent existence and validity of its own" (Daly, n.d.:1).

Nevertheless, the winds of change are blowing through some belfries. Recently, alternative theological visions and structural changes have been proposed.

New Religious Visions

Flowing from humanist and feminist concerns, new theological orientations have emerged during the last decade. One of the major assumptions of the Judeo-Christian heritage that is being challenged is the image of God as male.

Although the idea that God is male is not inherent in the Bible itself, "images have a way of surviving (such that) persons can speak of God as spirit and at the same time imagine 'him' as belonging to the male sex" (Daly, n.d.:2). The depth of this imagery is suggested in Diamond's exploratory dissertational research (1976). Using the game of charades as the research vehicle, he reports that when the word *God* is acted out, male charaders tend to take on Godlike qualities (such as puffing out their chests, looking stern, and pointing a mighty finger down from on high) whereas female charaders assume the supplicant role by kneeling before and praying to God. That is, male actors—but not female ones—become God.

The language of the church, the interpretation of the scriptures, and the all male leadership have perpetuated the "popular image of the great patriarch in heaven" (Daly, n.d.:2). This imagery has consequences for men and women. Reuther argues that the image of God-as-Father sanctifies both hierarchism and sexism. By casting God in a domination-subordination relationship to humanity, "allowing ruling-class men to identify with the divine father," they are encouraged "to establish themselves in the same kind of hierarchical arrangement to women and lower classes" (1975:65). That is, the imagery of God-as-Father not only helps perpetuate sexism but perpetuates the hierarchical arrangement of people.

Some argue that the notion that "*the* Supreme Being is male is the quintessence of sexism" (Hole and Levine, 1971:379) and call for "the death of God the Father" (Daly, n.d.). These men and women recognize that the solution is not to introduce an image of God-as-Mother," but to delete the notion of paternity-maternity entirely by conceptualizing God-as-Spirit.

The recognition that the theology perpetuates hierarchism of *all* kinds—not just sexual differential evaluation—is, perhaps, an even more radical view than those thus far discussed. It is proposing that the traditional theology perpetuates a class system in which not only women lose but many men do, too. Many people are now questioning the hierarchical structure of most churches and suggesting that alternative forms of ministry are necessary.

While some feminists and humanists are concerned with eradicating clergy ordination and with the development of alternative churches in which hierarchical organization is avoided, others are concerned with changing the existent church. For these activists, the ordination of women is seen as an imperative for both pragmatic and symbolic reasons.

According to Hole and Levine (1971:385–386), there are three primary reasons why some feminists seek the ordination of women. First, "women clergy are vital in order to reassess and counterbalance . . . [the] historically 'male interpretations and teachings' within the church." Second, because clergy play a major role in church policy formation (e.g., where to distribute funds, what curricula to teach, what position to take on social-political issues), "women in the clergy would put women into policy-making positions enabling them to shape the decisions that affect women's as well as men's lives." And third, because men traditionally have had the privilege to respond to the calling of the ministry, women should be accorded the same right.

In addition to these pragmatic reasons, the new visionists see important symbolic reasons for ordaining women. First, such ordination would symbolically transcend the dogma of the subordinance of women. "Ordaining women would . . .

symbolically ... purge the church of the 'eternal feminine' ... and force it to transform its image of women from mysterious and mystical creatures into people" (Hole and Levine, 1971:386). Second, a large proportion of women ministers would "visibly challenge the assumption that leader/follower is the only acceptable male/female relationship within the church structure" (Hole and Levine, 1971:386). And third, women in cleric roles would help dispel the latent assumption that only a male can be a direct link to God.

The transformation of the church is an exceptionally complex theological and structural question. It is difficult to assess just what the consequences would be if the radical alterations proposed by some feminists and humanists were enforced. Many church feminists believe that these changes would have a revolutionary effect on religion, and, because of religion's investment in the larger social order, the impact would have major ramifications for the entire society. They envision a church divested of the oppressiveness of sexism and hierarchism, a church dedicated to the individual's right to androgyny, a church actively allocating its energies and financial resources towards humanizing the society—stripping it of its worship of violence, cut-throat competition, and hierarchic arrangement of individuals.

However, because the question is so complex, we might ask, What can be some of the unexpected and negative outcomes of such a revision? Speculatively, if the theological and structural changes did occur, one potential consequence might be the total devaluation of the church and the virtual exclusion of the male laity. As was discussed earlier, the church fulfills many functions in the everyday lives of its members by providing solace and comfort, explanation of the unknown, a social community, a ceremonial marking of its important familial events, etc. It already services more women than men in these ways. Further, it currently has an aura of the "feminine." The church is a place where feminine values are sanctified. These values are not highly valued socially and are not socially ascribed to men.

If the theology were altered to limit God to spirit and to divest Jesus of his special divinity, and if the prestigious positions within the church were in actuality filled in substantial numbers by women, might not one of the outcomes be that males will view it as even a less desirable place for them than they already do? Because males now have few structural supports for incorporating the "softer" values and behaviors in their lives and few institutions in which they can seek aid, comfort, and communion, might the transformation of the church, in effect, remove even this source of support from the male? Is it not possible that church would become even more insulated and isolated from the "real" world by closing off even that institution to the male? That is, it is possible that the changes envisioned will only serve to further devalue the church, making it truly a female ghetto inaccessible to males.

No matter what our speculations concerning the effect of the radical alteration of the church on the lives of men and women, there is no doubt, that in its present form and content it plays a major role in adult social control.

In summary, then, the institutions of religion, law, and science have served as social control mechanisms for the adult population. The formulations of legal policy, religious creed, and scientific method have been consistent with the cultural biases.

Religion and law, together with the sciences of the social, psychological, and biological, have shared a common ideology of patriarchy. And many adults have been effectively controlled by them. However, within each of these preserves—the church, the law, the sciences—alternative views have been proposed to lessen the impact of the traditional teachings on adults and to increase their awareness of different perspectives and options. Perhaps it can be argued that in the arena of the intellectual and ideological, substantial changes have been accomplished. It is probably true that more people than ever before question the validity of tradition-al teachings, have raised their consciousnesses regarding sexism in the society, and recognize that their lives would be better if the pressures to conform to gender-role expectations were removed.

Assuming that more people are interested in greater freedom from sex stereotyping, we can ask, Can these people fulfill their desires? To answer this, we need to look closely at how the institutions of work, power, and the family are structurally and functionally linked such that most individuals are prevented from achieving this freedom naturally. We address this issue—institutionally structured inequality—next.

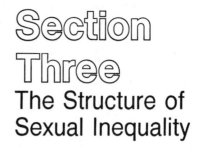

Section Three
The Structure of Sexual Inequality

What I seek to document in the forthcoming chapters is the institutionalized structure of sexual inequality—the unequal distribution of power, property, and prestige between male and female. I will document how the form, ideology, and dynamics that govern our political and economic institutions lead to the systematic exclusion and suppression of women. Further, I will argue that due to some of these factors a sense of failure is systematically produced in men, and, moreover, that the forms and processes within economic and political structures have direct and negative impacts on the intimate relationships between men and women.

In earlier sections of this book, I documented that the social prestige of women is less than that of men. Whether we were concerned with female personality, behavior, or social roles, we found women to be considered inferior to men. Further, I argued that *status* is both *chosen* and *prescribed.* That is, individuals have some ability to limit their psychological investment, to alter their behavior, to choose not to act in ways prescribed for their sex.

However, in this section, we will realize how limited those freedoms are, for now we confront the exigencies of the external, objective world. We can (and do) make choices regarding attitudes towards our subjective states. We can (and do) choose to do things that are not prescribed for our sex. But often our choices are difficult to implement. A woman can choose to be a bricklayer, but this choice will not necessarily provide her with the job of bricklayer. A man can choose to be a airline steward, but that choice will not necessarily guarantee him the position. The perpetuation of sexual inequality is not simply a "woman's issue." In short, we have reached a point in our analysis of sex and gender that to whatever extent our interpersonal lives might be changed if we choose to act differently, our subjective states are no match for the power of institutions and the interests of those who are already powerful.

9
Sexual Stratification

Social stratification is one of the central concepts in sociology. As might be expected, there are many different theories and perspectives to explain it. In the text that follows, I borrow from the work and insight of many scholars—Ernestine Friedl, Joan Huber, Gerhard Lenski, Karl Marx, Melvin Tumin, Max Weber—to name those most influential on me. I use their work to construct a framework that explains the universality of sexual inequality as well as provides a perspective for understanding how and why it is perpetuated in modern industrialized societies.

Social Stratification

All known societies have stratification systems, or the hierarchical arrangement of people. Members of a society are differentiated (categorized) on the basis of such ascribed characteristics as age, sex, race, and on the basis of such achieved characteristics as doctor, wife, bricklayer. The higher a person's position in the stratification system, the greater the socially valued rewards received.

Depending upon one's placement in the stratification system by virtue of one's age, sex, family, wealth, occupation, education, etc., a different probability exists concerning whether one will or will not receive the valued goods.

A particularly crucial factor is one's position in the division of labor. Division of labor occurs in all societies. It refers to the fact that no individual supplies all his or her own goods and services. Rather, labor is specialized, and the results of one person's activities are exchanged with others'. The more valued one's position in the division of labor, the more likely one is to receive rewards; and, further, if one is highly placed due to family, wealth, etc., then one is more likely to acquire such a position as an adult.

Social inequality, then, is both *a result of* and *perpetuated through* the unequal opportunity to control the extradomestic distribution and exchange of valued goods and services. If one receives scarce goods, one is in a better position to control their further distribution. Therefore, the stratification system has a kind of built-in feedback process, such that those who are more highly situated are more likely to control the distribution of scarce goods, which in turn reinforces and heightens their dominance.

Although almost anything can constitute a valued good, it must be something that is *publicly exchanged* and *socially scarce.* Valued goods can be classified under three major headings: *power,* or the probability that one's will will be done; *property,* or material or monetary compensation; and *prestige,* or respect and honor. These three—power, property, and prestige—are closely and reciprocally linked. They are conferred at the societal level rather than at the familial or individual levels. This is not to deny that a person may have domestic power and privileges by exchanging services and goods within the home. However, it is only when these are exchanged extradomestically that there is a public, social conferral of prestige and power. Stratification systems grow up around public exchanges, not domestic ones (Tumin, 1967).

In that power, prestige, and property are valued prizes in a society, it makes a greater deal of difference to the individual and to the society *how* these are distributed (Tumin, 1967). Consequently, all societies have norms for governing the distribution system—rules whose most salient feature is that they reflect the interests of those who are already in positions of power, even if the cost to the entire society is great. Regardless of one's position in the stratification system, adherence to the rules is usually forthcoming. This testifies not only to the strength of the established norms but to the power of the ruling group to enforce those norms.

Socially structured inequality is a fundamental feature of social life. Individuals are socialized to know their place, to accept the legitimacy of their role options and the rewards attached to their performance, and to recognize the rights and obligations they have as members of a particular group. Social order is partially maintained, then, by individuals accepting the options society offers them. In the United States, for example, we learn that it is or is not an option to be a nurse or a doctor, and that it is legitimate, moral, and just, after all, for a doctor to receive more power, prestige, and property than a nurse.

At the individual level, then, the induction into the stratification system begins young and is inextricably woven into the socialization process. However, conformity and acceptance is ensured by the ability of those who are more powerful to constrain the less powerful. They are able to do this because they control the distribution of the scarce goods and services. Such control means that they have the right to make the rules regarding the distribution and the right to enforce those decisions through negative sanctions and violence. But, just as there is a strong and overarching tendency for systems to perpetuate themselves, they inevitably are also subject to change. This change may be due to either alterations in the technological base or through recognition of the subordinate groups that their place in the system is unjust or through purposeful redistribution efforts by ascending power groups or through some interplay of these. In any case, to effect such change requires wresting control of the distribution of scarce goods and services.

Sexual Inequality

It is within the context of universal social stratification that sexual inequality occurs. In all known societies, there is a degree of male dominance—greater power and prestige bestowed upon the male than upon the female (Friedl, 1975:7). Although some scholars have postulated the historical existence of a matriarchy (a society dominated by women), there is no anthropological evidence to support that contention (Friedl, 1975:4). Indeed, most researchers and theorists, regardless of their ideological stance on issues of sexual equality, agree that male dominance is a fundamental and universal feature of social life. The question, then, is, "Why are men universally dominant?" In the past decade, considerable controversy over the answer to this question has emerged. Rather than reviewing the various viewpoints, I will discuss the arguments of two of the most popular explanations: the biogenetic and the bio-cultural.

The biogenetic explanation is based on the idea that, because male dominance is culturally universal, it must be genetically caused and it must play a major role in the survival of the human species. Males and females, the proponents argue, are physically and hormonally, different. Males have higher levels of androgens, the "aggressivity" hormone, whereas females have a monthly hormonal cycle. On the average, males are taller and heavier. Their skeletal structure and musculature are adapted to running and tasks that require sudden bursts of energy and strength. On the other hand, the female's skeletal, anatomical, and hormonal systems are not adapted for those tasks, but rather for her biological functions in childbearing and lactation. Because of these innate biogenetic differences between males and females, a *natural* division of labor occurs. Men are best suited for providing and protecting (the hunter and warrior roles); women, for childbearing and childrearing. Therefore, it is because of biological reasons that women are domestically placed and excluded from political and economic arenas. Women's lack of power and prestige is a natural consequence of this division of labor.

An alternative explanation, the bio-cultural one, argues that male dominance exists because men have greater access to the distribution of scarce goods and services. Their greater access, however, is not a result of genetic predisposition, but of a complex interplay among certain biological, technological, and socio-cultural factors.

To support their argument, they point out, for example, that the *degree* of male dominance varies cross-culturally, that the sexual division of labor varies between societies, that in some societies women do perform major public roles, and that the physical and hormonal variations *within* each sex is great. They reason that the diversity in cultural adaptations to biological differences is so great that deterministic genetic arguments are not sufficient explanations.

Recognizing that there is cultural diversity and that male dominance is one of degree cross-culturally, bio-culturists ask, Why is male dominance universal? In answering this question, they turn to the diversity of cultures and ask why is there male dominance within a *particular* society. Because biogeneticists tend to look at early forms of social organization to support their arguments, it is reasonable for us to look at those societal forms and ask, as bio-culturists do, To what degree and why are males dominant?

Friedl found sexual inequality in foraging (hunting and gathering) societies and horticultural (cultivation by hand or hoe) societies. These are the earliest and most developmentally "primitive" forms of subsistence technology. In these societies, the level of technology plays a major role in how inequality is structured. Although in both these societal forms males are dominant, the reasons for their so being depends upon the subsistence level.

In hunting and gathering societies, meat (protein) is scarce, and men have a monopoly on hunting and fishing. However, contrary to common opinion, men are the hunters not because they are physically stronger or more agile. Nor are women excluded from this role because they cannot wander far from the campsite (in fact, they do). Rather, it is primarily because hunting and carrying burdens are incompatible activities. Women not only carry fetuses *in utero,* upsetting their balance in the latter months, but they carry nursing infants. Compatible with the toting of babies is the bearing of other burdens—plants, roots, seeds—and other children. Therefore, although women supply the major source of subsistence in these foraging societies, they do not provide the most valued goods, meat. Further, because these societies are universally governed by a "generosity" norm—one should share scarce resources—the meat is publicly distributed. In that men are the providers, they have greater control over meat distribution and, therewith, greater dominance. (For a more complete discussion see Friedl, 1975.)

In horticultural societies, although women usually partake in the actual farm-ing, it is not the growing of food that is the scarce good. Rather, it is the acquisition and clearing of new land, after the old has gone fallow. Men are assigned these tasks because new land is usually at territorial boundaries where warfare is more likely. It is not because men are physically more able, however, that they are allocated these tasks. Rather, Friedl argues, it is because males are less neces-sary for the survival of the society; females, due to their role in reproduction, cannot be assigned high-risk tasks. Consequently, men are more likely to be involved in alliances and exchanges of valued goods with others and will more frequently acquire the rights to their distribution. (For a more complete discussion, see Friedl, 1975.)

Through agricultural (Boserup, 1970), industrializing, industrialized, and post-industrial economies (Galbraith, 1973; Huber, 1976), males continue to be more likely to acquire the rights over the distribution of scarce goods. For example, in societies where money, rather than protein or land is exchanged, males are encouraged to work outside the home and given more opportunities than women to acquire positions that are highly monetarily compensated (see Chapter 10). The system is structured such that the extradomestic advantages gained by men can be used to purchase the domestic services of women (see Chapter 11). Male dominance persists. Is it inevitable?

The Inevitability of Male Dominance?

If one assumes, as the biogeneticists do, that male dominance is the result of heredity and species survival, then it is, obviously, inevitable. Any attempts to alter it is either impossible or destructive for the individual, the society, and, ultimately, the species. Indeed, some would argue that the changes already wrought are damaging.

However, if one assumes that dominance is a result of the interplay among culture, biology, and technology, then it *may* not be inevitable. Indeed, from this perspective much of the current feminist agony and social unrest is a result of trying to limit the options according to some predetermined notion of biological suitedness. I hold to the bio-cultural assumption.

The dominance of males *appears* inevitable and immutable for many reasons. One of the primary ones is that, in industrialized societies, ideology has a significant impact on the distribution system (Lenski, 1966). The ideology that has supported the sexual stratification system in all industrialized societies—capitalist and communist, democratic and authoritarian—is that of patriarchalism, a belief that men are naturally superior to women and are entitled to greater power and prestige.

Why this ideology arose is difficult to say, although its underlying theme—the devaluation of women's work—is present throughout the world (Friedl, 1975). However, it is common for groups to propagate beliefs that aggrandize themselves, and it is equally common for the subordinated group to accept the dominant group's definitions. Further, it is a stance that meshes well with the demands of industrializing and industrialized nations. The important point, however, is that significant support for sexual inequality in contemporary nations rests on a set of ideas. Ideas are always culturally produced and are, therefore, always subject to social revision.

If, however, we are to refute the idea of the inevitability of male dominance, we must address the one indisputable difference between the sexes: no man can bear a child. As we have seen in earlier societal forms, women's lesser access to the control of extradomestic resources is directly related to her biological roles in reproduction. However, "Technology permits humans to transcend biology—people can fly although no one was born with wings" (Huber, 1976a:2). That is, although women have wombs, the technological level of industrialized societies is such that neither sex need be assigned to the role of child-rearer.

Consequently, the argument to be developed is that male dominance is not inevitable but that it will be sustained and perpetuated until two related social changes are accomplished. These are: (1) males and females are accorded equal access to the control and distribution of scarce goods and services, and (2) males and females have equal responsibility for child-rearing. We have reached a point in our technological development where these social changes can feasibly occur, although ideology and opportunity structure have not kept pace with technology.

We have reached this point of technological development for two primary reasons: rapid and long-term decline in fertility rates and widespread bottle feeding of infants (Huber, 1976). The fall in fertility has been a persistent pattern over the past 200 years in all industrialized societies. A major reason for the decline in fertility was that children were seen as economic liabilities to families. Currently, governments and individuals see a low fertility rate as desirable and the indications are that this will continue (Huber, 1976). Therefore, the average woman in industrialized nations will spend only two years or so of her entire life pregnant.

The importance of the widespread adoption of bottle feeding during the 20th century cannot be overemphasized. No longer is an infant's survival dependent upon a lactating mother. Consequently, the child-bearing function is technologically separable from the child-rearing function. Indeed, the average infant in the United States is not breast-fed; for those who are, best estimates are that three weeks is the median duration.

Since the average woman is only involved in child-bearing for a few months of her life, and because the average woman is also working outside the home, and because the average baby is bottle-fed, on what grounds can assignment of domestic tasks to women be socially justified (Huber, 1976a)? Such a division of labor made sense for our ancestors—the foragers and horticulturists. After all, fertility control was difficult then, and child-bearing and child-rearing were necessarily intertwined. But, this particular division of labor is no longer functionally necessary in industrialized societies.

Since the allocation of domestic tasks to women, and extradomestic ones to men, is the primary reason why men have achieved greater dominance and since it is no longer technologically necessary to retain this division of labor, male dominance is not immutable. It is retained, however, both through the ideology that states "Women's place is in the home" and through social structures that prevent men and women from sharing child-rearing–bread-winning tasks. Speculatively, Huber (1976a) suggests that if the decline in fertility continues, greater sexual equality may result: Inducing women to have children may require reallocating the primary responsibility for their care.

Large-scale social trends would seem to lend credence to a projected continuing decline in the birthrate: the proportion of singles is growing, the age at first marriage is increasing, the rate of remarriage is decreasing, the length of time between marriage and first child is increasing, and the divorce rate is burgeoning. Further, since one of the primary factors in reducing fertility is viewing children as liabilities, Huber postulates that we are reaching a point where not only the couple views children as economic liabilities, but where women view them as *personal liabilities.* Because women are still expected to raise the children, women are likely to weigh more seriously the gains of motherhood against the costs. If the low birthrate among educated and occupationally successful women is any indication, as more women aspire educationally and occupationally, we can expect more to choose to have few or no children.

If the fertility rates continue to dip, falling below the rate necessary for population replacement, Huber speculates that governments will intervene with policies and programs that will redistribute the responsibility for child-care. When the state has a vested interest in having more children, it may provide the necessary incentive: free day-care to all. By releasing women from the primary child-care duties, a redistribution of domestic responsibilities will occur. The result will be greater sexual equality. However, it seems unlikely that it will happen soon. Maintaining the outmoded and dysfunctional system is in the interest of those who already have power and prestige.

Sexual stratification, then, is universal but not inevitable. The particular shape and form such sexual inequality takes depends upon the society in which it exists. Let us look at modernizing and modernized societies generally, and specifically at the United States.

Industrial Economies

The hallmark of an industrialized society is its intense and widespread division of labor. With the advent of the factory system, goods usually produced in the home were produced outside. Workers in factories were assigned increasingly narrow and specialized tasks. As the population grew, the specialization of labor increased, leading to a more efficient output of goods and to greater profits for the industrialists. The economy shifted from agriculture to one of manufacturing, to—in advanced industrial nations—a service industry.

Paralleling the changes in the production of goods was a change in the manner in which the production was administrated. The administrative form that developed was that of the *bureaucracy*—a hierarchical structure designed to manage large-scale undertakings through the coordination of the work of many individuals, who are unequal in their positions in the division of labor (Weber, 1946; Coser and Rosenberg, 1976:353). The bureaucratic structure, therefore, is based upon specialization of labor within an organization in which both the *lines* and *levels* of authority are formally structured. Today, the corporate bureaucracy dominates the American economy (Baldridge, 1975:374). The corporation is a system jointly owned by many shareholders, but *control* rests in the board of directors and its high-level managerial staff (see Chapter 10).

During industrialization, due to increase specialization and hierarchism, the surplus of scarce goods increased. This meant there was more of the valued goods to distribute and more *levels* of decision-making. As a result *social mobility* —moving from one position in the hierarchy to another—became possible. In societies with service economies, the probability of such mobility is great, because service occupations are expanding and confer more rewards than blue-collar jobs.

Specialization of labor and bureaucratic structure have contributed to the economic growth of nations; however, they have also created groups of workers who could be categorized on the basis of their specialization and their position in the hierarchy and who could aspire to move up. Simpler and closed classification systems such as "peasant/lord" were replaced by more complex and open ones. In relation to complexity, for example, in the United States the classification scheme used by the Department of Labor (in descending order of prestige) is professional, technical; managers, officials, proprietors; clerical workers; sales workers, craftsmen, foremen; operatives; nonfarm laborers; service workers (e.g., household help). In terms of openness, individuals could not only move from one category to another (e.g., from sales to clerical) but could advance within a given category (e.g., from lawyer to Supreme Court Justice). One's occupation became, and continues to be, an excellent indicator of one's wealth, social prestige, life chances and lifestyle. The "better" the occupation, the greater the opportunity to control the distribution of scarce goods and services.

But does one's sex affect the probability of acquiring such control in an open classification system? In attempting to answer this question, I will focus on the structure of occupations in the United States.

Occupational Structure

Most men are gainfully employed; the unemployment rate for males currently hovers around 5 to 6 percent (Department of Labor, July 2, 1976). Even though most men work, they do not have a monopoly on the labor market and the edge they have had is rapidly receding. In 1950, for example, 70 percent of the labor force was male whereas in 1974 only 57 percent of the entire workforce was male. The growth of female labor force participation has occurred primarily since 1940, with sequential waves of women from various backgrounds—immigrant, young black, older married, and, most recently, young married women, many with preschool children. The demographic characteristics of women who work, have become increasingly similar to the characteristics of the entire population in terms of race, ethnicity, education, age, and marital and family status (Blau, 1975:218–219). That is, "it is becoming more difficult to consider working women as in some sense an unrepresentative or atypical group" (Blau, 1975:219). It is not atypical for a woman to work; nor is the working woman typically different on demographic characteristics than the nonworking woman.

Occupational Distribution

Although men are still more likely than women to have access to a position in the economy, the percentage differences in labor force participation are steadily decreasing. However, because the kind of job one holds determines to a great degree one's probability of acquiring control (as well as one's income and lifestyle), we need to know if, in fact, males and females have equal access to the different occupational levels. If there were no systematic differentiation by sex, we would expect males and females to be randomly distributed throughout the work world.

In all industrialized countries, however, we find males and females are distributed differently amongst the occupational categories. In the United States, in 1971, 28 percent of all working men were in professional and technical or managerial positions; only 20 percent of all working women were in these categories, and most of these were school teachers or nurses. More than one-third of employed women are in clerical positions—secretaries, file clerks, etc. The higher-paying, higher-status blue-collar jobs (e.g., fore*man* and crafts*man*) are predominately male occupations. Low-paying and low-status positions (e.g., household workers) are primarily held by women—more than 22 percent as compared to 8 percent by men.

The occupational placement of black women is especially skewed. Although 60 percent of white women employees are white-collar workers, only 30 percent of black women are at this level. "Fifty percent [of black working women] held service jobs in 1968, and fully half of this group were private household workers, the lowest-paying occupation" (Blau, 1975:22).

However, these data do not reveal the full extent of occupational segregation —the extent to which women are clustered in certain jobs. One of our cultural beliefs is that certain positions are appropriate for women and other positions are appropriate for men. As a result, occupations are sexually segregated, and, within mixed-gender occupations, certain job classifications are reserved for women, and others for men.

In 1971, more than half of the female labor force was in 21 occupations out of the 250 listed by the U.S. Census Bureau (Blau, 1975:221). Merely five occupations—elementary school teacher, secretary-stenographer, bookkeeper, waitress, and household worker—accounted for *one fourth* of the employed women (Blau, 1975:221). That is, "men are much more widely distributed throughout the occupational structure ..." (Blau, 1975:221). Further, "most women work in predominately female jobs" (Blau, 1975:221). For example, in a study of occupations in which more than 70 percent of the labor force was female, Oppenheimer found that more than 50 percent of all female workers were in these occupations (1973). And there has been no change in the distribution of workers from 1900 to 1960, only a greater number of occupations.

In an attempt to determine just how great occupational segregation was for each census year from 1900 to 1960, Gross devised an "index of occupational segregation." The index was constructed to measure the proportion of women who would have to change jobs in a given year in order for the occupational placement of men and women to be equalized. His conclusions were three-fold. First, the amount of occupational segregation had not effectively changed during this period—the difference between the high- and low-integration scores was only 4 percentage points. Secondly, the magnitude of the segregation was large. In order for occupational integration to be a fact, approximately two-thirds of the female labor force would have had to change jobs in any given census year

(Gross, 1968). And thirdly, sex segregation was more severe than racial segregation. (Whereas the index for sex segregation was 68.4 percent, the index for racial segregation was 46.8 percent. Because Gross has not reported a separate index for black females, we can surmise that that index is higher than either of those reported.) Gross concluded that "those concerned with sexual segregation can take small comfort from these figures." Women's entry into the labor force has been accomplished through expanding those occupations that were already female, the creation of new female jobs (e.g., keypuncher), or "through females taking over previously male occupations" (1968:202).

Oppenheimer (1973) concurs with this analysis, arguing that the great influx of women into the labor force is a result of the demands of industry for "women workers to fulfill 'women's jobs' "—service industries, clerical positions, etc. Sex segregation is an institutionalized practice within our occupational structure. The occupations that are sex-typed "female" not only are consistent with the culture's stereotypes towards women, but they are occupations that are unlikely to lead to rights to distribute scarce goods and resources.

Earnings

One of the valued goods to distribute in our economy is, of course, money. Despite the various measures employed by economists, one difference is clear: men earn more than women. The extent of the difference depends on how earnings are computed and what other variables are included in the study.

Considering only raw statistics, we find that white males earn substantially more than either black males or white or black females (see Table 8.1). For full-time workers, nonwhite males make approximately 70 percent as much as white males, whereas white females earn approximately 58 percent as much. Black females who share neither whiteness nor maleness with the dominant group, earn 50 percent as much.

TABLE 8.1   Average Salaries Earned by Working Men and Women, 1970

Workers	Average salary
Full-time, year-round	
White men	$9,375
Nonwhite men	6,598
White women	5,490
Nonwhite women	4,679
Full-time and part-time	
Men	$7,939
Women	3,785

Source: U.S. Dept. of Commerce, Census Bureau, **Current Population Report** (1970), Bulletin P-60, no. 80, p. 129.

The part-time worker fares even more poorly. As a group, women earn approximately 47 percent as much as male part-time workers. In addition, there are many more female part-time workers than males—and part-time usually means few fringe benefits and greater job insecurity.

But the raw statistics perhaps conceal more than they reveal, for one might think, "It makes sense that women make less; after all, they are less well trained and in lower positions than men." Consequently, we need to look at the income of males and females, while controlling for such factors as education and occupational placement.

When we consider just the major census categories for occupational placement (e.g., professional, clerical) we find, as Table 8.2 displays, that for each occupational listing men earn more than women.

TABLE 8.2   Median Annual Earnings of Full-Time Workers

Occupation	Women	Men
Scientists	$10,000	$13,200
Professional, technical	6,691	10,151
Proprietors, managers	5,635	10,340
Clerical workers	4,789	7,351
Sales workers	3,461	8,549
Craftsmen	4,625	7,978
Factory workers	3,991	6,738
Service workers	3,332	6,058

Source: U.S. Dept. of Labor, National Science Foundation, Data for 1968.

Moreover, because women are in various specific job classifications within each of the broad occupations, we will get a better estimate on income disparity if we control for specific occupations. In perhaps the largest statistical study of professors, Darland (et al., 1973) studied the yearly earnings of more than 13,000 faculty members at more than 300 universities. The researchers used many variables such as age, type and quality of employing institute, field of specialization, proportion of time spent teaching, number of articles and books published, research funding obtained, and length of academic service. They found that for almost every academic speciality and almost every type of institution, the salaries of women faculty members reflected discrimination. The greater discrimination occurred in the highest-status universities and in the physical and biological sciences (Darland et al., 1973).

Economists sometimes argue, however, that cross-firm analyses provide inadequate data, since organizations differ widely in their salary schedules, job classifications, etc. Therefore, it is suggested that one look closely at the salaries within a single institution in order to isolate the effect of the organization itself on salaries. In one such study of a single university, the author concluded that females receive fewer salary rewards for their experience than males (Katz, 1973). In another such study, the authors found that the differential earnings of men and women increased with age and rank (Gordon et al., 1973).

But, perhaps, women earn less because of the interplay of occupation, education, and the geographical region in which they work. These are all known to be interactive factors that influence a worker's income. Almquist (1973) set herself the task of estimating female income losses that could be attributed to these factors. She found that 32 percent of the black women's salary loss and only 12 percent of the white female's (relative to white males) could be attributed to educational, occupational, and regional factors. In dollar amounts, a $4323 salary differential between black women and white men and a $4570 differential between white women and white men could not be explained. These salary losses, Almquist argues, are direct measures of the extent of economic discrimination against women.

Consequently, whether one looks at gross incomes, particular occupations, a particular work setting, a sampling of specialities and work settings, or at other factors associated with income levels, the results are consistent: women earn less. Women are less likely to acquire positions with high monetary rewards. Further, when they do acquire such positions, they are paid less than men. Moreover, the higher the position the female obtains, the greater the absolute salary differential between herself and her male colleague. The more prestigious the occupation (e.g., physics) and the more prestigious the setting (e.g., Harvard), the greater the disparity. In addition, once entry into a job category has occurred, white women are more severely economically penalized than black women.

How can this economic discrimination be explained? Why are women not monetarily rewarded on a par with men? And why are white women more discriminated against than black women after job entry? Part of the answer to these questions rests in two elements of the ideology of patriarchy: women's work is not as valuable as men's; and women are provided for by men.

Viewing women's work as being not as valuable as men's work means that even when a woman is doing the same work as a man, it is not seen as identical; her sex status diminishes the value of her work in the eyes of her employer and he rewards her accordingly. Once the practice of paying women less is established, it becomes normative; unconsciously, succeeding generations of employers tend to follow such norms.

The second element in patriarchical ideology—"women are provided for by men"—suggests how employers justify discrimination against women, as well as why white women are penalized economically more than black women after job entry. It just might be taken for granted that "white men provide for white women, while black women provide for black men" (see Chapter 12). If this is so, employers will view black women as more committed and more in need than white women and reward them commensurately.

This assumption has little basis in the reality of women's lives. Neither black or white women can depend on being provided for by men. Most women work outside the home because they have to, because they need the money. Six and a half million women are single; they work to support themselves. The widowed, divorced, and separated constitute another 5.8 million female workers, most of whom support not only themselves but their families. Less than 30 percent of the income of the divorced or widowed women comes from any source other than her own labor (Amundsen, 1971:27).

Of those married and working, 7.8 million have husbands who make less than $5000 a year. Half of these have children. Of the remainder of the female labor force—approximately 11 million— "the majority have husbands whose incomes fall between $5000 and $8000 dollars per year—above the poverty level, but below the level defined as 'comfortable' by government economists" (Amundsen, 1971:3). The overwhelming majority of women work outside the home for economic reasons—not for pleasure, not for luxuries, not out of boredom.

Obviously, the belief that women are provided for by men decreases the probability that women's incomes will be viewed as exchangeable extradomestically. However, because the probability is three out of four that any woman will spend part or most of her adult life alone and because currently more than 20 million women are working for compelling economic reasons, denying the reality of why women work supports the present system and continues to allocate to men greater rights to control scarce goods and services.

10

The Work World: Organization and Process

Division of labor, specialization, and hierarchism, are characteristic of industrialized societies. One's place in the division of labor determines to a great degree one's probability of achieving power and prestige—the right to control the distribution of scarce goods and services. However, in addition to understanding the consequences one's work has on one's life, the organization of the work place itself must be addressed. This is so, because not only do people work to live; they live at work.

The everyday accomplishment of work is a socially structured activity that takes place in the context of a culture. It is at the social-interactional level—in the offices, factories, universities, stores, etc.—where the assumptions of the culture concerning gender differences are enacted. Consequently, we would be highly remiss if we did not address the organization and processes of the workaday world—the practices and rituals that are retaining walls of sexual inequality. Despite the work setting, level of training, and prestige of an occupation, the same basic rules and practices apply. We will discover that, ironically, the same processes and structures that serve to systematically exclude women systematically produce a sense of failure in men. A total and comprehensive documentation of such practices is impossible at this time, because researchers have only begun to view the occupational world from this perspective. Hence, what we will strive for is a consistent sociological framework through which old research can be viewed and new research designed.

Status Inconsistency

We have already seen how the work world is divided up so that women and men are sex segregated, so that women are clustered in low-paying jobs and rewarded less than men when they do advance. Earlier we discussed how the socialization process encourages males and females to have different occupational expectations. We need not review these data here, but should note, in passing, that some economists see this differential socialization as the primary for differential earnings, occupational placement, post-school training, labor force attachment, etc. (Kohen, 1975). We need to know, now, how these differential occupational outcomes are sustained through the everyday operations of work organizations.

Let us first of all examine the assumption that men's work and women's work is different. Whether a job is viewed as masculine or feminine is often quite independent of the work skills the job actually requires. For example, in the United States, medicine is seen as a profession that requires such masculine attributes as intelligence and assurance. In the Soviet Union, on the other hand, medicine is defined as a career that requires such feminine-defined traits as nurturance, service orientation, and humaneness. In the United States, 6 percent of the doctors are female whereas in the Soviet Union, 75 percent are women (Epstein, 1970:-154). That is, the Soviet Union and the United States share the same sex stereotype, but define the occupation in terms of different skills. Further, however, I would hypothesize that the social valuation of the physician is higher in the United States than in the Soviet Union and that the social organization of medicine in the United States, in effect, establishes medical care as a scarce service.

In the United States if women enter a predominately male occupation, they tend to be slotted into those positions that have the least prestige. For example, women in medicine tend to be in three low-status specialities: pediatrics, psychiatry, public health (Epstein, 1970:159); woman lawyers are disproportionately in the fields of domestic and public defense law (Epstein, 1970:160). It is generally true, throughout the occupational world, that the higher the position, the fewer the women.

On the other hand, men who enter predominately female occupations tend to be upwardly mobile. For example, in the predominately female professions of nursing, teaching, and library science, a higher proportion of males move into administrative roles than females.

Sociologists have paid considerable attention to the phenomenon of *status inconsistency*, or the fact that a person may hold different statuses which are inconsistent with the perspective of the culture. Examples are the Christian Science professor of medicine, the Jewish John Birch Society member, the black male domestic worker, the female judge, etc. Meeting someone of the "wrong" sex (or for that matter of the wrong age, race, ethnic background, class) for an occupation causes dissonance. The result is that students with a male professor of home economics, for example, tend to be distracted by the fact that he is male. Or, rather than assessing the worth of a female attorney's defense, the jury focuses on her femaleness. Although "sex—female" is irrelevant to the skills required to manage a board meeting, tar a roof, teach a class in physics, admonish a jury, or to minister to a parishioner, each of these occupational roles are sex-typed as male. Consequently, co-workers and others reduce their discomfort of dealing with a woman in these positions by focussing on the fact of her femaleness. In short, they make sex *salient*—when it is objectively irrelevant.

Persons who have status inconsistency tend to think of themselves in terms of their highest status and expect others to do the same. However, because people have a vested interest in elevating their own self-images, many unconsciously want to see others in terms of their lowest status (Lenski, 1966:86)—a kind of one-upmanship. The effect is one of "considerable stress for many persons of inconsistent status"; such persons find social interaction outside of their background area "somewhat less rewarding than does the average person" (Lenski, 1966:87).

The question then becomes, How is it that sex becomes salient in the organization of work? In what follows, we will look at three major structural components of occupations in the United States and analyze their effects on both women and men. These components are: (1) hierarchical networks, (2) sponsorship system, and (3) socio-emotional bonding.

Hierarchical Networks

With the exception of pure entrepreneurial enterprise, work in modern industrial countries is carried on in organizations. These organizations are internally hierarchically structured. Whether business, army, university, hospital, factory, or road crew, the practical way of knowing who is where is to look at order-giving and order-taking (Collins, 1975:62; Walum, 1975). The higher a person's position in an organization, the more orders given and the fewer orders received. Giving orders has profound effects on both the order-giver and the order-taker. The behavior, deportment, and litany of the order-giver reflects his or her position of power and prestige. And the order-taker "accepts one thing . . . to put up with standing before someone who is giving orders and with deferring to him at least for the moment" (Collins, 1975:63).

Receiving deference enhances a person's ability to use power successfully. But, to receive deference a person must be perceived of as worthy. According to Goffman (1967) receiving deference is primarily a function of a person's bearing, demeanor, and deportment—carrying oneself as a person who expects to be obeyed. It is through that presentation of self that others are convinced that authority rests within that person.

Further, where one fits in the organizational hierarchy determines to a great extent the amount and diversity of one's personal contacts. The more persons one knows, the more alliances and exchanges one can engage in. People can be asked to deliver support based on previous negotiations. The fewer personal contacts, the fewer the potential exchanges and the less the power. The structure of work viewed as a hierarchy of power-relations helps explain why and how women are excluded from management (order-giving) positions throughout the occupational hierarchy. Dominance is a trait associated with males: neither men nor women want to take orders from a woman. Women, consequently, are more likely to be professors than deans, lawyers than judges, doctors than chiefs and line workers than foremen.

Successful domination depends on carrying off one's authority through verbal and nonverbal communications. As we have already seen (Chapter 2), women are taught to communicate submissiveness. Few women have learned to style themselves as persons not to be questioned. This probably is especially true for order-giving to men. And even those women who have learned to act authoritatively still have a flaw—their sex—which continually affects others' reactions to them. Put another way, others respond to their lower status (female) rather than to their higher status (manager). In addition, by being removed from communication networks, women become increasingly submissive, subservient, and alienated from the goals of the company. Whatever commitment they may have had to career success is undermined by these structural features of work.

Several concrete examples will illustrate how these features are manifested in work situations. Michael Korda's *Male Chauvinism: How It Works* is particularly informative. He reports, for example, the reaction of a 50ish man to a 30ish woman—both famous lawyers. "When the man came in he smiled, turned to me [Korda] and said, 'Listen, you should have told me she was a great looking chick. . . .' " (1973:47). Rather than recognizing her professional status, he responded to her sex status. Imagine for a moment what would become of the male lawyer's bearing if the woman had said, "Hey, why didn't you tell me he was so well hung?" (Korda, 1973:47).

Publishing houses are notorious for their in-house power relations. For example, Time-Life was charged with 75 sex-discrimination complaints. One of the items focused on the practice of the magazines to hire college-educated women as researchers (nonwriting jobs) at 40 to 60 percent of the salaries paid to equivalently educated men who were hired as writers. Employed in nonwriting positions, they were ordered by the writers to perform such nonprofessional tasks as preparing coffee, and making plane reservations (Korda, 1973).

As these illustrations suggest, women are treated in terms of their sex-status within the organization of work and are, thereby, denied the authority that their positions might entitle them to. But, in addition, they are excluded from the network of communications and, therefore, access to the power base within the organization. The informal processes by which this occurs will concern us later, but we need to note here two kinds of formalized processes. First, the propensity of organizations to use architectural barriers to separate males and females (Walum, 1975). Factories often have separate male and female assembly lines, and some public schools have lounges labeled "Women Teacher's Room" or "Teacher's Lounge: Men Only." Korda reports corporate offices where female executives are placed in one corridor, male executives in another. Once the women are placed together in corporate purdah, each individual woman becomes invisible and can be treated as a member of the group *women* (Korda, 1973: 129–130). Soon, their status as executives can be ignored, and their functions within the organization can be limited and managed (Korda, 1973: 129–130).

The second major formal process is to encourage women to specialize in some small area of the corporate or research enterprise. With expertise in a minor area, their network communication lacks diversity, I would hypothesize further that the speciality probably is one that is neither highly valued nor one that is likely to lead to control over others in the organization.

Similarly, the typical organizational structure has direct consequences for the careers of men. Many men—due to ethnic or social class backgrounds—are not seen as having management potential by their supervisors. And many men who are not high in the hierarchy, nevertheless, carry around images of masculinity that require occupational success. The full impact of this structure on men will concern us shortly. But, we should note that those men who do succeed tend to perpetuate the same organizational structure through which they advanced. They do that through the recruitment and socialization of new members.

Sponsor-Protégé System

The saying "It is not what you know, but who you know" finds some reality in the second major feature of the social organization of work: the sponsor-protégé (master-apprentice) system. "Entry to the upper echelons of many professions is commonly gained through the protégé system" (Epstein, 1970:55), as is entry to top administrative posts, skilled trades, etc. For most elite professions and skilled trades, the sponsorship system is formalized; in others, such as in the corporate world, it is more informal, with the success of the sponsor determining the career of the junior.

The system is used to select candidates suitable for the skills of the trade. For many jobs, such as corporate law and neuro-surgery, the necessary skills can be learned only on the job. Only by being accepted into the field can one learn the trade secrets (Becker and Strauss, 1956). Entering the field, however, requires convincing the gatekeepers that one is already similar to, or is able to learn to be like, those already in the area. The more prestigious the speciality, the heftier the security guards, for greater care must be exercised in protecting its secrets.

Further, because sponsors probably already have greater authority and greater commitment to the organization's goals, protégés are those who will insure a continuity of leadership. The probability of such continuity is greater if the apprentice fits in well with the occupational peer group. Consequently, both internal desire for corporate immortality and external pressure from colleagues lead masters to recruit apprentices whose statuses are consistent with those of the occupation's membership.

The sponsorship system, therefore, functions within organizations to maximize in-group solidarity by minimizing the amount of dissonance and intra-group conflict. In addition, it functions to maintain the practices of the organization (profession, trade, etc.) by offering positions to those who are most likely to concur with those practices. In effect, the smooth transition of leadership ensures both the longevity of the sponsor's memory (research, power, etc.), and the maintenance of the organization's practices. Both personal needs of retiring elites and needs of the organization to maintain itself *as is* are favored through the practice of sponsorship. Consequently, there is a considerable amount of personal and communal interest regarding new recruits.

To the extent that the master-apprentice system functions to maintain an organization's practices, so does it function to limit women's economic rewards. Women are less likely than men to be acceptable as protégés due to their sex status. The status female is seen to be inconsistent with the status of neurosurgeon, bricklayer, and Dean. In the skilled-craft unions, women were explicitly barred. As late as 1942, seven of the American Federation of Labor unions officially excluded women, although women were employed in the industries covered by these unions. The most extreme example was in the construction of the International Moulder's Union, which stated that "any member, active or honorary, who devoted his time in whole or in part to the instruction of female help in the foundry or in any branch of the trade shall be expelled from the union" (Henry, 1923:100, quoted in Falk, 1975:256). In effect, wherever occupations are sex-typed as male, women are seen as not belonging and, therefore, as ineligible recruits.

Beliefs about women affect any given women's chances of being sponsored. One of these beliefs has to do with succession—handing over the reins (tools, methods, power, etc.) to one's chosen follower. In her study of professions, Epstein, for example, noted, that although a professional may even prefer a female assistant to a male, "he cannot identify her (as he might a male assistant) as someone who will eventually be his successor" (1970:170). In the trade labor unions, rigid apprentice rules have been established, requiring sponsorship by craft members and, in some cases, requiring that the apprentice be a son or nephew of the member.

The belief that women will not be good successors rests on assumptions about their psychological and biological natures. For example, it is assumed that a female will marry and have children, and thus is less committed to the organization (Epstein, 1970:170). Korda reports the threat of dependence on a good secretary is great enough ("What if she leaves me, what will I do?"), but clearly trivial compared to the threat of a groomed junior executive on maternity leave.

Further difficulties exist in the potential consequences that close relations between a male sponsor and a female apprentice might have on their personal lives. For example, the wife of a sponsor might be suspicious of the relationship; similarly, the pressures on the female worker, if a mother, are great in terms of role strains and familial obligations. Moreover, if men accept the competence of women in their offices and respect their desires for change, they may have to take seriously their wives' desires for change. And most threatening of all is that men may find that women are "far stronger and more resilient people than men" (Korda, 1973:60).

Finally, even when a women is able to enter a career through sponsorship, she is less likely to be promoted along a career path. This is so, primarily because it is assumed that women are not dependent, psychologically or financially, upon their careers. Consequently, male sponsors feel less responsibility towards them.

This is quite common in academics. For example, one academic woman reported asking her dean why two men whose vitas were less strong than hers were promoted and she held back. His response was, "You have a house and a husband here. You're not in a hurry." Three years later, when she was divorced, the same dean commented, "Now, you're promotable." The classic case, however, involves the academic history of Ruth Benedict, Chair of the Department of Anthropology at Columbia. Frank Boas, who was her mentor, recognized the value of her research but, nevertheless, regarded her as Mrs. Stanley Benedict. He considered her as "someone whose talents he must find work and a little money for, someone on whom he could not make extreme demands and for whom he need not be responsible." Only when she separated from her husband, was she given the position of assistant professor (Bernard, 1964:105–106).

Men, more than women, are expected to fulfill the American dream of occupational success. However, their background can limit their mobility as much as sex-stereotyping can limit women's. For example, one of the most striking and consistent findings in stratification literature is the extent to which high-prestige occupations are passed on from father to son. The son of a bricklayer who wishes to be a surgeon has little chance for such upward mobility; the son of the factory hand who wishes to be a typesetter similarly has little chance for such upward advancement. Sponsors aid persons with whom they feel an identity and a closeness. Ethnicity, race, family background all effect the possibility of being sponsored.

Women are viewed as inappropriate for sponsoring for certain positions, as are certain men. To understand more completely why, we need to look in more depth at the culture of occupations—at the practices that create a "consciousness of kind." To do so, we turn to the question of socio-emotional bonding as the third important element in the social organization of work.

Socio-Emotional Bonding

Because work is a network of interpersonal relationships, we would be highly remiss to view those relationships as only task-related interactions. Rather, where there are people, there are socio-emotional bonds. Work is a social activity wherein persons who are similar to each other come to spend increasingly more time together, at work and at leisure; they develop affective bonds. That is, the organization of work is built upon socio-emotional relationships between workers; and these work-originated relationships often develop into "after-hours" friendships. In turn, these provide further bases for work-related alliances. The relevance of the socio-emotional character of work, therefore, concerns both the internal dynamics of the organization and the external life of the workers. The theoretical dichotomy of work and pleasure, does not reflect the actual social life of persons. Work life and extra-work life are intricately related.

The kinds of socio-emotional bonding that occur in work settings is to a great extent determined by those who are in positions of dominance. For persons with power not only establish the instrumentalities of work, but also determine what kinds of emotional rituals and social climate will prevail. Hierarchies within organizations are visible in terms of those who create emotional ritual, those who follow, and those who are excluded (Collins, 1975:61).

Parallel to the role of ritual in religious institutions, the organization of work depends upon ritual exchanges that create a sense of emotional solidarity in the community of believers (organizationally committed persons). By partaking in the rituals through personal proximity, shared focus on an object, and coordination of activities, one's identity as a participant in the community is confirmed (Collins, 1975:58). The creation of the emotional solidarity based on the participation in the ritual activities of the organization provides the worker with a sense of belonging, just as exclusion confirms one's sense of alienation.

In addition, to these consequences for individual workers, control of the production of emotional solidarity has the consequence of perpetrating the organizational power of the order-givers, because it provides a very important vehicle for inculcating the work's culture. Through socio-emotional bonding, alliances are formed and intra-group struggles are defined as relevant or irrelevant. By establishing preferred emotional rituals, an ideal way of being is offered to others to emulate. If they lack the necessary resources to imitate the ideal, due to personal or positional traits, their exclusion from the network becomes a reality; and, most importantly, their exclusion is perceived of as *legitimate* by both themselves and the order-givers.

In the professions, this bonding is referred to as the "colleague system"; in the trades, the "buddy system"; and in business, the "old boy" system. To succeed, one must be able to participate in the socio-emotional rituals both within and outside the work setting. The greater the participation, the greater the commitment and potential for exchanges and alliances. The greater the exclusion from the rituals, the greater the alienation, the less the potential for alliances, and the less the chance for upward mobility.

This structural feature of socio-emotional bonding in the world of work has direct consequences on the participation of women in occupations that are sex-typed male. It has consequences for two primary and related reasons. First, most socio-emotional bonding is built upon the status male and its associated attributes, lifestyles, and preferred activities. The shared status male provides a set of rituals that are culturally defined as masculine—swearing, back-slapping, hand-shaking, girl-watching, etc. The rituals are used to transform the occupational class into a male status group. The occupation itself becomes associated with its masculine rituals. That is, these particular socio-emotional rituals, although in fact irrelevant to job performance, are seen as part of the job requirements.

Secondly participation in off-hours socializing is often requisite to career advancement. Some of these nonwork settings are such masculine preserves as the steam room, the golf course, the Men's Club, the local tavern. Others, become so defined. For example, one Midwest school district sponsors a Master Teacher's picnic each spring to which only male teachers and administrators receive invitations. One explanation offered for the exclusion of women is "the picnic wouldn't be as much fun with a bunch of school marms around" and "we (males) need a chance to let down and get to know each other" and "the women wouldn't like it anyway."

These two factors—masculine rituals within male occupations and the dependence upon the buddy system outside the job—not only create structural barriers to women's advancement, but also psychological barriers. If success requires emulation of the male model with its attendant ulcers, heart attacks, power-tripping, work-aholic mentality, women must ask themselves, "Is it worth it? Are the extra hours spent socializing with my colleagues worth the time I lose with my husband/lover/children?" And one must ask about the man who has his ulcers and heart attacks and still has not succeeded. Do the structural arrangements of work bring more satisfaction to him, or even to those who do succeed, than dissatisfactions?

Male occupations have been steeped in ritual for centuries. For example, the male social bonding of union members has a long history. In the early 1800s, the first trade unions were formed as an outgrowth of men's social clubs. They met in local saloons and were adamantly male. With the advent of the 20th-century labor movement, the earlier traditions were perpetuated and persist onto the present (Falk, 1975:225). However, we should not ignore the consequences that our cultural beliefs about sexuality may have for male bonding in occupations. Because the culture teaches that women are (should be) either sex objects or virgin mothers and that men should be sexually potent (see Chapters 2 and 8), we might wonder if these beliefs contribute to the development of masculine rituals within male occupations, and if so, how.

On the face of it, the sexual images of women and of men, which men are socialized to hold, are potentially anxiety-producing. If a woman is a sex object and a male is to perform, involvement with her exposes him to the potential humiliation of sexual failure; if she is a mother-virgin figure, then she holds the power to withdraw love and nurturance. If any particular woman represents all women, as Korda argues, then men need a place where they can escape from their own fears—a male haven. Accordingly, Korda argues, "An office is like a bazaar: it exists in part to reaffirm the bonds that exist between men" (1973:22). Through it and its associated masculine rituals, men can demonstrate to each other their potency; such rituals of power and success come to symbolize the male's masculinity without the threat of exposure by women. Male occupations, then, provide the safe harbor men are looking for. And to ensure the safety of the port, masculine rituals are emphasized. Construction workers whistling at passing women, male junior executives discussing sex at the water fountain, and professors comparing notes on "coeds," in effect are performing for each other without the concrete threat of failure.

The extent to which these speculations are true must await research. However we should not discount the importance of sexuality in the dynamics of work organizations. Sex in the office (or on the campus) is not new. The pattern of male bosses (professors) having temporary sexual liaisons with female employees (students), for example, is apparently quite common, although not carefully researched. But, the work arrangements now contemplated (and in some work settings accomplished) of males and females as colleagues present still another set of issues. As is well known from psychological research, the greater the interaction between equals, the more they like each other. Because our society increasingly condones sexual activity between persons who like each other, the probability of such sexual exchanges will increase.

In any case, although the reasons for the dynamics are not perfectly clear at this time, the male socio-emotional bonding structurally and psychologically excludes women from occupations that are sex-typed male.

In summary, then, we have seen how the social organization of work—its hierarchical arrangement, its sponsorship system, and its socio-emotional bonding reinforces a set of masculine values. As such, regardless of the hierarchy, women are likely to be at the lowest rungs with little chance for mobility. Their jobs lack glamour and meaningfulness and are supplemented by work at home.

Moreover, the social organization of work has degrading effects on most men. Men have been socialized to expect to work outside the home, to find fulfillment in their jobs, to achieve occupationally, and to find their basic sense of identity in their employment. In addition, they are expected to be autonomous, independent, capable of decision-making. In the eyes of the society and most men themselves, a man's worth is measured by his occupational success.

Work Lives of Men

The way in which work is socially organized makes it difficult for men to live up to the expectations they have been taught to have for themselves. Most work takes place in bureaucracies and factories. "With roughly 80 percent of the working population of the United States employed by someone else" (Brenton, 1976:-93), most men are in the positions of order-takers at work.

For the 50 percent who are blue-collar workers, alienation from work is becoming increasingly severe, in that blue-collar work is in the process "of losing its once distinct and always precious ability to affirm manhood" (Shostak, 1976:-100). Craft jobs still retain a sense of control, responsibility, and initiative. But, for the vast majority of blue-collar workers, work consists of simple assembly-line tasks, supervised as though the workers were children. And, indeed, in some plants the subdivision of labor has placed young boys and women on the same lines with the older men, depriving them of even the pretense that their work is "man's work". Mechanization of their work, further, tends to blur the distinctions between one's own work and that of the machine. "Blue collarites, in short, may find the meaning of work as often as not a negation rather than an affirmation of a basic sense of worthiness. . . ." (Shostak, 1976:101). As the meaninglessness of the work increases, commitment to it seems to grow less (Shostak, 1976).

Consequently, most men are alienated from the work that is supposed to provide them with a sense of self-identity.

Three dimensions of the alienation of the male worker are particularly salient. First, he is *powerless,* because he has little or no control over the results of his labor and he is subject to the demands of "the machine or the front office brass" (Brenton, 1975:93). Secondly, he may experience a sense of *meaninglessness* "because all he knows are his specialized little tasks, which he can't relate to the various other departments, to the organization as a whole" (Brenton, 1976:93). He is simply a cog in the bureaucratic or factory machinery; replaceable by another cog when broken or worn-out. Thirdly, is the experience of *isolation,* spawned from the understandable difficulty of identifying with the firm or its goals (Brenton, 1976:93).

Few men can find the fulfillment or self-esteem they have been socialized to expect to gain through their occupations. Few have the autonomy to make decisions. Most jobs do not contribute to a sense of autonomy, require one's best efforts, or provide a sense of accomplishment for one's unique service. Further, few jobs can be viewed as worthwhile ways to spend one's life. "Thus for the great ego investment a man makes in his job, the great emphasis he places on it in terms of his masculinity, the work he does, generally speaking, will not reward him commensurately" (Brenton, 1976:94).

To be sure, women also experience work as self-estranging. But the impact is often less for women, because they have not been reared to find their identities in their occupations. The relevance of an activity to a person's self-image is highly dependent on the amount of personal investment made to it. Men, much more so than women, have been taught to view their jobs as salient indicators of their worth.

Because work itself is unlikely to provide intrinsic rewards for most men, the only rewards possible are power, prestige, wealth. Men, therefore, frequently measure manhood by position in the organizational hierarchy, by the respect a job commands in the community, by the size of the paycheck, and by family lifestyle. That is, work is viewed as a means to gain extrinsic rewards, which confirm for men their masculinity. Unfortunately, a man's wife and children also tend to view him this way. Just as he is useful to his firm, he is useful to his family. "Utility," however, does not lead to deep, and intimate relationships, as we will discuss in Chapter 11.

Occupations in all societies are differentially evaluated. Some have higher prestige than others. In a society such as ours, where competiton is a virtue and "the best man wins" a man's prestige is a function of the particular career he pursues. With over 50 percent of the working male population in blue-collar industries, prestige is automatically denied. Because a hierarchical prestige system, by definition, limits the number of valued positions, the cards are stacked to produce a mass of "losers." Manual laborers are at the bottom of the hierarchy (Shostak, 1976:98). "Blue collarites begin and end the work day with the knowledge that their employ could hardly have less status [prestige]" (Shostak, 1976:98). Even blue collarites who enjoy their work, hold back on their positive estimation of themselves because their work is not middle-class (Brenton, 1967:95).

Nor can blue-collar workers expect upward mobility: *downward* mobility is more frequently the case. As they reach age 40, "most blue collar workers are frozen at the top salary they will ever reach. After this age they face job loss [due to injury or illness] and job demotion due to an inability to perform adequately with younger men" (Stoll, 1974:147). Although they have ambiguous feelings about white-collar work, "in the last analysis, many would rather have their sons follow the white collarite into a technical, professional, administrative or even clerical post than follow the 'old man' into the plant" (Shostak, 1976:104).

Even for those men who have obstensibly made it—those who have achieved a modicum of prestige—the problem is not settled, for prestige is a particularly unstable commodity in the work world. "Once achieved, it has to be maintained, leaving the man who banks on it at the mercy of all kinds of competitive pressure and changing circumstances" (Brenton, 1976:95). Part of the process of maintaining it is to hold others back; another part is to enhance one's own position. This means successful men cannot rest on their laurels. Continuation of the in-fighting, jockeying for positions, expending of energy to enhance one's position, and to picking off those who might rise above one become daily preoccupations. And as the novel *Something Happened,* by Joseph Heller (1974), makes clear, fear is a compelling emotion in high-prestige persons in bureaucratic organizations, as they struggle to enhance their own position and power.

Although moving women into positions now held by men might help many women financially, it by itself will not alter the deleterious effects of the social organization of work. Why is work structured in such a way as to exclude women and dehumanize men? And who benefits? In whose interest is it to perpetuate this particular structure of work? We now turn to some answers to these questions.

Who Benefits?

The social organization of work takes shape in the context of the American culture. It is not isolated from the values of that culture or its other institutions—particularly, the family. Therefore, it is not surprising that such values as achievement, competition, individual success, and male superiority are represented as they are in organizational structures. The structure of the family (male breadwinner, female housekeeper-and-supplementary-breadwinner) meshes with the structure of work. (The full extent of this relationship of work and home is the concern of Chapter 11.) Evolving since the industrial revolution, the pattern of work organization have been consistent with the culture's values. But why has this pattern been perpetuated?

The corporate economy requires three primary classes of workers: (1) dependable cogs, (2) executive decision-makers, and (3) a temporary reserve labor force. The perpetuation of a class of persons, men, who view themselves as required to work to support their families and/or to fulfill their role expectations provides industry with its first two classes of workers; the perpetuation of a class of workers, women, who view themselves as supplementary breadwinners provides industry with part of its third category of workers.

Men who have executive aspirations are willing to spend from 70 to 90 hours a week to advance their careers. Their advancement, however, is dependent on what profits they bring to the company. Their success may bring personal gratification, but for the company it brings greater financial dividends. The most substantial portion of these financial benefits do not go directly to the executive, but to the owners of the corporation.

Most men, however, fulfill coglike positions in bureaucracies and factories. Increased financial gains depend upon the increased output that mechanization ensures the owners. The routine and monotonous labor of these men, while systematically destroying their sense of human dignity, systematically increases the wealth of the business elite.

The categorization of women in the third pool of workers—the reserve labor force—provides considerable financial benefits to employers. The use of women as temporary workers—whether as full-time or part-time employees, whether in the canning factory at harvest time or in the university as visiting lecturers, "is one of the most profitable arrangements available to employers in contemporary times" (Amundsen, 1971:56).

Hiring women as temporary help is economically profitable for the institution. Not only do temporaries receive lower wages, they are not entitled to fringe benefits—retirement, health plans, sick leave, vacation pay, etc. Maintaining a skeleton staff of full-time workers and supplementing them seasonally with temporary help, according to economist Joan Jordan, has become a common industrial pattern (Jordan, 1969). Incidentally, the local unions have supported this industrial pattern. Temporary help are expected to pay union dues; but, if their positions are lost within 90 days, they are not considered union members and, therefore, are not entitled to support during their lay-offs.

The profits from withholding fringe benefits, however, are slight compared to the extra profits derived from paying women lower salaries than men for the same work. In 1950, Hutchins estimated that 23 percent of the profits of manufacturing companies ($5.4 billion) were the result of paying women less money than men for similar work (Hutchins, 1952:9). Because wage differentials for men and women have not lessened in the quarter of the century since that research, we can estimate that a similar proportion of the profits are still based on differential wage scales. When we review the differential salaries of the male and female workers at each occupational category and sub-category (see pp. 148–50), we can see that the personal cost of lower wages for women amounts to a considerable gain for institutions.

Further, occupational segregation serves to maintain lower wages for women and, most importantly, to prevent a restructuring of occupations. For example, the manufacturing industries tend to be of two kinds: the labor-intensive and the automated. The labor-intensive industries (e.g., textiles) have a greater need to control wages than do the automated ones (e.g., chemicals) because "higher labor costs in the former industries would reduce the profits and raise the prices and potentially destroy the ability of the industry to compete with foreign exports" (Amundsen, 1971:59). As might be predicted, the less automated the industry, the greater the proportion of female workers. In textile and clothing industries where women constitute 70 percent of the workers, weekly wages in 1969 were $78; in chemicals, where males are 70 percent of the work force, weekly salaries were $139 (Amundsen, 1971:60). This pattern of extra profits applies wherever females are the majority of an occupation. The female sex-typed professions of nursing and teaching are the lowest paid professions. Service workers, which are predominately women, barely earn subsistence incomes. For example, in Ohio in 1975, the minimum wage for a waitress was 60 cents an hour, and current minimum wage laws do not cover domestics.

Institutional sexism is not only a problem for women, but is intricately tied to the demands made upon men. Viewing women as supplementary breadwinners necessitates that men view their work as primary in their lives. In addition, it has a direct financial impact on men, because they are closely related by marriage and kinship to particular women. It is highly unlikely that a male would wish these women to receive fewer rewards than a male holding the same job. This is not to deny that controversy may exist over a wife's work, but to conclude that men would, therefore, prefer female family members to be treated inequitably seems to assume that males sacrifice their rationality to service their fragile egos. In reality, it economically benefits individual men to have female family members whose economic contributions can lessen their own toil. Although a man may receive a psychological lift from the taken-for-granted inferiority of his wife, such a personality dynamic only underscores how brutalizing and dehumanizing work is for many men. For those men who do not fulfill the masculine dream, the perpetuation of a lower class of persons who cannot be successful gives them at least some sense of relative success. Wives viewed as economic scapegoats profits not the marriage, but it helps to retain the male worker in debasing jobs.

Consequently, the maintainence of the myth that women are working only for pleasure does not profit men or women—either economically or personally. By continuing to structure the occupational system so that women are not likely to control the distribution and exchange of scarce goods and services, and so that most men will not achieve those rights, the already powerful continue to remain so.

11
The Political Economics of House Life

The self-contained worlds we live in as single adults with or without children, as wives or husbands, as mothers or fathers, or as cohabitors, are not insulated from the institutional arrangements of our society. Rather, it is when we address ourselves to private lives that we can perhaps see most clearly how culture, socialization, and the institutions that socially control adults are integrally intermeshed.

The social institution of the family in its various forms is probably universal. "No society has ever existed without some kinds of social arrangement that may be labeled kinship or familial" (Scanzoni and Scanzoni, 1976:4). Most sociologists would argue that the family is the major institution upon which the rest of the society depends. And, there is every indication that "family patterns of some sort will continue to exist in all modern and developing societies" (Scanzoni and Scanzoni, 1976:4).

My primary focus will be upon the marital pair, the adult male and the adult female who expect to maintain an ongoing sexual and economic exchange. I limit my scope for two reasons. First, to discuss all the various forms and functions of the family, and the interpersonal relationships within it, is well beyond the province of this book. (For such discussions, see Skolnick, 1973; Scanzoni and Scanzoni, 1976). Second, although some persons do not ever marry and many are unwed during a substantial portion of their adult lives, most people (93 percent), at some point in their lives, are married.

Marriage is not isolatable or separable from the other social institutions. At the structural level, the ideology, legal system, and opportunity structure that support and perpetuate the assignment of domestic responsibilities to women is one of the primary ways through which sexual inequality is maintained in the political and economic institutions. And, correlatively, the maintenance of sexual inequality in those institutions contributes to a division of labor in which "women's place *is* in the home." Power and privilege go to those who control the extradomestic distribution of scarce goods and services. The ideology and structural avenues are such that the kinds of interpersonal relationships that men and women can develop are affected.

On the individual level, as well, home and work are not insulated from each other. People do not live one life on the job and another at home. One's employment has an impact on one's behavior at home. For example, a husband who is powerless at work may exert dominance over his wife and children. Or, an employed wife may exert more rights to decide how to spend the family income than one who is not working outside the home.

Although marriage as a social form has been studied for many years, there are three major research obstacles to understanding it: *familiarity, mystification,* and *moral sacredness.* Familiarity involves the fact that persons are raised in families which they enter when they are young and vulnerable. Their objectivity is blurred and their perceptions of what marriages are and should be like are influenced by their own experiences. That which is most familiar is the most elusive. The second major obstacle, mystification, arises because married couples conceal information about their interaction from outsiders. An example of this is the frequent surprise of friends and associates when they learn of a particular couple's separation or divorce. Perhaps the need for secrecy stems from the moral character of it, the third major obstacle. This is probably particularly true if the marriage does not live up to the ideals that flow from the Judaic-Christian tradition, and are reinforced through the media and legitimated through laws specifying the division of labor.

Marriage, therefore, in one sense, is within the public domain; it is the concern of ministers, legislators, social-workers, etc. The religious and legal institutions have an interest in it. But, in another sense, marriage is private, a secret social arrangement. Consequently, what we have to come to know about the marital union has primarily been in the realm of norms and values regarding what married life should be like. Any one particular couple knows how their marriage differs from the ideal, but they are unlikely to know how others depart from that standard.

Consequently, the intent of this chapter will be to focus the sociological lens in such a way that the major obstacles to understanding married life can be overcome. That process is begun by considering the problem of conceptualizing marriage.

Conceptualizing Marriage

As argued earlier, the way in which marriage is conceptualized does have important consequences for people's lives. The assumption that one marital form is not only the ideal one but the actual one, limits the kinds of questions we might ask, established social policies to correct labelled pathologies, and social-psychologically affects the self-image of persons who live differently (see Chapter 6). Further, it prevents the investigation of possible negative outcomes of married life.

When marriage is defined as a legally joined adult male and adult female intent to have children, then consensual unions, childless marriages, homosexual unions, single parent homes, etc. become social problems. Similarly, if the division of labor within the house is determined by stereotypes of male role and female roles, then househusbands, working mothers, illegitimacy, etc. become problematical. On the more personal level, individuals whose marriages do not meet the idealized standards of love, emotional interdependency, and individual freedom tend to view their marriages or themselves as lacking. Further, the insistence upon incorporating both the *household* (economic arrangement) and the *marriage* (kinship arrangement under the same rubric, marriage and family) limits the solutions to problems generated by individual needs—such as the simultaneous fulfillment of both spouses' careers, which may require separate households in different cities (Kirschner, 1976). "Many of these [social] problems derive from what are essentially political assumptions about the normal sex and power relationships within the family, and how people should live" (Skolnick, 1973:22). Although atypical living arrangements may create problems for the participants, explaining those problems by viewing the arrangement as deviant, only obscures what the real difficulties are. As Rodman asks, Should we view the deviancy from the social norms "as *problems* or as *solutions* to more basic problems" (1964:450)? Are childless marriages and two-location couples, for example, problems or attempted solutions to the career vs. family dilemma? Further, are we to interpret the few full-time househusbands and the few full-time career women as natural and commendable? Or, are they to be viewed as indicators of cultural and economic obstacles that need to be removed?

As should be clear from the above, how one sees the marital institution in great measure depends on the lens one chooses to look through. (For a review of models of marriage, see Glazer-Malbin, 1976.) I have chosen the perspective that asks: What are the structural flaws of the marital institution? This question has not been particularly popular in sociology; nor is it an especially pleasant way to view one's intimate environment. Yet, it is the one which must be asked if our understanding of social life is to move beyond idealized versions of familial harmony and if our understanding is to rise above the "personal problem" approach to social issues. For example, the fact that nearly one in every three marriages ends in divorce is normally attributed to the vagaries and immaturities of the individuals involved. However, as C. Wright Mills argued, such a high rate of divorce must reflect something of the structural problems of the marital institution itself and of the others which are impinging upon it. Rather than viewing divorce wholly as a personal problem, Mills suggests that sociologists should consider how the institutional structure, itself, generates strain for its members. He proposes the major sources of marital strain stem from the demands of the corporate economy upon the male, and the stultifying homemaker role assigned to the female (1959:10). Because these strains are a result of external influences, the development of satisfactory marital institutions remains beyond the realm of the personal solution.

Although marriage experts have argued that the problems of marriage can be solved by improving the communication patterns between the couple, no matter how well the couple does succeed in communicating, they will not have changed the political and economic structures that impinge upon their marriage. They may, indeed, find greater personal peace, happiness, and growth by improving their communication skills; but, those skills will not allow them to escape the structural constraints placed on their marriage by the institutions external to it.

Intimately living with another person, regardless of sex, age, or race is likely to lead to disagreements and conflicts. Because people differ in tastes, lifestyles, preferences, and moods and because their ideas and attitudes change over time, disharmony is inevitable. But, the question is, over and above this predictable strain in any intimate relationship, are there particular strains involved in the cross-sex one? More concretely, do particular strains arise precisely because the status of males is higher than the status of females? To what extent does the power and prestige of "male" serve to perpetuate a power imbalance within the marriage? How do the rights to extradomestic distribution of goods and services, which accrue to males, affect the relationships between spouses?

Marital Power

Power, or the probability that one's will will be done, is greater if one controls the distribution of scarce goods and services. Historically, in the United States, when women entered into marriage they legally surrendered many rights, such as the right to inherit property, to make a will, to control their property or salaries. If children were born, the husband was granted full authority over their education, religious upbringing, as well as their guardianship. In consonance with the religious belief system, a man was deemed master of his home and property, which included his wife, children, and slaves.

More recently, the laws and social customs surrounding the institution of marriage have altered, providing women greater access to their inheritances, wage, children, and husbands. In fact, many marriage and family experts characterize the modern marriage as "democratic" or "equalitarian." However, there is little evidence to support these claims. Rather, as I shall argue, the distribution of power within marriages has not substantially changed in modern times; the power that has historically rested in the hands of the husband continues to reside there.

Over the past decade and a half, the research of Blood and Wolfe (1960) on marital power has been especially influential. They argue that, in modern America, husbands and wives are "potential equals—with the balance of power tipped sometimes one way, sometimes the other" (1960:29). In that this claim is a strong one and their conclusions have influenced many students and researchers, it is necessary to review in some detail how Blood and Wolfe have conceptualized and measured power.

For their study, they selected eight areas of marital decision-making that they considered important and typical. They asked: Who makes the final decision regarding:

1. What job the husband should take.
2. What car to get.
3. Whether or not to buy life insurance.
4. Where to go on a vacation.
5. What house or apartment to take.
6. Whether or not the wife should go to work or quit work.
7. What doctor to have if someone is sick.
8. How much money the family can afford to spend weekly on food.
   (Blood and Wolfe, 1960: 19–20).

Viewing the list leads one to question the way Blood and Wolfe chose to measure power (Safilios-Rothschild, 1969:297–298). All areas of decision-making are given equal weight in the scoring, although clearly some areas are more important than others. The husband's job, for example, has greater consequences for the entire family than which doctor to call. Further, the frequency with which decisions are made in each area differs—food budget may be negotiated frequently, whereas a new car purchase may occur seldomly. In addition, there is a kind of naivete in the questions themselves, which belies the nature of human interaction. Although a final decision is made when, for example, a husband accepts a new job, there were probably many smaller negotiated decisions leading up to it. Focusing on the final decision eliminates the processes of decision-making. Finally, decisions on complex issues are usually not unidimensional. For example, one spouse may decide *when* to get a new car, while the other may choose the color.

But, perhaps most telling, is that Blood and Wolfe's conclusions on marital equality are not supported by their own research findings, which are shown in Table 11.1.

TABLE 11.1   Husband's Mean Power in Family Decision-Making Areas
(5 = Total Power; 0 = No Power)

Area	Power
Husband's Job	4.86
Car	4.18
Insurance	3.50
Vacation	3.12
Wife's Job	2.69
Doctor	2.53
Food	2.26

That is, according to the findings of their study, rather than their interpretation of their results, husbands have substantially more marital power than wives (Gillespie, 1971:447).

Although asking who decides is appropriate when discussing power, Blood and Wolfe's discussion ignores important issues. An example of this is their explanation of why husbands do more decision-making regarding their own and their wives' jobs than wives do. They reason that the husband may want her to work to help out with financing a new home, children's college educations, etc. Or, he may not want her to work because of the repercussions on him. For example, he "will have to help out more around the house." If he is a small business man, "he may need her services in his enterprise"; if he is an executive, he may "prefer her" to expend her "energies on entertaining prospective clients." In brief, Blood and Wolfe suggest that because the work role is so central to the male, even the wife's work "is but an adjunct to his instrumental leadership, leaving this decision in his hands" (1960:22).

In effect, Blood and Wolfe are providing justifications for why the husband would want more power in a particular arena. "The basic assumption ... is that he can have it [power] if he wants it" (Gillespie, 1971:448). The more important question of "Why is he able to get it if he wants it?" is not even raised (Gillespie, 1971:448).

I will argue that husbands can get more power if they want it, *because* the sexual stratification system has ramifications for the marital union. The placement of women in that stratification system lessens their chances to control the distribution of scarce goods and services; the political and economic inequality contributes to a power imbalance within marital unions. The power, prestige, and property which accrue to males as a category are carried with them into marriage, allowing the male to "dominate *without* a definite effort to do so" (Goode, 1963:70).

Sexual inequality, as should be clear from the first section of this book, is partially sustained through the socialization process. Women are expected to find their greatest fulfillment within the roles of housewife and mother. The personality traits attributed to them are those that are consistent with servicing roles within the home. Men, on the other hand, are expected to find their identities in the occupational sphere; the skills they are expected to master are those that are compatible with occupational success. Consequently, the two partners are differentially socialized towards marriage as an institution.

In effect "the principle of least interest" is operable here. In all human exchanges, economic or romantic, the person who has the least interest in the exchange has the greater power, because he or she can more easily withdraw from or terminate the exchange. Males are socialized to have "least interest" in marriage. Consequently, at the social-psychological level, women are socialized to be less powerful than men in marriage. And, the greater their perceived need for marriage, the greater their psychological powerlessness. Adult control mechanisms such as religion, law, and the social and psychological sciences reinforce this early socialization. Whether by religious creed or legal doctrine or scientific findings, the man is the head of the house.

These major social processes of socialization and adult social control, then, have direct impact on the social-psychological power relationships within a marriage. But in addition to these, the structure of the political and economic system have a direct impact. We have already seen how barriers to women's occupational success are erected and maintained and the consequences of those barriers: the higher the position, the fewer the women. Now we need to turn the question around: Does a man's greater occupational success lead to greater power within his marriage? The answer appears to be "yes."

A man's place in the stratification system external to the marriage does have consequences for the balance of power between the spouses. From the research in this area, three generalizations appear to be warranted. First, the higher the occupational status of the husband, the greater his marital power. Second, the higher the husband's income, the greater his power. And third, the higher the husband's overall social status (based on occupation, income, education, and ethnic background), the greater his marital power (Gillespie, 1971).

Although these are general conclusions, there are interesting differences between the social classes. White-collar husbands have more power in their marriages than blue-collar workers. This is not surprising, given the society's preference for professional rather than manual achievements. Nor is it surprising that there is a direct association between income and amount of power. It was only when social status was considered that an unexpected relationship was discovered. The lower blue-collar laborers had more power than the upper blue-collar workers, followed by ascending levels of power as a man's social status increased.

Despite greater claims to equalitarianism by middle-class men, in practice, their wives obtain fewer rights than the lower class wives. In middle-class families, women and children are not expected to make demands that might interfere with the husband's work. "He takes preference as a *professional,* not as a family head or as a male; nevertheless, the precedence is his" (Goode, 1963:21). In effect, the doctrine of equality has little impact on the distribution of marital power (Goode, 1963:21).

Although it is unquestionably true that males do profit in their marriages by dint of their social status, occupation, and income, it would be inaccurate to discount the costs to them. One of the costs is the continued expectation that they achieve occupationally—whether they want to or not. Loss of job, demotion, retirement, or employment in a less socially valued occupation, affects the self-esteem and longevity of the male. If his position as "head of house" is dependent on his external statuses, as it is, then loss of one often means he loses on all fronts—home and work.

In that a husband's power in a marriage is related to his extradomestic power, it is reasonable to ask whether a wife can increase her marital power by increasing her extra-domestic power. Both anthropological (Friedl, 1975) and sociological evidence indicates that it does. Reviewing the research concerning the effect of wives' work, educational, and organizational experiences, Gillespie concludes that these have an impact on the distribution of marital power (1971:452. Wives working outside the home, regardless of class, have more power than those who do not; the longer their labor force participation, the greater their power.

In the early stages of the marriage, the wife is frequently working and the power is not as unequally balanced as it is when children arrive. During the time following the birth of the first child through the preschool years, the husband's power is the greatest. Because it is common for women to stop working during these years, she tends to become highly dependent economically, socially, and emotionally upon him. Her husband's world is expanding while hers contracts. Despite the fact that women are contributing full-time work in the home during the early years of their children's lives (Chase Manhattan Bank estimates 99.6 hours per week), this work is so little socially valued that in reality her power within the family diminishes to meet the social worth attributed to that role. Domestic labor not only does not bring one power and prestige in the stratification system, it lessens ones power within the home. In addition to employment outside the home, participation in organizations enhances the woman's influence in the decision-making process. Further, amount of education plays an important role. In white-collar and upper blue-collar marriages, if the husband's education is less than his spouse, he tends to have less power, although this relationship does not hold for the lower blue-collar marriages (1971:452).

The conclusion, therefore, is that if a wife is to gain more power in a marriage, she must have access to external resources. Paid labor force participation, superior education, and greater organizational involvement than her husband will increase her power position. "Equality of resources leaves the power in the hands of the husbands" (Gillespie, 1971:457).

As has been argued earlier, however, women do not have equal access to these external sources of power. The sexual stratification system of the country structurally restricts women from obtaining the necessary resources upon which equalitarian marriages might be built (see Chapter 9). Despite the intentions of husbands—who may indeed want equal partnerships—such marriages will remain mythic ideals until women have the same access to the control of the distribution of valued goods as men enjoy. Until then, the likelihood of any couple achieving an equalitarian bond remains slim. No matter the good will or intentions of the partners, the institutional arrangements reach down in the living rooms of couples and affect the context of their marriage lives. Although women can achieve more power than their husbands by being superior to them in education, income, employment, and organizational experience, more power is not the same as equal power.

It may well be argued that power is not necessary for "marital happiness"; that, indeed, individuals choose to give up some of their influence and autonomy in exchange for a satisfying home life. This issue must be addressed.

Happy Housewife: Myths and Realities

The social theorist, Emile Durkheim, concluded more than a half century ago in his study of suicide that marriage is more debilitating for women than for men, because "the regulations imposed on the woman by marriage are always more stringent. Thus, she loses more and gains less from the institution" (1951:271). Intrigued by Durkheim's conclusion, Jessie Bernard reviewed an extensive literature on marital satisfaction, marital happiness, and mental health. Her analysis of these materials, "The Paradox of the Happy Marriage," (1971) is worth reporting at length.

Bernard argues that every marriage is really two marriages: his and hers. The research rather consistently supports the contention that "wives' marriages look less happy than their husbands" when specific areas of marital problems and dissatisfactions are surveyed (1971:147–148). However, paradoxically, a large proportion of married women contend that they are happy. Indeed, more married women than single women make such self-reports (1971:150). Further, research indicates that married women strongly associate their overall happiness with their marital happiness (1971:148), and the strength of these correlations is higher for wives than for husbands (1971:150).

From the surveys on mental health and behavior, Bernard suggests that serious doubts must be raised about the housewife's actual personal happiness. For example, more married women than single report that they experience depression, were afraid of death, thought they might go to pieces, and were bothered by body pains and ailments. Further, when the mental health of married women is compared to that of single women, more of the former are reported to be phobic, depressed, or passive. In brief, married women appear to suffer more psychological disability than single women.

But not only do they show greater psychological difficulties than single women —despite their stated greater happiness—they have more psychological distress than married *men:* married women are more likely to feel a nervous breakdown is imminent, feel inadequate in the marriage, have negative or ambivalent self-images, and see their physical appearance as a deficit (Bernard, 1971:152–153). Although married women may view their husbands as the cause of their problems, "they feel their own inability to adjust to them to be [their own] . . . shortcoming" (Bernard, 1971:153). In terms of major psychological problems, married men are less damaged than married women.

Therefore, one can't help but wonder about the effects of marriage itself on women. A quarter of a century ago, Bernard proposed a "shock theory of marriage" to account for unexpected findings from a survey of 1400 upper-income persons. Her data suggested that either more psychologically disturbed women married than did not marry or else that marriage had a destructive impact on some women. Because the difference in psychological damage increased with age, she concluded that marriage "has a traumatic effect on personalities of women" (quoted in Bernard, 1971:153). More recently, Mulligan, in a study of 457 wives of professional men, reports that self-esteem was inversely associated with the amount of time spent in the home (1975).

The shocks of marriage are potentially many for women. These include the loss of her individual identity as symbolized in taking her husband's name; the exchange of her status as student, teacher, secretary, etc., to that of housewife; the loss of her independent network of social alliances with the role of wife being supercedent; the recognition that her husband's career not only has preference over her career but also over her homelife—while she may have been the most important thing in his life before marriage, his work afterwards takes on greater importance; the gradual realization that if they have children she is responsible for them while he continues to grow in adult contexts; the discovery that her husband does not meet all the sex-role stereotypes—he is not always strong, capable, and rational—and correlatively, that she is frequently called upon to be the strong one in the relationship; the equally disturbing discovery that she does not meet all the stereotypes; the threat or use of physical coercion by her spouse; finally and most compounding, the belief that what she is experiencing is unique, private, and personal, unshareable with others, and perhaps, best not even thought about.

Because the structure of marriage itself seems to be so destructive to the mental health of women and because it is difficult to reconcile the depressed and anxious characteristics of married women with their reports of happiness, Bernard asks, "Why do women who present such a far-from-happy picture nevertheless think of themselves as happy? (1971:55) Bernard suggests that perhaps these "happy housewives" are confusing happiness with adjustment. Women who are living up to the expectations of their culture by making life comfortable for their husbands and children are conforming to its norms. Female happiness is culturally defined in these terms. Therefore, "Could it be because married women thus conform and adjust to the demands of marriage, at whatever cost to themselves, they judge themselves happy?" (Bernard, 1971:156).

This kind of adjustment may have been necessary in the past; but given the kinds of options and alternatives increasingly available to women, "Adjustment at what cost?" must be asked. Conforming to the feminine sex-role stereotypes (dependent, cautious, indecisive, etc.), enhances a woman's chances of viewing her marriage as happy. However, "in fact, adjustment to the demands of marriage may greatly impair mental health" (Bernard, 1971:157). Indeed, clinicians are beginning to ask whether many happily married women are so, precisely *because* they have poor mental health (Bernard, 1971:157). To view married women's poor mental health not as a personal defect of the individual, but as a direct result of the institution in which they have been socialized to breed within, raises new avenues for social research and social change. To recognize that married women's low self-esteem is a function of their dependent position in a power system leads one to suggest that these women are not neurotic but oppressed. As Bernard concludes, "It may come to seem increasingly anomalous that we must make women sick in order to fit them for marriage. Could it be that marriage itself is 'sick'" (1971:158).

But what about husbands? Does marriage have an equally deleterious effect upon them?

Unhappy Husband: Myths and Realities

Well-tended to over the centuries in legend, story, and humor is the notion that marriage is a repugnant but necessary noose which women slyly place around men, tethering them to a life of restraint. Cartoon strips (e.g., Maggie and Jiggs, Dagwood and Blondie, The Flintstones), stand-up comedians, and parlor witticisms repeat century-old themes like: "Women (wives, mothers-in-law) victimize men: marriage is an unnatural state." Through these, women become convenient scapegoats.

Does marriage have deleterious effects on men? And, if so, are these consequences a result of the marriage (and by indirection their wives) or a result of the demands made upon marriage by society?

Bernard concludes: "There are few findings more consistent, less equivocal and more convincing" than the superiority of married men over never-married men on almost every index—medical, social, psychological, demographic (1972:16–17).

Despite the image of the marital bond as a prison contract, married men have better physical health after middle-age, are less likely to commit crimes or suicide, show fewer signs of psychological difficulty, and enjoy better credit, insurance, and banking privileges, etc. Further, once divorced or widowed, men are more likely than women to return to the married state. "Once men have known marriage, they can hardly live without it . . . Indeed, it may not be too farfetched to conclude that the verbal assaults on marriage indulged in by men are a kind of compensatory reaction to their dependence on it" (Bernard 1972:18).

Of course, it is difficult to determine whether it is marriage itself that improves the life chances of men, or whether those who never marry constitute a population of men whose life chances were fewer anyway. One way of determining whether or not marriage has positive effects on men is to look at what happens to widowers following the death of their spouses. They show higher rates of psychological distress, suicide, and greater frequency of death than either never-married men of their age or widows (Bernard, 1972:19).

In addition to married men's life spans being longer, judging from the statistical research, their lives are also happier than unmarried men (Bernard, 1971:21). The happiness in marriage that men report, unlike that of their wives, is not associated with psychological deterioration.

There are, however, costs that men often mention in regard to leaving their bachelorhood. The two major ones expressed are the economic responsibilities of marriage and its sexual restrictiveness (Bernard, 1972:23). Men report that their marriages would be happier if their economic responsibilities were reduced and their sexual freedom was greater. According to Bernard, both of these are realizeable in the near future.

The economic support of the family is already shared in more than a third of the family population, and this trend is continuing. And, according to Bernard, the "way is being prepared for a growing acceptance" of greater sexual freedom for married persons (1972:24). If these trends continue, and there is every reason to believe that they will, the deficits of marriage for men will be further decreased.

However, let us look again at the complaint men have regarding their economic responsibilities. Although wives are contributing to the support of the home, I would argue that her contributions have not substantially lessened the economic burden felt by the husband. This is partly so because the wife's work tends to be viewed as supplementary and incidental. Despite the actual needs of the family for her economic contribution, both the husband and wife are still likely to define her contribution as secondary. That is, the couple tends to see the husband as the breadwinner and the wife as the cakewinner. Because they define the situation in this way, it has real consequences for the man's continuing to feel economically burdened.

Nearly half of all male workers are in the manual trades—factory work, construction industries and semi-skilled crafts. The fact that their labor is physical rather than mental, hazardous rather than safe, supervised rather than supervisory, means that, although certain elements of their work life are "masculine," on balance, they do not meet the culture's standards for male success. Rather than leaving their home and entering a world in which they are in control, they perform monotous, routine, and unimportant tasks. There are few intrinsic or extrinsic rewards. With little autonomy and dignity arising from their work lives, the belief that they are the economic strength of the family is an important rationale to hold on to.

White-collar workers have a similar need to validate their work. According to Filene (1976:398) two-fifths of these workers report they would prefer a different job. Home life and the symbols of affluence become important to these men as justifications for their employment. In the upper-middle classes, there is an especially insidious pattern—such that the more successful the male is occupationally, the greater the conflict and dissatisfaction within his marriage (Dizard, 1972). If men choose to try to fulfill the culture's expectations for occupational success, they spend a greater proportion of their time on their career and participating in community organizations. This leaves less time for enjoying their home and for sharing life with their families. In addition, the skills which men develop in the pursuit of occupational success (e.g., individualism, competitiveness, aggressiveness) are particularly unsuited for developing and sustaining intimate relationships (Dizard, 1972:196–198).

The poignancy of this trap is illustrated by the results of a 1973 survey of business and corporate executives. Four-fifths of them reported that "their attitudes toward achievement and success were changing: they located their basic aspirations not in the companies that employed them, but in their families and private lives" (Filene, 1976:393). However, although they stated such changing beliefs, there is little evidence to suggest that they are willing or able to act on those beliefs. "The tug of man-work expectations [is] hard to resist" (Filene, 1976:393). When it comes down to the nitty-gritty of risking the economic and psychological security that serious commitment to a career offers men in exchange for spending more time at home, few men are prepared to do so (Filene, 1976:393).

Ironically, then, the interconnectedness of home and work seems to ensure that most men will lose in at least one of these spheres, and many in both. The more occupational success they attain, the more conflict ridden their marriages and the more difficult it is for them to diminish their career-oriented activities. If they are not occupationally successful, they experience doubt about themselves—doubt which is carried home with them. The economy is ensured its labor force of highly committed professionals and executives and its dependable laborers. Perpetuating the present ideology and structure of work with greater importance placed on occupational success than interpersonal pleasures irretrievably places most men in a "no win, no way out" situation. The full implications of this, however, can only be understood in the context of the division of labor based on the allocation of child-care responsibilities.

Child Care

Sexual inequality in all industrialized societies is sustained by assigning the child-rearing role to women and the economic-provider role to men. This social arrangement meshes well with the demands of industry. Moreover, this pattern is the basis for "most of the sex-role divisions and of their consequences in modern society" (Grønseth, 1972:175). Without a major restructuring of this division of labor, "it will be impossible to achieve an end to other destructive sex-role divisions" (Grønseth, 1972:175).

This sex-role division probably originated in the biological differences between men and women: only women bear and nurse children. However, it is technologically no longer necessary to assign women the child-rearing role. Due to the bottle feeding of infants, it is feasible to allocate primary child-care responsibilities to the father, the mother, both parents, the extended family, or child-care centers. The sexual division of labor in modern societies is a matter of societal *choice* and, therefore, is subject to alteration (Huber, 1975). The ideology that still supports sex-role division is so persistent and deep that it is almost unconscious. Consider for a moment why fathers are not asked, "Well, if you don't want to stay home and raise the children, why did you have them?" Or why mothers are not asked, "Have you made economic provisions for your child in the event of your death?"

Even our language reinforces these ideas about child-rearing. For example, the expression "maternal care" is used generically to refer to the child-rearing activity. The use of the feminine generic is not accidental. Consider, the connotative difference between the following two sentences:

1. The baby was fathered by X.
2. The baby was mothered by Y.

The first sentence implies biological paternity; the second, tender loving care (example drawn from Polatnick, 1975:204).

Further, the language blurs the two meanings of *nurturant*. The first meaning is simply to provide food or nourishment; the second is to promote the development of another through education, training, rearing, etc. Through language blurring, the physical ability to lactate is enlarged to incorporate the second meaning of nurturance and therewith the responsibility for rearing children. Through an even greater semantic leap, women are then held responsible for nurturing (feeding, taking care of, etc.), the entire family.

In addition to the language that identifies women with child-rearing, biological arguments are widely proferred. "Of all the social 'roles' associated with the female sex, the one most bolstered by references to nature, biology, and anatomy is undoubtedly that of the mother" (Polatnick, 1975:202). Many of these arguments rest on the fact that only women can bear and nurse children. In other words, the argument states that because women bear children, they have the physiological and emotional capacity to rear them. And, in a companion belief, it is assumed that men are social-psychologically and physiologically unsuited to such an endeavor.

But, we might equally as "logically" argue that males should be responsible for child-rearing because women cannot force men to have intercourse through which the sperm is supplied and because women fulfill their obligation by providing prenatal nurturance. Because this logic is obviously spurious, why is it so difficult to recognize the equally spurious nature of arguing based on female biology? It does not follow that the impregnator or the bearer should *ipso facto* be responsible for the raising of the child.

The biologically based argument concerning why women rear children goes beyond the anatomy of the female and suggests that women have a natural instinct or predilection for such activities. However, there appears to be little biological evidence to support this claim and a great deal of sociological evidence to the contrary. Research has failed to find hormonal evidence to substantiate the nurturance-as-destiny claims (Essig, 1974). Investigation of primates also contradicts the nature hypothesis. For example, when primates are viewed in natural settings or in zoos, we find an interesting fact: those monkeys we see "mothering" infants are frequently males. In fact, there are 27 species of monkeys in which the nourishment function is fulfilled by the female and the physical contact function is fulfilled by the male (Williams, 1975).

Consequently, nature has not destined women to be child-rearers. Rather, the way we socially structure child-rearing creates a self-fulfilling prophecy. "Mother becomes the source of security and comfort *because* she provides the security and comfort. Who would be the focus of gratification if father provided those ingredients?" (Polatnick, 1975:207).

Clearly, socialization plays an important part in the continuation of the sexual division of labor. The role models presented to most children are those of father-breadwinner and mother-child-rearer. Fathers are frequently emotionally removed and usually physically absent during the day. Nurturant play for boys is negatively sanctioned, teaching them to feel self-conscious and inept around infants. Girls, on the other hand, see the sex-role model mother-housekeeper, which they are encouraged to imitate.

In addition, the major agents of adult social control—religion, law, science, psychology, and the mass media—all converge on adults with the same messages: children need their mothers. Mothers need their husbands to economically provide for them and their children.

Because there is no biological basis for the sex-role division nor any compelling social need at this point in history to perpetuate it, we must conclude that continuing to assign child-rearing to women and child-supporting to males, is a societal choice. Who profits from assigning child-rearing to women?

Persons with greater power can enforce their decisions more readily than those who are relatively powerless. The structure of sexual inequality is such that males as a group have more power than females. Consequently, they are in the position to both make and enforce decisions. One of these decisions has been to continue to assign child-rearing to women. "Men as a group don't rear children because they don't *want* to rear them" (Polatnick, 1975:213). If they did want to, they could. Rather "it is to men's advantage that women are assigned child-rearing responsibility, and it is in men's interest to keep things that way . . . ," (Polatnick, 1975:213).

This is so because the child-carer loses power both domestically and extra-domestically. There are several reasons for this. First, in terms of society's values, child-caring is not a high-prestige occupation. In fact it has low status, is vacationless, pensionless, isolated, full-time on-call, and financially uncompensated. Although child-rearing may be a superior activity to many of those available in the labor market it is not viewed as real work, because it is outside the market economy.

Second, full-time child-rearing limits what else one can do. It especially diminishes one's ability to pursue a professional career. The 70 or so hours required for a high-level business or professional career are not available to the full-time child-rearer; nor are the 50 hours for middle-management success. Even if one does not have the professional aspirations, the exigencies of child-raising are such that the one charged with the responsibility has virtually no private time or space. The child's needs and desires are ever-present and unpredictable.

Moreover, the spouse who takes care of the children forfeits bargaining power within the marital union. Once a formal or informal pact has been made allocating child-rearing to the wife, she becomes even more disadvantaged in future negotiations. This is especially so in terms of negotiating her right to work outside the home. Although fewer husbands forbid their wives to work, many still believe it is improper for a mother of small children to be employed (Walum and Franklin, 1972); and they have the power to enforce that belief. Most telling in all of this is that the power to make the decision as to who will raise the children does not reside in the hands of the person who almost invariably has that task—the mother. For most women today, the choice is to have children and rear them or not to have them at all (Polatnick, 1975).

In a particularly compounding way, sex-typing the occupation child-rearer as "women's work" ensures that it will continue to have low prestige. Insidiously, it signals that the culture does not value its children as highly as it does its economic growth, despite the folklore to the contrary. For, if one universal pattern does exist cross-culturally, it is that the work deemed most important is assigned to men (Friedl, 1975).

As further evidence of the society's disregard for child-rearing—and therefore for children—neither government, business, nor labor have shown any interest in rewarding women who have raised children; or in altering work so that men can take a fuller part in their children's lives. If we value motherhood at least as much as war, as is often claimed, why aren't there programs such as the G.I. bill with its attendant benefits of medical care, advanced education, occupational hiring preference, early retirement, and loan benefits, for women who have served their countries in the capacity of mothers?

Men, as a class, then, gain certain power advantages from assigning child-rearing to women. However, for many individual men, the losses far outweigh the gains. Some individual men suffer losses because they may be unexpectedly cast into the role of child-rearer; others are denied the right to fulfill that role; and still others feel the cost of the emotional estrangement from their children.

An example of the first is reported in a sensitive account of a sociologist, Jerry Boren, after his wife left him and their eight-year-old son. He writes:

> I began to wonder if I had ever really known how to be a warm nurturant parent. I know how to be a firm but fair authority figure. I knew how to have fun . . . in a playful way. And I knew how to push him [his son] to explore and test his mind, strength, and agility. But that was no longer enough . . . I felt inadequate (1976:427).

But even more, individual men lose who want to rear their children but are denied that role. For example, men following the break up of their marriages are almost invariably denied the custody of their children. Even in states that have modernized their domestic law, fathers have to demonstrate, in effect, that they are more qualified than the mother to even hope for temporary custody. If parents are "equally qualified," the court will assume the children belong with their mothers.

It is likely that many of these men—men who have strong desires to be with their children, whether or not they have engaged in a custody battle—will lose a great deal and have their future lives controlled in great measure. This is so, because it is likely that these divorced men are deeply concerned that their children's financial and emotional disruptions be minimized. Therefore, they are less likely to risk incurring the displeasure of their ex-wife for fear of consequences to the children or to themselves. Such divorced men, further, are probably the ones most desirous of limiting the time and commitment they have to their careers in order to have more time with their children; unfortunately, however, they are also the ones least likely to be able to diminish their work time, because two households are more expensive than one. Consequently, it is a likely hypothesis that those divorced men who care the most about their children are the ones who lose the most as individuals, because of the advantages gained by men as a class.

And there is a third category of fathers who do not benefit. These are the men who at some point in their lives question the value of how they have lived and sense an acute loss of something no longer attainable: a reciprocal emotional bond with their children.

Even though the present sex-role division of labor costs many men, it, nevertheless benefits men as a group. The primary assignment of child-rearing to women perpetuates sexual inequality. Moreover, and more relevantly, this power imbalance is in the interest of the business and political elite. By perpetuating the sexual division of labor, the corporate economy is provided with a family structure that is subordinated to the demands of the occupational structure and with a family structure that contributes to the powerlessness of both males and females vis à vis the elite.

Family life is subordinated to the demands and requirements of industry. On the day-to-day basis, the industrial economy depends on some variation of the traditional two-parent family, with the mother in the home (Boren, 1976:226). The industrial time clock is not calibrated with the public school one; nor is it designed to fit the physical and emotional needs of children.

On a year-to-year basis, the role division ensures industries of their major labor pools: executives and professionals (male) and dependable laborers (male), and marginal and temporary workers (female). The ready supply of these workers and the profits that are built through them are more likely to be ensured if the traditional child-care pattern persists. For the occupationally striving family, "the crucial concern . . . is the male involvement in work." This means that the family life is molded by and subordinated to his work—"moving when the male's 'future' requires it, regulating activities so that the male is free to concentrate on his work," etc. (Miller, 1976:380).

Moreover, there is another major reason why it profits the business elite to subordinate the family structure to the occupational one—namely, the political control of its workers. "The control mechanisms through which the political domination of family occurs . . . is through the husband economic-provider role aspect of the husband-occupational role" (Grønseth, 1972:184). By diverting men's energies into economic pursuits, they become politically immobilized. As a corollary, the physical isolation of the mother-child alienates them from other families. Objectively, this alienation limits political participation; and subjectively, the feelings of apathy and desperation that follow help maintain political noninvolvement. Because they are powerless, "they have to adjust their family life to the demands of the economic-political system" (Grønseth, 1972:184).

The current family is suited to the needs of the economy. But, at what cost? And who is to decide "which of the competing interests shall be said to represent the interests of the total society?" (Grønseth, 1972, 190). Shall the family lives of people be subordinated to the needs of the economy? And, because this

> family structure is the producer of the type of male achievement-motivated personality that is adequately socialized to function in the present widely exploitative, competitive, and alienation-generating occupational and economic life, then not only this type of occupational and economic system but also this family structure . . . are in the long run *not functional* but dangerous for the total society (Grønseth, 1972:190).

For what "the achievement-oriented power elites" define as chief values may in the long run lead to the disintegration and destruction of the society" (Grønseth, 1972:190).

Increasingly, persons have come to question the roles assigned to them at work and in the home. Many are seeking alternative lifestyles. For most, if they wish to change their private lives, the psychological or economic costs are too great. Recognizing the awesome difficulty facing individuals who wish to live alternatively, let us look at what some of the necessary conditions might be for increasing the probability of persons achieving more satisfying and emotionally meaningful lives.

Alternative Lifestyles

A great deal has been written recently about alternative lifestyles. Under this rubric have come discourses and empirical studies on such diverse topics as homosexual unions, swinging, dual-career marriages, childless marriages, singlehood, single-parent families, communes, collectives, etc. Rather than reviewing the new forms of intimacy (since I am not convinced that the new forms necessarily lead to more humane and equalitarian relationships), I will attempt to delineate in a quite tentative and speculative manner some of the most strategic factors that must be considered if individuals hope to create truly alternative lives within the existing political economic system.

One of the chief considerations is for the individual to decide whether or not to marry at all. At the present time, there are approximately 49 million Americans of marriageable age who are single. Nearly one-fourth of women under 24 were single in 1974 compared to 16 percent in 1960 (Scanzoni and Scanzoni, 1976:-153). Among both males and females the rate of singleness under age 35 has increased approximately 4 percent since 1960 (Scanzoni and Scanzoni, 1976:-154). It is too soon, however, to determine if the increase in singleness represents delay in marriage or a life-long commitment to singleness as an alternative lifestyle.

Although the least educated of both sexes for both blacks and whites are the least likely to ever marry, among white women the *greater* the education and occupational success, the less likely they are to marry. In the past, the high rate of singleness among educated women was attributed to their lack of "femininity," their undesirability to men. More recently, sociologists have begun to view it differently. They suggest these women are *choosing* not to marry. For educated and occupationally successful women, the costs of marriage may exceed the rewards. By remaining single, they have a better chance to retain their autonomy, to move geographically, to spend their income as they please, to commit energies to career without the constraints of marriage.

Increasingly, both males and females are expressing a belief that singleness is a more preferable state than marriage. Fewer of the singles see themselves as misfits or "leftovers." Many have found that marriage is no longer necessary in order "to find emotional support, sex, and an active social life" (Stein, 1976:420). By never marrying or not remarrying, the structural problems that marriage presents for individuals can be avoided. However, unless the proportion of singles radically increases, there will be little, if any, effect on current interrelationships between home and work.

If the option chosen is to remain single, then the individual has additional alternative decisions that can be made. For example, living with another person has become an increasingly common pattern among the older (social security recipients), the younger, and the more liberal members of the population. Living together for some persons provides a sense of emotional security and predictability without the full constraints of marriage. However, living together as a structural alternative to marriage may not, in practice, be much different from a marriage (Macklin, 1972); individuals easily fall into prescribed roles. Other alternatives such as establishing same-sex or cross-sex communal or collective homes can provide singles with the sense of "family" without the encumbrance of a spouse. Similarly, sharing an apartment or home with a friend with whom there is no sexual liaison can offer companionship and autonomy.

If persons choose to marry, the question becomes, What factors are associated with the development of equalitarian marriages? Because those factors are probably many and complexly interrelated and because they undoubtedly include the psychological, biological, as well as the sociological, I shall not attempt anything approaching a complete inventory. Rather, I shall discuss a few of the sociological factors that seem especially pertinent.

Although only two states require a women to take her husband's name upon marriage, most women do so. This probably has ramifications for the spouses' marital and extra-marital interactions, as well as for their careers. To assume the man's name, to submerge one's personal identity linguistically (to become Mrs. John Doe), cannot help but set the stage for the couple to be seen by themselves and others as "Mr. Couple." Breaking with convention by retaining separate names, probably indicates the partners' intention to build a marriage that is satisfying to them rather than one that conforms to the social norms.

The consequences for the wife's career are probably positive. By continuing to work under her maiden name, colleagues and employers are probably more likely to consider her a career-committed person. Further, whatever recognition she has received under one name may not be easily transferred to a new one—and if she changes her name each time she marries in the course of a lifetime, she may acquire three or four different ones. (Changing names is particularly dysfunctional in cosmopolitan careers such as academia, writing, show business). The consequences for the male's career may not necessarily be detrimental. For example, one vice president of a large business firm commented, "*Because* my wife has not taken my name, my associates see her as an interesting person to get to know. . . . Unexpectedly, she has helped rather than hurt my career." Clearly, research on marriages where the wife does not adopt the husband's name is needed.

A second factor is the relationship each member of the couple has to the occupational system. I would hypothesize that equality is more easily achieved if each spouse has a similar relationship to the economy: either both work or neither do; and, if both are employed, then the occupational statuses and income should be similar.

However, I would argue that similar relations to the work place, although probably a facilitating condition, is not a sufficient one. In addition, equality is more likely to be achieved if the couples' careers are viewed as equally important. The research on dual-career marriages (Holmstrom, 1972; Rappoport and Rappoport, 1972) finds that equalitarianism is not even achieved when both partners are highly trained professionals. Rather, the pattern is to give preference to the husband's career. Because the tendency to favor the husband's career is probably, in part, unconscious and because the political and economic structures are such as to favor men, achieving an egalitarian marriage may require placing the woman's career before the man's. To treat each career as equally important, then, may require implementing decisions that are *preferential* to the wife.

Closely intertwined with the relationship to work is the couple's allocation of domestic responsibilities. If the wife continues to be held responsible (through her own or her husband's expectations), for the routine cooking, shopping, and cleaning, as well as for decision-making in these areas, then the marriage will perpetuate an imbalance of power. Not only are those duties time- and energy-consuming, their performance lessens one's domestic power. What is needed is a division of labor in which both partners are responsible for domestic decision-making and task-performance.

Although balancing career opportunities and domestic responsibilities may lead to greater equality, it will not necessarily maximize the emotional interchange between the couples nor sustain an equalitarian marriage. Dizard reports that emotional closeness is more easily achieved if both partners *decrease* their emphasis on occupational achievement. When both are primarily committed to occupational success, "concerns about competitiveness and getting ahead dominate the relationship" (1972:198). Miller concurs, stating, "Egalitarian relationship cannot survive if people are not somewhat equally involved with each other and if the major commitment is to things outside the relationship which inevitably intrude on it" (1976:380).

Recently couples have attempted to codify their rights and responsibilities by writing their own marriage contracts. Marvin Sussman, Hugh Ross, and Betty Cogswell have been engaged in a major research project on the nature and content of these contracts. In a preliminary analysis of 1300 such documents, Sussman (1975) reported the major provisions in the contracts centered on economic, career/domicile, children, extra-marital sexual and nonsexual relationships, and termination issues. Partners vary widely as to whether they codify their contract in general expectations or in very concrete and specific ways. Although such contracts, which the partners view as reflecting their own aspirations and as morally binding, are not yet widespread, the very process of negotiating their intimate lives may lead to either a decision not to marry, or to a marriage that is more egalitarian.

Most people enter marriage and careers at approximately the same time in their lives. For couples committed to equality, the compounding strains of a new marriage and new job may be difficult to surmount. Speculatively, I would hypothesize that equality is more likely to be achieved by delaying marriage until both partners are firmly entrenched in their professions, or until they have reduced their desire to achieve in that sphere.

But perhaps the factor that most impedes equality is the addition of a child. Although folklore about parenthood contends that child-rearing is fun, children are sweet and cute (there are not bad children, only bad parents), that the sacrifices are worth it (Le Masters, 1976), and that children bring a couple closer together, there is little or no evidence to support any of these beliefs.

In fact, children have a strong and often negative impact on the marital relationship. Children take an incredible amount of time, energy, money, and emotion; they radically alter a couple's life. The addition of children "makes even a low-level decent relationship [between the parents], let alone, an egalitarian one, difficult" (Miller, 1976:380).

If the husband is expected to have a high degree of participation in child-rearing, then he may feel resentment, as Miller reports he did in his "Confessions of a Middle-Class Father". Child rearing "seemed to interfere terribly with the work I desperately wanted to achieve. . . . To make matters worse I did not know of other work-oriented husbands who were as involved as I was with their children" (1976:-376–377). Although Miller saw himself intruded upon by the demands of his children and the expectations of his wife, he notes that his disruptions were considerably less than those his physician-wife experienced. Despite his "good intentions," his marriage became a "typically upper-middle-class collegial, pseudo-egalitarian American one." Although he "helped his wife," he recognized

> that is not the same thing as direct and primary responsibility for planning and managing a household and meeting the day-to-day needs of children. . . . The more crucial issue, I now think, is not the specific omissions or commissions, but the atmosphere I create. . . . In the long run I have undoubtedly lost more . . . but the long run is hard to consider when today's saved and protected time helps meet a deadline (Miller, 1976:378–379.)

Having children, then, can have a serious negative impact on couples. Childlessness, on the other hand, can have "benign effects on marriage" (Bernard, 1976). Contrary to all clichés, childless marriages that do survive are happier than marriages with children" (Bernard, 1976:323). Childlessness releases both parents from the prescriptive sex roles of father-breadwinner/mother-child-rearer.

For those who choose to marry and have children, it is probably true "the fewer, the better." Delaying the birth or adoption of the children—until both individuals are more certain regarding their own self-images and goals, until the financial burdens that children bring can be minimized, and until both are established in their professional lives—probably diminishes the negative impact of children upon the marriage.

For those who do so choose—choose to marry and have children—and also want a more egalitarian and meaningful life together, considerable energy, time, and strength must be devoted to finding a path that takes them where they want to go. All too frequently, "individual attempts to resolve the dilemmas posed by competition and hierarchy, in combination with the subordination of women, have failed to sustain meaningful lives" for the persons involved (Dizard, 1972:200). Although some individuals and individual couples manage to establish a new path, for most, such cannot be trod until the society undergoes a major reorientation. Such a restructured society requires change in the institutional structure as well as in the ideological underpinnings. If one wants "a future in which family, community, and play are valued on a par with politics and work for both sexes, for all the races, and for all social classes and nations which comprise the human family" (Rossi, 1972a:353), one must recognize the necessity of understanding the connection between home and work, the interplay of the domestic and the extra-domestic. Only through the restructuring of the current sexual stratification system is there hope for the great majority of people to achieve more equitable and humane lives. And restructuring the stratification system requires a redistribution of power.

12
The Question of Power

Power—the probability of having one's will done despite oppositon—is a complex phenomenon. Although there is general agreement that certain items, such as money, numbers, access to the creation and dissemination of knowledge, are power resources, political sociologists and political scientists continue to disagree as to whether power in the United States is located in the hands of a few—a governing elite—or in the hands of many competing interest groups.

I take as my theoretical starting point that power resides in the hands of those who control the extradomestic allocation of scarce goods and services. In the United States, this power rests in persons who hold key decision-making positions (in corporations, labor, universities, foundations, the mass media, government, and political parties) and in those who control great wealth. For want of a better word, I will refer to them collectively as the "establishment."

When the system by which values, goods, and services are distributed to members of the society remains unchallenged, the probability is high that the interests of the establishment are those that will be served. Only when interest groups become politically active in relationship to particular issues does the potential for impact on decision-making on those issues shift away from the dominant group. This political activity may take the form of the social movement or that of a coalition between diverse pressure groups. Without such political activity, however, the system will *de facto* profit those who are in positions to make decisions that are in their own interests.

My intent in this chapter is to accomplish three primary goals: (1) to explain the processes by which power is retained in the establishment and obtained through social movements; (2) to document the extent of the exclusion of women from decision-making, and (3) to discuss the structure and effects of the Women's Liberation Movement. In the following chapter, men's liberation, black liberation, and coalition politics will be explored.

Although the focus of this chapter is women, to view it as concerned with only female issues is to miss the message. First, the theoretical analysis is essential for an understanding of power—whether one is a male or female. Secondly, the substantive concern with women is not merely an oversight of men. Certainly, most men do not achieve the positions of prominence discussed in this chapter; and certainly, more men due to their socialization, are more likely to view this as a personal defect or failure than are women. However, although the probability of any man achieving substantial influence in the policy making arena is slight, the possibility of any women achieving such is practically zero. That is, women are in a *qualitatively* different category than men when it comes to the question of power. Most observers recognize the saliency of race in relationship to power questions and would not equate the difficulties of most white men in achieving prominence with the experience of black men. Why, then, is it so hard to recognize that the situation is analogous for women?

One note of explanatory introduction is perhaps necessary. There are people who deplore the power game that's so prevalent in American life; to them, it is dehumanizing and corrupting. This may be so; however, the social reality is that there is power being exercised in the world. Eschewing it personally will not make it go away. It is imperative that we understand it whether we want more of it or less of it, or want to restructure the entire society so that power is de-emphasized or distributed differently.

Establishment Power

Corporate Economy

Wealth is a power resource if its owner controls its investment. Despite the common myth that women control the wealth, in fact men "earn, own, and control most of the wealth in this country" (Bernard, 1975:241). Fifty-eight percent of stock shares are owned by institutions whose boards of trustees and brokers are almost exclusively male. Individually, women own approximately 18 percent of privately held stock shares; men, approximately 24 percent (De Crow, 1974:173). In terms of privately held real estate holdings, only 39 percent belong to women, despite the fact of female longevity (De Crow 1974:143). Approximately 60 percent of persons with financial assets over $60,000 are male (Bernard, 1975:241).

These statistics are probably quite liberal estimates of the wealth of women, because it is common for men to place holdings in the names of their wives, daughters, or mothers for tax purposes (De Crow, 1974:143). Women are neither wealthier than men, nor are they situated to use their wealth as a power resource.

Rather, it can be argued that the control of the wealth in this country rests in the hands of a very small elite—approximately 1 percent of the population composed of owners and managers of the megaconglomerates. Members of this elite "own 25 to 30 percent of privately held wealth in America, own 60 to 70 percent of all privately held corporate wealth" (Domhoff, 1974:82), 40 percent of the federal bonds, 36 percent of all mortgages, and about 30 percent of the currency (Baldridge, 1975:172). They receive about 24 percent of the nation's yearly income (Domhoff, 1974:82). Further, the amount of wealth held by these people has been increasing over the past few decades; and moreover, "there is a remarkable continuity in the families that hold wealth ... thus preserving intact the radical concentration of power and money" (Baldridge, 1975:172).

Our nation's "upper crust" belongs to interlinking social, financial, and governmental networks. They attend the same prep schools and universities, revel at the same men's clubs and resort-retreats, and marry into each other's families. That is, not only do these persons share common financial interests; they are socially and familially bound to one another.

The policy decisions of this elite are discussed informally in board rooms and social clubs, and concensus is reached in their major policy-setting organizations, which themselves are "directed by the same men who manage major corporations and financed by corporation and foundation monies" (Domhoff, 1974:93).

In turn, these decisions affect our government through a number of channels. First, many of the members of these corporate organizations serve in high-level government offices, commissions, and committees (Domhoff, 1974:134–135). Secondly, "hired experts intimately identified with these organizations serve as government advisors" (such as Henry Kissinger and Herb Stein) (Domhoff, 1974: 98). Third, these organizations provide experts for testimony at congressional committees and for advising those committees. Fourth, many members of these corporate organizations are large contributors to campaigns and have, therefore, easy access to politicians (Domhoff, 1974:98).

For those readers who question the control of the corporate elite over politics in this country, I would suggest that they follow the news for the next week or so with two questions in mind: "In whose interest is this policy?" and "What is the social and corporate background of this appointee?"

The relationship of corporate executives and politicians is developed through informal modes of interaction. And these modes are exclusively male. One of the settings for the development of this social cohesion, which Domhoff has recently studied, are exclusive retreats—The Bohemian Grove, Rancheros Visitadores, Round Up—which "women are strictly forbidden to enter" (1974:24). Activities at these retreats such as boozing, hi-jinxs, calf-roping, cross-country horseback caravans, stag movies, the Bulls' Balls Lunch (donated yearly by a cattle baron following the castration of his herd) liken the retreats to a transplanted "college fraternity system" or "an overgrown boy-scout camp" (quoted in Domhoff, 1974: 23). But apart from the stereotypically masculine orientation of the fun-and-games, these retreats provide a context of intimacy wherein the corporate rich cement their social bonds with governmental officials, university chancellors, and presidents of television networks.

Within these encampments, policies are suggested, proposals are made, and appointments are discussed. One way of understanding the consequences of the establishment structure is to consider simply the numbers of women in key positions in the economy. Because the members of the corporate elite are interested in increasing their own profits as well as enhancing their lifestyles, to what extent does their policy of men-only-meetings pervade the world of the establishment power?

The weight of the evidence seems quite clear that the corporate economy is effectively controlled by a few megacompanies—banks, insurance corporations, and conglomerates. And that, further, the major decisions of these companies are made by only a few persons—the boards of directors (Domhoff, 1967:38). Amundsen reports that, of the 884 persons who served on boards of these top corporations in the early 1960s, none were women (1971:91). In a survey of the top 15 insurance companies in 1969, she found 8 women seated among 201 men. That is, women are not in positions to direct the corporate economy at its highest levels. Nor are they situated to direct it at high-level executive positions. Amundsen, for example, points out a *Business Week* survey of 1969 that found that the number of women executives in the corporate world had not changed in the past decade—approximately 2 percent of the top-level executives being women (1971:92). Corporate lawyers, similarly, are almost exclusively male. De Crow summarizes her analysis of the corporate world by noting that "women are conspicuously absent from the ranks of stockbrokers, financiers, corporation and bank presidents—and other elements of control over the wealth of our country" (1974:144).

Another access to influence in the corporate economy is through organized labor. Over the past 50 years, labor unions have demonstrated their veto power and their ability to initiate legislation. Despite the historical origins and rhetoric of union leaders, organized labor is oligarchical. Major policy decisions are made at the national level; the rank-and-file are ruled from the top down. In effect, unions both agitate and govern their members. Leadership determines which issues are non-negotiable—and which can be sacrificed.

Although women constitute approximately 12 percent of the union membership, they have not reached important decision-making positions. They rarely rise beyond assistant to department chiefs, and what little strength they have is at the local level. "Women are rarely found as officers of the intermediate bodies, the joint boards, and district councils, and almost never appear on major negotiating teams, on national executive boards, on national staff, or among the national office-holders" (Shortridge, 1975:260). Even in the two unions that are overwhelmingly female, the leadership is male (Amundsen, 1971:97).

The lack of power of women in the union leadership is undeniable, although researchers dispute the causes (Shortridge, 1975:261). According to Shortridge, the explanation rests on an interaction of factors. Women, due to domestic duties, have little time for union activities, which provide rungs up the leadership ladder; and both men and women tend to see such leadership positions as more appropriately belonging to the male (Shortridge, 1975:261). But for whatever the reasons, the ramifications for women workers are that their particular interests, such as child care and maternity benefits, are the first things bargained away at the nego-tiating table.

Women have no power in the corporate arena. They neither sit on boards of directors nor hold high-level executive positions in management or positions of leadership in organized labor. The corporate economy, although dependent on the work of women, does not offer them positions of influence or control.

Knowledge Creators and Disseminators

Knowledge is clearly a power resource (see Chapters 5–7). There should be no question regarding the relevance of the intellectuals' wares to the political arena. The intellectuals' works legitimize practical politics. The universities provide the resources through corporate- and foundation-sponsored research, and through the students they train to take positions of leadership in the government, corporate economy, and the media. The knowledge-makers, the intellectual's, and the knowledge-distributors, the managers of the mass media, exercise considerable influence.

The power within the university rests primarily in the hands of the trustees, the board of regents, and the president or provost. In a review of the 1975–76 catalogs for the big-10 universities (Iowa, Ohio State, Minnesota, Wisconsin, Indiana, Pur-due, Northwestern, Michigan State, Illinois), data revealed that no females occupy the top posts of president or provost. And 15 women out of 114 persons sit on these university board of trustees. For the most prestigious universities (Harvard, Yale, Princeton, and Chicago), the ratio is even smaller.

Another power resource for the creation and dissemination of knowledge rests in large philanthropical foundations. These control billions of dollars, and their network of influence pervades the university, the media, and the arts and sciences. In a survey of the boards of directors of four major foundations (Ford, Carnegie, Danforth, and Rockefeller), 10 members of their boards of directors were women, 61 were men.

The mass media has the ability to define our perception of reality—what is, what should be, and what is enjoyable. It has the ability to limit the boundaries of public discourse, to determine that which is newsworthy and that which is not. There seems to be little doubt about its ability to reinforce already existent belief systems or its abilities to transmit the culture to children (see Chapter 3). As such, it has considerable influence on the institutional arrangement of the society. For example, it can report a news item as serious or trivial; it can boost a candidate, co-opt a social movement, and publicize a political scandal. Its influence is so pervasive and effective, because we all depend on it to learn what we should know and how we should think. The media has the power to influence our political persuasion. Such power is not to be treated lightly in a democratic system, which ultimately depends on the support of its citizens.

What role do women play in the media? Do they hold positions that permit *them* to decide what shall be communicated and by whom? In reviewing the major television networks (ABC, NBC, CBS), out of the total of 47 members of the boards of directors in 1974, three were women (one for each network). At the executive level of these television channels, only a handful of managers have been female.

We might also wonder if the lack of female leadership in the media is reflected in its content as well. Television, which is watched an average of six hours a day in American households (Gutman, 1973) presents consistent stereotyped images of males and females throughout its programming—commercials (Bartee et al., 1974), soap operas (Katzman, 1972), prime-time shows (De Fleur, 1964), and comedy hours (*Columbus Dispatch,* July 12, 1974). De Fleur (1964) systematically analyzed the portrayal of occupations on television during peak hours of childrens shows. He included programs that depicted people interacting in modern settings in which occupational activities were being carried out (cartoons, quiz shows, commercials, and news programs were excluded from the analysis). He found that "overall, the world of work on television is a man's world. . . . Among the televised workers, 83.9 percent were males and 16.1 percent were females" (1964:65).

Television content is duplicated in all studies conducted on mass media. Content analyses of magazine fiction (Flora, 1971), advertisements (Courtney and Lockeretz, 1971), sports reporting (Grunden, 1973), and popular music (Freidlander et al., 1973), all reach similar conclusions. In brief, all media forms duplicate each other, each affirming and reaffirming power differentials between males and females.

Persons who hold key decision-making positions in the media can and do, effect its content. It seems reasonable to hypothesize that women in those positions would alter the content, judging from the greater diversity of roles and images that occurs when women have some control. (The most notable examples are the programs controlled by Mary Tyler Moore ("The Mary Tyler Moore Show," "Rhoda," "Phyllis"), the soap opera "Mary Hartman, Mary Hartman" directed by a woman, and magazines such as *Ms., New Woman, Womensport,* which are editorially supervised by women.

Government

An institution that obviously must be considered when discussing differential power in the representation of males and females is the government. Although it is simplistic to assume that a man will represent the interests of men and that a woman will represent the interests of women, it is a place to begin. As the black political force has recognized, there is greater likelihood of a black representing black interests than a white, and the likelihood of those interests being met increases with the number of black representatives. What, then, is the differential access to the legitimated power of the government office? We will first consider elected positions and then turn to the appointed ones.

No woman has held either of the top two executive positions—the presidency and vice-presidency—nor has any woman been a party candidate for these offices. The Senate has been overwhelmingly male; only in the House of Representatives have women fared slightly better. Table 9:1 shows the total number of women members of both houses in the federal government from 1947 to 1976. The representation is small, and there is no clear pattern of growth. Nevertheless the process of entry may be altering, particularly in the House. Before 1949, congresswomen entered via the right of widow's succession: "If power is thrust upon a woman by her husband's death, she may accept it without blame" (Lynn, 1975:376). Although female senators are still more likely to be appointed than elected to their first term, new women representatives are more likely to run on their own professional and political merit (Lynn, 1975:378). However, simply being elected to the halls of congress, does not insure the representative an active role in legislating. Influencing budgets, initiating legislation, taking part in investigative functions, responding to the particular needs of one's constituency, all depend upon one's seniority, committee assignments, and access to the informal communication network (Amundsen, 1971:69).

TABLE 12.1   Women Members of Congress, 1947-1976

Congress	Year	Senate	House
80th	1947-48	0	8
81st	1949-50	1	9
82nd	1951-52	1	10
83rd	1953-54	2	11
84th	1955-56	1	16
85th	1957-58	1	15
86th	1959-60	1	16
87th	1961-62	2	17
88th	1963-64	2	11
89th	1965-66	2	10
90th	1967-68	1	11
91st	1969-70	1	10
92nd	1971-72	1	12
93rd	1973-74	0	16
94th	1975-76	0	19

Source: Adapted from Lynn, 1975, with permission of author.

Longevity in office is one of the primary ways by which a representative moves along in the power hierarchy of the Congress. As one 67-year-old male freshman representative remarked upon his choosing not to run again for office, "Nobody listens to what you have to say until you have been there 10 or 12 years. . . . There are only about 40 out of the 435 members who call the shots. They're the committee chairmen and ranking members" (Quoted in Amundsen, 1971:69).

It is not until the 5th term in the House of Representatives, that a member of congress might expect to have influence (Lynn, 1975:378). From 1918 to 1973, only 17 women have held their seats in the House for the minimum 5 terms (Lynn, 1975:378). The major exception in the Senate was Margaret Chase Smith who served nearly a quarter of a century. (She entered politics by running for the House seat that her husband vacated due to serious illness.)

Committee assignments and leadership positions are further avenues to power within the congress. No woman has held the important leadership positions such as majority leader, Speaker of the House, party whips. Further, not all committees have equal power and importance. In a study of committee assignments, Geblen found that women were assigned to low-prestige and uninfluential committees. She concludes, "Indeed, the women do not participate equally with the men" (Geblen, 1969:40)—even when they are elected representatives.

The third path to successful influence in congress is through the informal social network. As is true of most important policy-making in business, much of the important work of government takes place on the golf course, the steam room table, and the men's clubs. These informal settings not only provide safe contexts for negotiating problems, they provide environments in which personal allegiances and friendships can be built. The importance of these informal contexts in developing friendships has lead at least one male administrative aide to contend, "No woman can quite make it. So much of the power is built [in the male-only preserves]. I doubt that the best of most able women can ever get to the inner circle, where there is complete acceptance" (quoted in Lynn, 1975:379).

When we further consider government's close relationship with industry, we see the probability of women obtaining power shrinking even more. However, before we conclude that this lack of female representation is somehow a function of their biology, we should briefly contrast the United States with other nations. Although it is true that women are underrepresented in all nations, it is also true that "the United States has one of the worst records for having women in national public office. . . . Among the few nations to match the low United States percentage of 2.4 percent in 1970 were Guatemala with 2 percent and Thailand with 2.2 percent" (Lynn, 1975:379).

Federal Appointments and Employment

Decision-making in government goes on not only at the legislative and executive levels but in a wide variety of bureaus, the functioning arms of the government. Emanating from these bureaus are policies, practices, and programs that encompass the entire dictionary of our social life, from atoms to zoos. Individuals in positions to make decisions at this level have either been appointed to or have worked their way up through civil service. The question is, Do males and females have differential access to these positions? Let us look at the highest-level appointments first.

The president's Cabinet has access to the president and, presumably, the power to influence decisions at the executive level. Only two women have ever held Cabinet rank. No woman has served as a member of the Supreme Court, and only in the last few years has such a possibility even been suggested. The Circuit Court of Appeals currently has one woman. However, the treasurer of the United States is usually a woman—this position is largely honorary, the primary function being signing the currency. Ambassadors and ministers to foreign states have been predominately male. Through 1976, only 18 women have held those positions. And, of the 1700 federal positions considered to be key policy-making positions, 39 were filled by women in 1972 (Lynn, 1975:380).

However, because much high-level positions are, in actuality, unavailable to most people, male or female, we will gain a better grasp of the differential access to decision-making by looking at the federal bureaucracies. The federal government is the single, largest employer in the country. Including the military, it employs more than 20 percent of the labor force. Equally worth noting is the fact that the government is viewed as a model for the employment practices in the private sphere (De Crow, 1974:47). In theory, the employment system is a fair one. Persons take government service exams, qualify at particular levels of competence, and, if positions are available, they can begin their civil service careers. The greater the expertise, training, and knowledge, the higher the level and the greater the salary obtained.

In 1961, when President Kennedy established the first Commission on the Status of Women, approximately 1 percent of persons in supergrade positions (above 18) were females. Prior to the establishment of the committee, request for personnel could specify sex preference. In one six-month period that was studied, 94 percent of the requests for grade levels 13–15 were for males (Lepper, 1974:113). Consequently, the commission created a Committee on Federal Employment Practices and Policies. Succeeding presidents to the civil service commission then gave further executive orders to abolish sex discrimination in every agency and department of the federal government through affirmative action.

The outcome of these executive orders in terms of occupational placement within the upper reaches of the federal government has been examined by Lepper (1974). Has the access to decision-making—that is, the placement of females in high-level government employment—changed?

Table 12.2 provides the distribution by sex in 1967 and 1972 of persons employed in grades 13 or above. As is clear from the table, the structure of employment did not change much during those 5 years; the total proportionate gain of females was only .3 percent.

Further, it is only at levels 15 and above that persons are considered executives within the federal government—that is, persons charged with the responsibility and duty to make decisions. In 1972, 2.3 percent of the persons listed in the federal executive inventory were female (Lepper, 1974:115). In raw numbers, 34,700 executives were male; 838 were female. And, as might be expected, most women in these positions are at the bottom level—87 percent of female federal executives are at level 15 (Lepper, 1974:115). Further, 71 percent of all female executives are clustered in three occupational groups and these occupations are those "traditionally associated with women" (Lepper, 1974:117).

TABLE 12.2   Employment in Federal Agencies by Sex in Government Service Ratings 13-18: 1967 and 1972

	1967			1972		
Grade	Total	Number of Women	Percent of Women	Total	Number of Women	Percent of Women
13	85,308	3,632	4.2	102,968	4,797	4.7
14	42,938	1,583	3.7	50,257	1,924	3.8
15	22,901	577	2.5	27,373	883	3.2
16	6,321	124	2.0	5,356	98	1.8
17	2,349	35	1.5	1,869	30	1.6
18	756	5	0.7	1,334	14	1.0
18 (above)[1]	609	15	2.5	299	6	2.0
Total	161,182	5,962	3.7	189,456	7,752	4.0

Table from Lepper, 1974:112, with permission of author and publisher.
[1]This category includes persons who are not part of the career service.

Party Power

To a great extent, modern government is party government. The route to political positions is through the party system. One position that may provide some form of power is that of committee person within the Republican or Democratic parties. The process by which persons hold those positions, however, affects both the amount of influence they hold as well as the kinds of issues they choose to push within the party organization. Most committeewomen hold their positions because they were selected by men—this is particularly true at the national committee level (Wells and Smeal, 1974:62). It apparently is true even at the local level, where in one study approximately 50 percent of the committeewomen were recruited for reasons other than their interest or involvement in politics (they were wives, mothers, and friends of party officials and candidates) (Wells and Smeal, 1974:-62). Of those women selected by the party to run for committee member, only 28 percent had any opposition. Wells and Smeal conclude that "the current recruitment of women into party positions is much like that of Uncle Tom blacks in the past. They are window dressing and not expected to promote themselves or other women in higher positions of power." And, if this is so, "the women already holding office in the party are not likely to provide leadership in the drive for raising the status of women in politics" (Wells and Smeal, 1974:62).

One way in which power can be expressed in the party system is through representation as a delegate to the party's convention. Such individuals, in fact, stand as the representatives of the electorate in a crucial stage of the electoral process—the nominating of candidates. Males make up a much greater proportion of party delegates than females, although both parties are moving towards greater equity in representation. However, of particular note is how delegates happen to be selected. In one study of the Michigan delegates to national conventions, the researchers found that the males were more likely than the females to be self-employed or employed at the professional level, to have completed college, to have held key appointments, or to have run for elective office. More than half the female delegates were not employed outside the home, and half of these women were wives of politically prominent men. Further, they were more likely than the male delegates to believe they should go along with the party's decisions rather than on their own personal belief systems (Jennings and Thomas, 1968). Men achieved their delegate positions in the political arena, while many women had their position donated to them with the expectation that they would be agents of the party's position rather than agents for change.

The lack of female representation in the government at all levels and in all branches, in both elected and appointive positions, is not the result of lack of female participation in politics at the level of voting. In fact, as Jaquette comments, the differential voting turnout of men and women is so slight as to bring forth a studied "ho hum" from political scientists (1975). Nor can it be explained by differential engagement at the campaign level. The women volunteers—in their canvassing, phoning, typing, and mailing—are the real armies of the night; they provide the free labor upon which campaigns depend. Rather, the differential representation is the result of the long-term differential socialization of males and females.

To the extent that women do not see themselves as a group that is clearly discriminated against, they will not recognize common issues and the necessity for bloc voting. If women do not see themselves as capable of administrating the country or the town, they will not run for office; if women do not have a collective conscience simply by virtue of being women, they will be excluded from political power.

Because they are not influential members of the corporate elite or any of its subsidiaries and partners—government, mass media, universities, and foundations—their access to power, if they choose to have it, is through social movement and coalitions. We turn to these arenas next. First, we shall discuss the Women's Liberation Movement and then the Men's Liberation Movement. We need to discover whether, at this point in history, the social movement route is differentially available to men and women.

Social Movements

If unchallenged, the political system will represent primarily the interests of the governing elite. However, it is likely that the interests of the elite run counter to the interests of other groups. For example, "What is good for General Motors is good for the country," was an oft-spoken slogan of the 1950s whose shamfulness has been recognized in the 1970s. Or, directly to the point, is the 1960s bumper sticker "War is Good for Business—Invest your sons." Fortunately, the republican political system is designed not only for the perpetuation of elites, but to allow the interests of less well-placed persons to have an impact on the political arena through "anti-system" activities such as boycotts, strikes, mass demonstrations, and social movements. Indeed, it is a primary function of the disenchanted groups within a democracy "to hold a democratic system to its own pretensions" (Lowi, 1971:56).

Social movements directed towards political change will be the primary concern of this section. Social movements are a part of the democratic political process—a necessary part in that they tend to restrict the oligarchic tendencies of the system by presenting alternative ideologies. Successful movements can change laws, provide for their implementation, and organize their membership to receive greater benefits (Freeman, 1975:2).

At the psychlogical level, involvement in movement activities tends to transform one's self-image. Part of this self-redefinition involves the recognition that what one previously thought to be personal problems are in fact experienced by many others. Sharing private realities counters social myths and helps politicize the problems. That is, perceiving personal problems as public issues leads to the need to influence public policy. "If such private recognitions are translated into public demands . . . the movements enters the political arena" (Freeman, 1975:5); if not, personal growth may occur, but the political institutions will remain unchanged.

Not all social movements enter the political arena; and not all that do are successful in achieving their goals. Increasingly, researchers are attempting to understand the structural conditions that lead to a movement's success. Because the study of social movements is a complex one that contains many competing theories, I will limit this discussion simply to the conditions under which movements are likely to emerge, grow, and succeed.

Social movements emerge slowly, and usually painfully, when two preconditions exist: "a long period of discrimination and oppression coupled with a short period of progress that generates rising expectations in a particular substrata" (Baldridge, 1975:207). It is not the absolute hardships of oppression alone, but the perceived relative deprivation—the gap between rising expectations and reality—that are prerequisite conditions for the emergence of a social movement. For example, although blacks have suffered long-term and absolute oppression in this country, it was only after they compared their position to that of whites that the Black Power Movement arose.

However, in order for conditions to lead to the emergence of a social movement, there is a need to recruit and link together members. One effective way of accomplishing this is to locate an existing communications network connecting the potential recruits, one that is "co-optable to the new ideas of the incipient movement" (Freeman, 1975:48). This is most likely if the persons linked in the network have similar backgrounds, experiences, and social status. If such a network does not exist, more energy must be expended on initial organizing activities.

Further, for the movement to emerge, a precipitant is necessary. The precipitant may take the form of a crisis—an event (such as the refusal to serve blacks in a restaurant) that symbolizes the general discontent. Or, the precipitant may be the formation of an organization that both disseminates the new ideology and provides an association with which the disenchanted can identify. "If a co-optable communications networks is already established, a crisis is all that is necessary to galvanize it. If the network is organizationally rudimentary then an organizing cadre of one or more persons is necessary" (Freeman, 1975:49).

At this point, the movement is ready to flourish or flounder. If it is to grow, the leadership must be able to perform both administrative and ideological functions. Administratively, it is necessary for the leaders to coordinate and develop organizations that meld the "followers into a strong political force toward concrete goals" (Baldridge, 1975:319). Moreover, it is necessary for the intellectual leaders to specify the ideology of the movement—its ends, its enemies, its utopian vision—in such a way that the "feelings, hopes, frustrations, and dreams" of its members are translated into action. (Baldridge, 1975:319).

Success is largely determined by the movement's ability to mobilize resources as well as the responses of other groups and agents of social control. Those who are in positions of power can respond in different ways: co-opt the movement, grant the demands, or suppress the activities. Few movements are successful in having their demands fulfilled; even fewer see their goals enshrined as social policy and law. And, there is an irony here, for if the movement does indeed succeed, it must die.

With these ideas in mind, let us look at this particular avenue to power, the social movement. It is a legitimate path open to the discontented, male and female alike. In the past decade, it has been the route chosen by women interested in altering institutionalized sexism. More recently, it has been tried by men similarly interested in liberating themselves from cultural and institutional restraints.

The Women's Liberation Movement

The 1960s witnessed a flourish of political activism—the Civil Rights Movement, student protests, and mass demonstrations for peace. The political activity of the 1960s sensitized many women to their second-class citizenship and led some to seek redress through political activity. Because the demographic statistics available concerning women active in the origination of the women's movement are very scant, it is difficult to determine the degree of deprivation they were experiencing. Some of these women were college-educated yet receiving fewer monetary rewards for their labor than were their husbands or male college friends or male co-professionals. Further, they were experiencing fewer chances for professional success and were cast into the two roles of housewife and supplementary breadwinner. A second, for the most part younger, group of women were enrolled in college and immersed in the university street community.

Given the two different social bases, it is not surprising that the women's movement has had two distinct origins representing two different strata of society, with two different styles, orientations, and forms of organization. And it is only in the last few years that these two branches have begun to merge.

The older branch of the movement—both historically and in terms of the average age of its members—is most prominently associated with the National Organization for Women (NOW), although other organizations such as the Women's Equity Action League (WEAL), Federally Employed Women (FEW), and the National Women's Political Caucus (NWPC) are also part of this branch. A major force for NOW's formation began in 1961, when President Kennedy established the first Commission on the Status of Women. The report of that commission in 1963 documented extensive legal and economic discrimination against women and proposed that commissions be established at the state government level. These commissions were composed of talented, politically active women. Their research not only supported the conclusions of the federal report, but convinced other women that the situation required redress. Further, the existence of the official reports raised expectations that corrective action would be taken at the state and federal levels. The women who served on these commissions exchanged communiqués and reports and attended national meetings, thereby, forming "an embryonic communications network among people with similar concerns" (Freeman, 1975:53).

Two important events occurred during this period. First was the publication of Betty Friedan's *The Feminine Mystique*, in 1963. The book described the "problem that has no name"—the malaise, frustration, and boredom of the middle-class, middle-aged woman. Unpredictably and almost immediately, it became a best seller. The second event concerned Title VII of the Civil Rights Act of 1964. In what was referred to as "ladies day" in the House of Representatives, Representative Howard Smith (D., Va.) introduced an amendment to include "sex" in Title VII, thereby, making discrimination in employment illegal. The amendment, ironically, was introduced in order to defeat the bill in its entirety by splitting the liberal vote. The debate had a circuslike atmosphere and was an occasion of much laughter. However, through the determined activity on the part of its supporters including Representative Martha Griffiths (D., Mich.), the amendment passed, only to have it described as a "fluke . . . conceived out of wedlock" by the executive director of the agency charged with its enforcement, the Equal Employment Opportunity Commission (quoted in Freeman, 1975:54). Subsequently, Representative Martha Griffiths attacked the agency on the House floor for their disrespect and ridicule of the law (Freeman, 1975:54).

The Citizen's Advisory Committee on the Status of Women rejected the resolution from nondelegates that the EEOC (the Equal Employment Opportunity Commission) "be urged to treat sex discrimination as seriously as race discrimination" (Freeman, 1975:55). And, on June 30, 1966, 28 women, including Betty Friedan, decided the time had come to try to bring women into full participation in American society; thus, the National Organization for Women was founded.

NOW was conceived of as a kind of NAACP for women, with a general focus on economic and legal equality. It was (and is) a top-down, hierarchically structured organization with a formal constitution, officers, boards of directors, etc. The initiators of the organization were drawn from women who had served on the state commissions and their friends, disgruntled employees of EEOC, and a Betty

Friedan contingent. These women had few skills in organizing masses of people, but considerable expertise in using the media. "They could create the appearance of activity but did not know how to organize the substance of it. As a result, NOW often gave the impression of being much larger than it was" (Freeman, 1975:56).

NOW's goals were clearly within the mainstream of the American value system and thereby provided an organization with which women could identify. Their initial goals were specified as a Bill of Rights and were adopted at the first NOW national conference in 1967. These were:

I.   Equal rights constitutional amendment
II.   Enforce law banning sex discrimination in employment
III. Maternity-leave rights in employment and in social security benefits
IV.   Tax deduction for home and child-care expenses for working parents
V.   Child day-care centers
VI.   Equal and nonsegregated education
VII. Equal job training opportunities and allowances for women in poverty
VIII. The right of women to control their reproductive lives

Meanwhile, the second branch of the movement drew from women who had worked in other movements concerned with civil rights, peace, or socialism. Despite these latter movements' ideology of freedom and participatory democracy, their women members were cast into the traditional roles of serving men coffee, sex, food, and typed copy. Further, these movement organizations refused to consider the issues of women relevant. For example, in December, 1965 (*after* the passage of the Civil Rights Act), the question of women's liberation was laughed off the floor at the Students for Democratic Society's (SDS) convention. Requests of SDS women to place a resolution in the organization's newsletter, *The New Left Notes,* were honored by "decorating the page . . . with a freehand drawing of girl in baby doll dress holding a picket sign and petulantly declaring, we want our rights and want them now" (Freeman, 1975:58).

At the 1967 National Conference on New Politics in Chicago, although women succeeded in gaining the last place on the agenda, the chairperson refused to recognize them. Irate women rushed to the podium demanding an explanation. The chairperson "just patted one of the women on the head and told her, 'Cool down, little girl, we have more important things to talk about than women's problems.' The 'little girl' was Shulamith Firestone, future author of *The Dialectic of Sex* (1971) and she did not cool down" (Freeman, 1975:60). These incidents repeated themselves throughout the radical community.

Soon, women began to form caucusses and to use the underground press to communicate with each other. Spontaneously and independently of each other, at least five women's liberation groups formed in 1967 and 1968. Although these women lacked the resources and desire to form a national organization, they were skilled at local organization and at using the existing structure of the underground press. This branch was originally referred to as Women's Liberation. Structurally, it is composed of many small autonomous groups linked together by the feminist press and friendship networks. The groups are characterized by the exclusion of males, shared tasks, lack of formal leadership, and an emphasis on participation. The value system and organizational structure are a direct consequence of the concerns of the radical community for participatory democracy.

Let us look more closely at these two branches of the movement in terms of conditions necessary for a successful social movement. First, the two branches had available to them social bases from which membership could be drawn. The membership bases were different, but probably both had experienced long-term discrimination and recent rising expectations relative to significant reference groups. Both branches had pre-existing communications networks: the older women through the states commissions on the status of women; the younger, through the radical community. Further, these networks were co-optable in that they linked together like-minded people. The older branch was highly sensitized to the unjust treatment of women due to their own involvement in research on the status of women. The radical women shared an ideology of liberation for oppressed people. The sexist behavior and attitudes of their male counterparts highlighted their own exploitation. Both groups were confronted with crises. The older branch was spurred on by the refusal of EEOC to enforce the sex provision and the nonchalant attitude toward it by federal officials. For the younger branch, the crises were frequent, each one serving to further symbolize the discontent and to focus it on the need for change. Given these conditions, the need for organizing the discontented into social movement organizations was requisite. In the older branch, organizers were virtually absent, which its slow growth of members evidenced. In the younger branch, organizers were the major reason for the rapid growth and spread of the Women's Liberation Movement.

By 1970, the women's movement exploded in the media. Major stories appeared about it in the newsmagazines, magazines, telecasts, prime-time specials, etc. Since that time, the movement has continued to mushroom: Not only have more members joined the existent organizations, but more importantly, more organizations drawing upon different social bases have been formed. Virtually no social category of women or social institution has been left untouched. Within religious institutions, many activist groups have formed—the National Coalition of American Nuns, the Women's Board of the Methodist Church, Church Women United of the National Council of Churches, the Unitarian-Universalist Women's Federation, to name a few. Professional women have organized associations and caucuses within practically all professions and academic disciplines, which are united under the Federation of Organizations for Professional Women. Within government and politics, organizations such as Federally Employed Women (FEW) and National Women's Political Caucus continue to try to develop bloc voting. Labor women have organized the Coalition of Labor Union Women (CLUW), and black women, the Black Women's Liberation Movement.

Not all of these organizations have been equally successful in organizing or achieving goals. However, their existence proves that the women's movement is no longer exclusively white or middle-class. Although the earlier organizations retain those characteristics, the new organizations draw from different social bases and have increased the numbers and kinds of women concerned with their status, class, and power.

The diversity of the women's movement—particularly the differences between the older and younger branches of the movement—rather than tearing it asunder has provided it with a particular strength. Freeman argues the younger branch has skills in organizing at the local level and in providing feminist analyses, while the older branch has been prodded on by these analyses and been able to implement change at the governmental level. In effect, a symbiotic relationship between the two branches has developed. The symbiosis has led to an irony: the older, more conservative branch has become increasingly radical, whereas the younger branch has become increasingly reformist in activity (e.g., establishing local self-help clinics, women's media centers, rap groups, and cooperative garages. However, the symbiosis has led to considerable change at the policy-making level of government.

To chronicle the successes of the women's movement to date requires an examination of policy and legislative changes. At these levels, the gains have been substantial. Before the development of the women's movement, there was virtually no national policy on women. Since the emergence of the movement, however, a national policy has been created to favor legal equality of rights and protection for men and women. Much legislation has passed, including (1) the Credit Bill, prohibiting discrimination in loan eligibility based on sex or marital status; (2) Title 7 of the Civil Rights Act, prohibiting discrimination in employment based on sex; (3) Title 9 of the Education Amendments Act, which witholds federal financial assistance to any educational institution or program which discriminates by sex; (4) the Equal Rights Amendment at the federal level and a comparable law within some states; (5) the legalization of abortion; (6) the revision of the income tax laws; and (7) the revision of some state criminal codes towards more sexual equity.

Much of this legislation has been a direct result of the ability of the women's movement to mobilize its constituency into effective political participation through demonstrations, letters, lobbies, etc. What is particularly remarkable about these achievements is the speed with which the notoriously slow legislative apparatus has moved.

The first step toward social change, legislation, has been accomplished for some of the goals of the movement. More equal-rights laws than ever before are on the books at both the federal and state levels. As such, a legal-moral climate is provided by them, and legal recourse for redress is open. However, what is lacking is the full enforcement of these laws. Legislation makes social change possible, but without monitoring and enforcement what we are left with is simply the illusion of change.

This illusion of change, unfortunately, has also contributed to the belief that the women's movement is no longer necessary. Several other conditions as well have emerged to suggest that the Women's Liberation Movement is dead. First, many original concrete goals have been achieved; second, many remaining goals have been co-opted by the establishment, leaving the more radical and less easily articulated demands to the movement; third, the mass media has instituted a "brown out." The flurry of news items of the early 1970s has been replaced with near silence. Fifth, powerful counter-movement interests have mobilized their resources to undermine gains already achieved (e.g., legal abortion) and to prevent the attainment of others (e.g., ratification of the ERA). Sixth, fragmentation and fighting between the leaders of the movement, which is characteristic of movements after achieving major successes, have replaced unification—if only temporarily. However, I would hypothesize that the movement will re-emerge within a few years—when young women enter the work world with high hopes only to discover a severe gap between their expectations and reality.

Women have pursued the social movement alternative as a path to power. Their successes are visible in terms of the raised consciousness of Americans regarding the injustices of sexual inequality, the feminist-inspired revisions of social and psychological sciences, the creation of some nonsexist children's materials, the personal growth of its members, and certain policy and legislative changes. However, the core problem is that those successes are yet to be translated into positions of power within economic and political institutions. The power structure has not been changed. In other words, we have come full circle, back to the problem originally faced in this chapter: The interests of women will not be served until they have control of key decision-making positions.

There is one other possible path: the formation of coalitions with other groups interested in altering the power relationships in this country. Both the Black Liberation Movement and the Men's Liberation Movement are interested, but is such a coalition possible?

13
Coalition Politics: Men's, Women's, and Black Liberation

In all known societies, systems of stratification exist; that is, groups of people are arranged in a hierarchy such that those on top have greater access to scarce resources—prestige, power, and opportunity—than those on the bottom. In the United States, part of the stratification system has developed along two dimensions: gender and race. Consequently, when considering race and gender there are four distinct groups—white males, white females, black males, and black females—and a complex pattern of power relationships among them. (Franklin and Walum, 1972:242–253).

Traditionally, all members of this society have been socialized to believe that white malehood is the superior status and that white males as their legitimate birthright should receive the greatest power, prestige, and opportunity. Socialization, however, is never complete, perfect, or omnipotent. Although the norms and values of the society are formally inculcated into its members, compliance is not always forthcoming. The more people perceive these norms as unfair, the less likely they are to comply. Because the demands made on subordinates are great and the rewards few, individuals located low on the social hierarchy have more reason to question the legitimacy of the norms that govern their lives.

Noncompliance within each of the four groups becomes even more predictable when we examine the gap between society's values and their own, society's images of them and their images of themselves. For example, a black girl may be taught by society that black women are irresponsible and lazy, yet experience the black women around her as competent, hardworking, and highly motivated. Or, she may learn that women are to be protected and pampered, yet, vicariously experience her own mother's exploitation.

In order to function, it is psychologically necessary to make sense out of the inconsistencies of the experiential world and the formal dictums of the society (Festinger, 1975). One way to make sense out of the dissonance, to reduce the contradictions, is to strive towards changing the norms of the system—the rules of the game. We are in the midst of such a change now. The major subordinate groups—black men, black women, and white women—are questioning definitions of their groups as weak, dependent, and worthless; and trying to reduce their dependence and increase their own power. And unless the total amount of power in the society can be increased, those with less power have to improve their positions by lessening the power of those groups above them in the hierarchy.

But in addition to the redistribution of power being accomplished through the activities of subordinate groups, it can also be achieved through the voluntary surrender of power by the dominant group. The latter balancing mechanism is currently being explored by persons within the Men's Liberation Movement. We turn to that movement, now, before readdressing the question of power within the black community and between the black and white communities.

Men's Liberation

When the Women's Liberation Movement was reaching its crescendo in the press during 1970–71, a new movement began to emerge on college campuses: The Men's Liberation Movement. According to its scant chronology, (Pleck, 1973) predominately white, middle-class males met together initially in reaction to alterations of their lives or psyches due to their involvements with newly emergent feminists. One such Chicago group, Men Against Cool (MAC) stated, "[We] are a group of guys who, almost to the man, have come together out of confrontations with women over the nature of our sexism" (1970). But quickly these goups began to focus on two other issues—namely, how they related to other men and how they related to work. One such group, The Berkeley Men's Center issued a Manifesto that included the following statements:

> We, as men, want to take back our full humanity ... We no longer want to feel the need to perform sexually, socially, or in any way to live up to an imposed male role, from a traditional American society or a "counterculture."
> We want to relate to both women and men in more human ways—with warmth, sensitivity, emotion, and honesty.... We want to be equal with women and end destructive competitive relationships between men.
> We are oppressed by conditioning which ... serves to create a mutual dependence of male (abstract, aggressive, strong, unemotional) and female (nurturing, passive, weak, emotional) roles.
> We believe that this half-humanization will only change when our competitive, male dominated, individualistic society becomes cooperative, based on sharing of resources and skills. We want to use our creative energy to serve our common needs and not to make profits for our employers (n.d.).

As with women's consciousness-raising groups, there is no reasonable estimate of how many men's groups are in existence, although undoubtedly there are many fewer of these than of the women's groups. Few though they may be, these men are seeking alternative ideologies for their lives in a supportive atmosphere. Although some of the spokespersons for the men's movement focus on the need for institutional change, the groups themselves seem to have adopted the model of the younger branch of the Women's Liberation Movement—small, autonomous, and, theoretically, leaderless. As the reader will recall, in order for a social movement to emerge there must exist both long-term oppression and rising expectations. If the movement is to progress beyond the incipiency stage, it is necessary to have a pre-existing communications network which the new ideology can co-opt, followed by a precipitating event which activates the potential membership. If the communications network is embryonic or nonco-optable, a cadre of organizers is necessary.

Although most men have suffered long-term sex-role oppression—as chronicled in the Berkeley Men's Center Manifesto—this has been primarily psychological oppression. Men have been discriminated against because they are poor or black or uneducated or rural or non-Wasp; but, they have not been economically or politically discriminated against because they are *men*. That is, the discrimination is not a result of sexual inequality. As to rising expectations, it probably can be argued that the feminist movement provides some of these men with the hope that they too could effectively alter their lives. Indeed, much of the ideology of the Men's Liberation Movement is phrased in terms of their deprivation relative to women in such areas as support, nurturant behavior, emotional expressivity, etc. However, it is difficult (for me at least) to see that the primary prerequisite social conditions exist either in reality or in the perceptions of very many men.

Further, there is no doubt that a male communication network exists—the tavern, the ball park, the fraternity, the union, the men's club, the economy, the state. But this network is designed to exclude individuals, regardless of their sex, who do not share the same proclivities and predilections of those already part of the network (see Chapter 10). Consequently, although there are seemingly ample communication structures, on the face of it, these are not co-optable to the ideas of men's liberation. Barring this resource, the formation of an organization with an active cadre of leaders is essential. Although several men have emerged at least as spokespersons for the movement, a national organization (such as National Organization for Men) has not been a part of their programmatic goals. Even if a major precipitating event were to occur, without formal organizational structure or a co-optable network, the event would not crystallize the potential social base into a social movement.

But is there a potential social base? In that women are inconsistently socialized, it is easier, once the myths are shared, to organize the discontented and relatively deprived around political and social issues. The complexity of the demands of the women's movement, further, allows various people to plug into it at different times. For example, the goals of equality of opportunity and the right to be rewarded for achievements are within the mainstream of the American value system.

But, parallel supportive arguments cannot be made for the men's movement. White males are consistently socialized to view themselves as valuable and to achieve within the system. Their privileged position within the system does not give them the structural advantage of challenging their own treatment as unfair. Most of the goals of the men's movement are not easily politicized. Analogously to those goals of the women's movement that are still seen as "personal" (housekeeping and child care), most of the aims of men's liberation have not been perceived as truly political. Although one of these goals, men's relationship to their work, has a great potential for politicizing—particularly in times of economic uncertainty—the men's movement has not chosen to treat it as a public issue, capable of alteration through political action.

Not only does the Men's Liberation Movement lack the essential structural forms for the development of a viable social movement and an active social base to mobilize, it is notably hindered by major social-psychological obstacles within the male population. Women who feel comfortable and protected are not likely to join the women's movement. Analogously, most men, even if they don't feel they "have it made," are living in a society where to admit disillusion is to suggest that there is something wrong with them—as men.

But, perhaps, the most important barrier to the success of the Men's Liberation Movement is the fundamental dilemma which any anti-power group faces. Farrell has articulated this dilemma well: "On the one hand they are attempting to obtain enough power to stop a system (capitalism) which only recognizes power from its tendencies toward power aggregation. However, in the process of gaining this power, they are faced with the prospect of individuals in the new system becoming power hungry themselves" (1975:172–173).

Men's Liberation—striving as it does to wrest its members from the tyranny of power and competition—faces this dilemma. How can it engage in the political sphere without reinforcing the power in the psychology of its adherants?

What, then, can men do—men who are interested in altering the social arrangements among the sexes in this country? The Berkeley Men's Center Manifesto suggests that "every group must speak its own language, assume its own form, take its own action, and when each of these groups learns to express itself in harmony with the rest, this will create the basis for an all-embracing social change" (n.d.).

While recognizing the vision of the manifesto, that harmony is not soon upon the land. In the meantime, I would argue that the disaffection with the system felt by men, can be channeled. The continuous development of self-help and support groups is one such valuable enterprise. And, if the power dilemma can be laid aside or personally solved, there are at least three viable options for the Men's Liberation Movement at this time. The first is the clear alignment with the Women's Liberation Movement in terms of coalition formation. The second is to use their privileged positions and greater opportunities to *directly* alter the administration of political and economic institutions; this may require acting in a more powerful way than some men do now. And the third is to politicize the structure of work—a goal the Black Liberation Movement and the Women's Liberation Movement can fully share.

The Race and Gender Hierarchy

What, then, is the race and gender hierarchy in this country? As stated earlier, white males have historically and contemporaneously enjoyed the greatest power and prestige. Further, the distribution of power among the subordinate groups is largely controlled by the values, ideology, and policies of the superordinate groups. Being "white" in the eyes of the dominant group, is superior to being "black," and consequently, white women have enjoyed greater power than either black men or black women.

The distribution of power between black women and black men is a more complex problem. Objectively, black men have had greater access to educational and employment opportunities (Jackson, 1971:3—41). In terms of occupational placement and income, black men fare much better than black women (see Chapter 11). Black men, in fact, have greater rights to distribute key resources than black females. But black females are generally perceived as being more powerful. This is so for several reasons. First, white policies have been such that, historically and even currently black females are defined as more powerful than black men. In the words of Thomas and Znaniecki, "If you define a situation as real, it is real in its consequences" (1918:76). The consequences have been the perpetuation of the belief that black women are dominant in black society—the "myth of black matriarchy." By defining reality in this way, black women have gained an unsought psychological advantage. It is profitable for the white male group to define black males as powerless, thereby lessening threats to their own masculinity. It is even more profitable to produce discord in the black community by favoring the black female. And it is most profitable if the black male, then, diverts his rage away from the white community toward the black female.

Second, more social-psychological power accrues to the black female than to the black male as a result of relative deprivation (Runciman, 1966). The black male, like all individuals in this society, has been taught the ideal role model is the white male. Although he makes more money than the black woman, the black male is not measuring his performance in relation to the black woman, but to the white male. And compared to the white male's status, the black male experiences a sense of very real deprivation. The psychological response is to see himself as even less powerful than he is, leading to "a self-fulfilling prophecy."

Consequently, the power hierarchy might most profitably be viewed as two separate hierarchies. There is an objective one, which places groups in descending order as follows: white males, white females, black males, and black females. But there is also a subjective or social-psychological one, which views the power order as follows: white males, white females, black females, black males.

In that the white female's positions on both the objective and subjective power hierarchies are consistent, she can increase her power by lessening her dependence upon the white male and by increasing her own power resources. Consequently, she has fought for access to educational and employment opportunities to reduce her financial dependence and has engaged in consciousness-raising activities to lessen her psychological dependence. In addition, she has developed alternative sources of gratification, such as sisterhood and career involvement. And she has sought through social movement activity to acquire access to decision-making positions. Some white men have aided this process either through involvement in the Men's Liberation Movement or through using their positions within organizations.

However, because the objective and subjective power hierarchies are not consistent in regards to blacks, the question is, Where has the Black Liberation Movement directed its energies? The primary orientation has been along the objective power axis. Blacks have struggled to lessen their dependence upon the white structure through such techniques as black separatism, black capitalism, etc., and they have worked to increase their access to key decision-making positions within the white structure. However, black males have played a predominant role in the Black Liberation Movement, and part of their energies have been directed toward lessening the perceived psychological advantage of the black female. A recent episode at a large state university is illustrative. The following letter (excerpted) signed by "a black sister" appeared in the student newspaper.

> Why, black brothers do you continue to rap the white man and his establishment but continue to date his women? This is certainly having a double standard (what are we fighting against). The black brother who strolls on campus with a beautiful natural hair style and colorful dashiki with a white is hypocrisy personified.
>
> Let's be absolutely frank about what is at stake . . . equality, better education, better and more jobs, decent housing, essentially a better society . . . It certainly cannot be done by dating whites to prove to the white man that you are "equal" (*The Lantern*, April, 17, 1970).

Subsequent to its publication, the writer was subjected to threatening phone calls and physical harassment by black males, which resulted in her request for police protection. The reason given for the harassment was that "a black woman had no business telling a black man what to do."

Lessening the power of the white male, then, has been an object of white women, black men, and black women. But, in addition, black men have been seeking to increase their psychological power within the black community and reducing the advantages of black women in the white power structure.

Black Women in Women's Liberation

Why, then, when one of the outcomes of black liberation is to lessen her power and one of the outcomes of women's liberation is to increase her power, do so few black women elect to join the women's movement? Of course, there is no singular prototype black woman. Consequently, there are various reasons for not joining the women's movement depending on socialization, perception of reality, and goals. In what follows, I offer five major reasons why black women refrain from involvement. These are based on student's journals, reading, and discussion. It is understood that not all black women will share the same reasons, but I believe this to be a fairly complete accounting of the important factors.

1. *Race is a more salient variable than sex.* Despite the claim by Shirley Chisholm that she has experienced more discrimination as a woman than as a black (Chisholm, 1970:43), this is not the common perception of black women. Subjectively, in our society, race has been a more important variable for experiencing power, prestige, and opportunity than sex. The black experience as it confronts the black woman in its intensity and everydayness is far more relevant than her sex-role experience. As one black woman recorded in her journal, "As a woman, I am *suppressed.* But as a *Black* Woman, I am *oppressed.* How can I turn onto Women's Lib? What can it do for me as a Black?"

The black woman's experience is qualitatively different from the white woman's experience. The impact of blackness is omnipresent, and totally structures the life chances of black women. Consequently, although the power of black women is diminished in the Black Power Movement, progress toward increased power in the society is more readily realized through black identity. For example, one student writes,

> The view of black women and men in a very real struggle, for survival on the physical level makes it necessary to lay to rest the myth that the black woman needs to join the Woman's Liberation Movement. . . . The black man and woman can work together against the system.

That is, black women perceive more at stake due to their blackness than due to their femaleness.

2. *Black male and black female relationships.* Just as the black experience is different than the white experience, the relationships between the sexes in the black substructure have been different than those in the white substructure. As one black woman stated, "We don't join women's lib because we're already liberated." Or, as Toni Morrison writes, "In a way, black women have known something of the freedom white women are now beginning to crave. But oddly, freedom is only sweet when it is won. When it is forced it is called responsibility" (Morrison, 1971:64). Stated another way, these women are saying that they have had a psychological advantage within the black power structure. And, further, this arrangement foisted upon them by the policies of the white substructure has led to intolerable relationships between black men and black women. The black woman, by being defined by the white culture as more competent and responsible than the black man, has acquired an increasing lack of respect for black males (Morrison, 1971:64). Black males, in turn, vent their rage on black women, seeing them as Geraldinesque enemies or "cobras" (Cleaver, 1968). The problem for black women is not to gain more power, but to come to terms with the black male, to restructure new role relationships between them. And further, the restructuring between the sexes in the black community is, as one student puts it, "a family concern . . . and outsiders [white women] aren't invited."

3. *Political orientations.* Because black oppression is severe and intense, any

alignment with the women's movement will only serve to minimize the importance of black liberation. Politically, the women's movement is a late-comer in liberation struggles, borrowing black ideology without being black, and at least latently, attempting to co-opt the black woman from her struggle in the Black Liberation Movement. Many black males are strongly opposed to black woman's involvement in women's liberation. As one black male student wrote, "We certainly don't need our women growing even more aggressive than they already are. It is not only counter to *my* struggle, it is counter to *our* struggle."

4. *Attitudes toward white women.* Attitudes toward white women held by black women are decisively important in their reticence to join the movement. I will discuss two of the most crucial attitudes—namely, *distrust* and *distaste*. White women are, first and foremost, white; although they may not have been the ideological presenters of racism in this country, they have been ideological supporters. Why should they be trusted? Many black women believe that if they did join white women's caucuses, they would simply be used by them. There is nothing in the history of white women that can alter the basis for this belief. Secondly, many black women have a distaste for white women. This distaste comes from two different sources. On the one hand, they have been taught that white women are the standard of beauty and behavior against which they are to be measured. Association with these images of femininity taught long ago serves to court in the black women feelings of worthlessness, ugliness, and inappropriateness—and their offspring, rage. Black women in pure sanity voluntarily choose not to associate with persons who make them feel "down" or angry. On the other hand, black women have a distaste for white women because they don't respect them. Toni Morrison writes,

> Black women have found it impossible to respect white women . . . Black women have no abiding admiration for white women as competent, complete people. Whether vying with them for the few professional slots available to women in general, or moving their dirt from one place to another, they regarded them as willful children, pretty children, mean children, ugly children, but never as real adults . . . They were totally dependent on marriage or male support (Morrison; 1971:64).

To align with white women, then, is to align with a group that is neither trustworthy nor desirable. To feel sisterhood is difficult, insane, or impossible.

5. *Opposition to goals.* Opposition to the goals of women's liberation comes from at least three very different directions. First, some black women, as alluded to earlier, see the goals of the movement as completely irrelevant to their life experiences. Getting into medical school, getting a seat on the stock exchange, getting lunch at the Men's Grill are not very pressing problems compared to getting medical services, getting a job, and getting food for the table. "Escaping motherhood" is not relevant compared to how to successfully *be* a mother (Morrison, 1971).

Secondly, as implied earlier, there is opposition to the women's movement on the grounds that if it does succeed, it will only push the Black Liberation Movement further behind. The success of the women's movement will mean only greater competition for scarce rewards such as employment. Whites being white will reward white women with the positions. Further, the persons who will profit by the women's movement will not even be the radical women who spearheaded it, but rather the late-comers, the more traditional women. These traditional women once vested with power will continue the policies of the white men. In this struggle, neither the black nor the radical women will win; instead, the fruits of their struggle will go to continue the power imbalance.

Thirdly, black women, like white women, have been socialized by the dominant culture, which declares that "woman's place is in the home." Many black women are seeking at this point what the white women is turning her back on. Some black women choose it for politicized reasons like "having children for the revolution" or "getting behind her man." But many choose it for glamourized American ideological reasons. For example, one black student wrote the following:

> To the White Women in this Class: The way you talk here, you seem to want what I've had all along. Well, you can have it. As for me, I'm going to marry a black brother, stay home, raise flowers and children and read recipes. You don't know what you're giving up . . . and what you're going to get isn't worth it.

The American ideal of pampered womanhood, for some black women, is the preferable goal, not liberation *from* the home, but liberation *to* the home.

These reasons for not joining the movement are clearly interwoven; and when the weave is examined it looks like a proper fabric for shrouding women's liberation. The black woman, regardless of her ideological viewpoint, has little to gain in direct or indirect advantages by participation in the woman's movement and potentially a great deal to lose. It should not be surprising then that there are so few black women in the women's movement.

Although few black women have joined the Women's Liberation Movement, the women's movement has had an impact on black women and can play a role within black liberation. As discussed earlier, one of the chief problems within the black liberation struggle is the role relationship between black males and black females. The black power struggle has been directed not only to the white system but to increasing the power of black males in the black community. One of the outcomes, as Linda LaRue suggests, is that:

> The Black Liberation Movement has created a politicized, unliberated copy of white womanhood. Black women who participated in the struggle have failed to realize for the most part the unique contradiction between their professed renunciation of capitalist competition and their acceptance of sexual colonialism (1970:61).

Consequently, LaRue argues, black women ashamed of their strength and competentency seek to suppress it, adopt white notions of femininity, compete fiercely for black males, and rationalize the adoption of traditional domestic roles by politicizing them. In redressing the imbalance of power within the black community, then, black women have been politicized to imitate white woman's roles, roles which white women in women's liberation have been casting aside.

The Women's Liberation Movement, therefore, has a striking contribution to make to the black struggle. "The birth of Women's Liberation Movement, is an opportunity for the black movement to come back to its senses" (LaRue, 1970:61). Black men and black women need not adopt worn-out white role relationships, nor retain worn-out white policy based role relationships. Unlike the dynamics within the white power structure, where the white male is both dominant and threatened by the white woman's moves towards equality, the black woman is not threatened by the black man's increasing ability and competency. She welcomes it. Therefore, they are in a unique position to move toward an equality of respect, responsibility, and companionship.

The Women's Liberation Movement, then, serves to keep alive the notion that other roles are possible, that the traditional white role relationship is faulty, and that persons can uniquely define and redefine themselves.

Coalition Politics

I have argued that black women have little to gain from direct involvement with women's liberation and potentially a great deal to lose. I have further argued, however, that the Women's Liberation Movement has certain indirect contributions to make to the black women's struggle to restructure the role relationships with black males. I have also argued that men's liberation, if it so chooses, can gain political goals through alignment with the women's movement and the black movement. Will it be possible, then, to create a coalition between women's liberation and men's liberation, as predominately white movements, and black liberation?

Coalitions are possible when two conditions are met. First, each of the parties believe they can gain more through their joint efforts than they can separately; and secondly, they trust that the benefits reaped will be shared. Currently, neither of these conditions are fulfilled. The black movement has gained through black identity. More rewards are seen emanating through a united black front than through a coalition with white women or white men. White women, on the other hand, have benefited by the liberation struggle of the blacks, which has opened doors for them they've never opened themselves. Secondly, both white men and white women have to weigh the advantages they might receive in coalition with the black liberation against the losses they may incur. If white women did indeed join with the black coalition, they would have to be prepared to welcome as equals black men and black women. The unconscious racism among whites stands in the way. Although they might gain through the alliance, they have to be prepared to loose their privileged positions as whites. The risk of being judged by whom you associate with against retaining at least some privileged sanctuary works especially against white women joining into coalitions with blacks.

White men stand to lose both sources of privilege: sex and race. Although men's liberation holds this as a positive end, at this point in history, such a goal seems unlikely to be met. Further, as is well recognized by liberated men, the subtle forms of domination that they have habitually practiced over women re-emerge during public encounters (Farrell, 1975). To remain loyal to the goals of their own ideology almost requires them to remain outside the women's struggle.

The lack of trust of white women among black women has already been discussed. The distrust by the black community of white men is probably even greater. Analogously, the same factors of distrust that psychologically prevent black women from joining women's liberation operate to block any coalition between black liberation and the women's movement. White women and white men may not trust the black community either. In this case, though, it is primarily through their unconscious racism, fear of the unknown, and magnification of the six o'clock news.

Given, then, that the attitudes of both white and black women and men are such as to prevent effective coalitions, at this time, who profits? One of the oldest techniques in history that superordinate groups use is to propogate competition, distrust, and distaste among subordinate groups. If subordinate groups are kept as competitors rather than as cooperators, the dominant group's power is enhanced. In this case, the white male profits from the anti-power base of men's liberation and the noncoalition of women's liberation and black liberation.

What can be done? There is no way to erase the attitudes of distrust that have been generated over centuries. But, perhaps, there is a way to convince each group that, at this particular point in history, there is more to be gained through coalition on specific issues than either group can gain alone. An example will illustrate the problem:

At one large state university, ten university fellowships for minorities were established five years ago. For the first four years it was tacitly understood that these fellowships were to go to blacks. In the fifth year, one was awarded to a white Appalachian woman on the grounds that under HEW guidelines she also qualified as member of a minority and could not be discriminated against. The net impact is that the positions won by the struggle of blacks over the last decade for employment and education were now being distributed among all named minority groups—American Indians, Chicanos, women, blacks, etc. The number of positions haven't increased, only the number of "qualified applicants." Further, and especially destructive in view of the earlier discussion on the struggle between black males and black females to find satisfactory role relationships, black women were given the highest priority, because as they say in the bureaus, "we can kill two birds with one chick."

The acceptance of shared quotas as legitimate, then, is profiting black females and white females to a greater degree than black males. But the profit is really only apparent. The major ones who gain from the competition are the dominant white male group.

Therefore, a coalition at this time between liberationists aimed towards specific goals of, for example, increasing the proportion of educational and employment opportunities in a particular institution, can essentially profit these interest groups. By increasing the size of the pie, the subordinate groups can have absolutely a larger slice. And secondly, if such a coalition regarding just one school or one employer works, then both the model of its possibility will exist and some of the barriers to trust may be broken.

The Black Liberation Movement is now at the crossroads. As said earlier, getting into medical school, or getting a University Fellowship is just not very important compared to the demands of getting through the daily life of being black in America. The value of coalition on these basically elite problems is a decision to be made within the Black Liberation Movement. Are coalitions for such minor goals worth the time, energy, and people-power when survival looms so heavily? It is a shame to lose to women and other minorities what the black struggle has already won for itself; but the decision as to where to allocate resources and which tactics to take must remain a black decision. The women's movement will and has profited without the coalition. Must the black community lose? Divided and conquered, we now stand.

A Final Note

The maintenance of sexual inequality does not depend entirely on the socialization process that teaches it, the institutional arrangements that foster it, or the ideology that legitimizes it. In the final analysis, it is not institutions or ideas that act—it is you and I. Through the daily and often unconscious acceptance and compliance with the norms of the society, we create intimate and public environments that perpetuate sexual inequality. Thus, to truly create an egalitarian society requires the personal commitment and energy of individuals to alter their own everyday lives *and* the public commitment and energy of many to change the political and economic institutions of our society. Only when the nexus between the personal and the public is achieved, may we hope to see the demise of sexual stratification.

References

Abrahams, Roger. "Joking: the training of the man of words in talking broad." Pp. 215–240 in Thomas Kochman (ed.), *Rappin' and Stylin' Out: Communication in Urban Black America*. Albuquerque, New Mexico: The University of New Mexico Press, 1972.

———. "Negotiating respect: patterns of presentation among black women." Mimeographed. Austin, Texas: University of Texas, n.d. Abbreviated version in *Journal of American Folklore* 88(1975):58–80.

Adler, Freda. *Sisters in Crime: The Rise of the New Female Criminal*. New York: McGraw Hill, 1975.

Almquist, Elizabeth M. "The income losses of working black women: product of racial and sexual discrimination." Presented at American Sociological Association. New York: August, 1976.

Almquist, Elizabeth, and Angrist, Shirley. "Role model influences of college women's career interests." Pp. 301–323 in Athena Theodore (ed.), *The Professional Woman*. Cambridge, Mass.: Schenkman Publishing, 1971.

Amir, Nebachem. *Patterns of Forcible Rape*. Chicago: University of Chicago Press, 1971.

Amudsen, Kirsten. *The Silenced Majority*. New York: Prentice-Hall, 1971.

Angrist, Shirley; Dinitz, Simon; Lefton, Mark; and Pasamanick, Benjamin. *Women After Treatment*. New York: Appleton-Century-Crofts, 1968.

Argyle, Michael; Salter, Veronica; Nicholson, Hilary; Williams, Marilyn; and Burgess, Phillip. "The communication of inferior and superior attitudes by verbal and nonverbal signals." *British Journal of Social and Clinical Psychology* 9(1970):222–231.

Baldridge, J. Victor. *Sociology: A Critical Approach to Power, Conflict and Change*. New York: John Wiley and Sons, 1975.

Ball, Donald W. "The 'family' as a *sociological* problem: conceptualization of the taken-for-granted as prologue to social problems analysis." *Social Problems* 19(1972):295–307.

Bandura, Albert, and Walters, Richard H. *Social Learning and Personality Development*. New York: Holt, Rinehart and Winston, 1964.

Bardwick, Judith, ed. "Psychological conflict and the reproductive system." Pp. 3–28 in *Feminine Personality and Conflict*. Belmont, Calif.: Brooks/Cole Publishing Co., 1970.

Barron, F., and Leary, T. "Changes in psychoneurotic patients with and without psychotherapy." *Journal of Consulting Psychology* 19(1955):239–45.

Bart, Pauline. "Women's self-help: a new medical concept." Presented at the North Central Sociological Association Meetings, 1974, in Windsor, Canada.

――――. "The loneliness of the long-distance mother." Pp. 156–170 in Jo Freeman (ed.), *Women: A Feminist Perspective.* Palo Alto, Calif.: Mayfield Publishing Co., 1975.

Bartee, Debbie et al. "Sex and television commercials." Mimeographed. Columbus, Ohio: Ohio State University, 1974.

Becker, Howard. *Sociological Work: Method and Substance.* Chicago: Aldine, 1970.

Becker, Howard, and Strauss, Anselm. "Careers, personality and adult socialization." *American Journal of Sociology* 62(1956):253–63.

Bell, Robert R., and Chaskes, Jay B. "Premarital sexual experience among coeds: 1958–1968." *Journal of Marriage and the Family* 32(1970):80–84.

Bem, Sandra. "Psychology looks at sex roles: Where have all the androgynous people gone?" Paper presented at University of California-Los Angeles Symposium on Women, May 1972.

――――. "Sex role adaptability: one consequence of psychological androgyny." *Journal of Personality and Social Psychology* 31(4)(1976):634–643.

Bem, Sandra; Martyna, Wendy; and Watson, Carol. "Sex-typing and androgyny: Further explorations of the expressive domain." *Journal of Personality and Social Psychology.*

Bentzen, Frances. "Sex ratios in learning and behavior disorders." *National Elementary Principal* 46(1966):13–17.

Berkeley Men's Center. "Berkeley Men's Center Manifesto, The." Mimeographed. Berkeley, Calif., n.d.

Bernabei, Rita. "Can you tell me how to get to Sesame Street?" Mimeographed. Columbus, Ohio: Ohio State University, 1974.

Bernard, Jessie. *Academic Women.* University Park, Pennsylvania: The Pennsylvania State University Press, 1964.

――――. "The paradox of the happy marriage." Pp. 145–63 in Vivian Gornick and Barbara K. Moran (eds.), *Woman in Sexist Society: Studies in Power and Powerlessness.* New York: New American Library, 1971.

――――. "The benign effects of childlessness." Pp. 322–352 in Judy Blankenship (ed.), *Scenes from Life: Family, Marriage and Intimacy.* Boston, Mass.: Little, Brown and Co., 1976.

Bernard, Shirley. "Women's economic status: some cliches and some facts." In *Women: A Feminist Perspective,* edited by Jo Freeman, pp. 283–241. Palo Alto, Calif.: Mayfield Publishing Co., 1975.

Bettelheim, Bruno. "Dialogue with mothers: what makes boys masculine." *Ladies Home Journal,* September 1967, pp. 41–42.

Bird, Phyllis. "Images of women in the old testament." In *Religion and Sexism: Images of Women in the Jewish and Christian Traditions,* edited by Rosemary Reuther, pp. 41–88. New York: Simon and Schuster, 1974.

Birdwhistell, Ray L. *Kinesics and Context: Essays on Body Motion Communication.* Philadelphia, Penn.: University of Pennsylvania Press, 1970.

Blau, Francine D. "Women in the labor force: an overview." Pp. 211–226 in Jo Freeman (ed.), *Women: A Feminist Perspective.* Palo Alto, Calif.: Mayfield Publishing Company, 1975.

Block, Herbert, and Geiss, Gilbert. *Man, Crime and Society.* New York: Random House, 1962.

Blood, Robert O., and Wolfe, Donald M. *Husbands and Wives: The Dynamics of Married Living.* New York: The Free Press, 1960.

Boren, Jerry. "The single father." Pp. 423–434 in Judy Blankenship (ed.), *Scenes from Life: Family, Marriage and Intimacy.* Boston, Mass.: Little, Brown and Co., 1976.

Boserup, Ester. *Women's Role in Economic Development.* London: Allen & Unwin, 1970.

Branscom, Ruth. Personal communication. July 18, 1976.

Brend, Ruth M. "Male-Female intonation patterns in American English." Pp. 84–87 in Barrie Thorne and Nancy Henley (eds.), *Language and Sex: Difference and Dominance.* Rowley, Mass.: Newbury Press, 1975.

Brenton, Myron. "The paradox of the American father." Pp. 125–138 in Louise Kapp Howe (ed.), *The Future of the Family.* New York: Simon and Schuster, 1972.

_____. "The breadwinner." Pp. 92–98 in Deborah David and Robert Brannon (eds.), *The Forty-Nine Per Cent Majority: The Male Sex Role.* Reading, Mass.: Addison-Wesley Publishing Co., 1976.

Brim, Orville G. Jr. "Family structure and sex role learning by children: a further analysis of Helen Koch's data." *Sociometry* 21(1958):1–15.

Brisset, Dennis and Lewis, Lionel. "Guidelines for marital sex: an analysis of fifteen popular marriage manuals." *The Family Coordinator* 19(1970):41–48.

Brody, Carol. "The Beacon curriculum on sexuality." Presented to Sex Roles Seminar (April 1973). Columbus, Ohio: The Ohio State University.

Broverman, I. K.; Vogel, S. R.; Broverman, D.; Clarkson, F.; and Rosenkrantz , P. S. "Sex role stereotypes and clinical judgements of mental health." *Journal of Consulting and Clinical Psychology* 34(1970):1–7.

Brown, Claude. "The language of soul." Pp. 134–139 in Thomas Kochman (ed.), *Rappin' and Stylin' Out: Communication in Urban Black America.* Urbana, Ill.: University of Illinois Press, 1972.

Brown, H. Rap. "Street talk." Pp. 205–208 in Thomas Kockman (ed.), *Rappin' and Stylin' Out: Communication in Urban Black America.* Urbana, Illinois: The University of Illinois Press, 1972.

Brown, Roger. *Social Psychology.* Glencoe, Illinois: The Free Press, 1965.

Browning, Ruth. "Women in religion." Presented to Sex Roles Seminar, Department of Sociology. Columbus, Ohio: The Ohio State University, 1974.

Brownmiller, Susan. *Against Our Will: Men, Women and Rape.* New York: Simon and Schuster, 1975.

Brunner, Jerome. *Toward a Theory of Instruction.* Cambridge, Massachusetts: Belknap Press, 1966.

Calderone, Mary S. *Release from Sexual Tensions.* New York: Random House, 1960.

Cameron, Paul. "Frequency and kinds of words in various social settings or What the hell's going on?" Pp. 31–37 in Marcello Truzzi (ed.), *Sociology for Pleasure.* Englewood Cliffs, N.J.: Prentice-Hall, 1974.

Campbell, Angus; Converse, Phillip; Miller, Warren E.; and Stokes, Donald. *The American Voter.* New York: Wiley, 1960.

Carlson, Rae. "Understanding women: implications of personality theory and research." *Journal of Social Issues* 28(1972):17–32.

Cartwright, R. D., and Vogel, J. L. "A comparison of changes in psychoneurotic patients during matched periods of therapy and no-therapy." *Journal of Counseling Psychology* 24(1960):121–27.

Cheek, F. "A serendipitous finding: sex role and schizophrenia." *Journal of Abnormal and Social Psychology* 69(1964):392–400.

Chesler, Phylis. *Women and Madness.* New York: Doubleday and Company, 1972.

Chesney-Lind, Meda. "Judicial enforcement of the female sex role: the family court and the female delinquent." *Issues in Criminology* 8(1973):51–69.

Child, Irwin; Potter, Elmer; and Levine, Estelle. "Children's textbooks and personality development: an exploration in the social psychology of education." Pp. 292–305 in Morris L. Haimonitz and Natalie Reader Haimonitz (eds.), *Human Development: Selected Readings.* New York: Thomas Y. Crowell Co., 1960.

Chisholm, Shirley. "Racism and anti-feminism." *The Black Scholar* 43(1970):40–45.

Christensen, Harold T., and Gregg, Christina. "Changing sex norms in America and Scandinavia." *Journal of Marriage and the Family* 32(1970):616–627.

Cicourel, Aaron, and Kitsuse, John. "A note on the use of official statistics." *Social Problems* 11(1963):131–139.

Cleaver, Eldridge. *Soul on Ice.* New York: McGraw Hill, 1968.

Cohn, Yona. "Criteria for the probation officer's recommendation to the juvenile court." In Peter G. Garabedian and Don D. Gibbons, *Becoming Delinquent.* Chicago: Aldine Press, 1970.

Coleman, James S. *The Adolescent Society: The Social Life of the Teenager and it's Impact on Education.* Glencoe, Illinois: The Free Press, 1961.

Collins, Randall. *Conflict Sociology: Toward an Explanatory Science.* New York: Academic Press, 1975.

Columbus Citizen Journal. UPI; May 30, 1973.

Columbus Dispatch. July 7, 1974.

Comfort, Alex (ed.). *More Joy of Sex: Lovemaking Companion to the Joy of Sex.* New York: Simon and Schuster, 1972.

Congressional Record. February 24, 1972 (Dr. Peter Breggins).

Constantin, Edmond, and Kenneth, Craig. "Women as politicians: the social background, personality, and political careers of female party leaders." *Journal of Social Issues* 28(1972):217–236.

Cooley, Charles Horton. *Human Nature and the Social Order.* New York: C. Scribner's Sons, 1902.

––––––. *Social Organization: A Study of the Larger Mind.* New York: C. Scribner's Sons, 1909.

Cooper, David. *The Death of the Family.* New York: Pantheon Books, 1970.

Coser, Lewis A., and Rosenberg, Bernard. *Sociological Theory: A Book of Readings.* New York: Macmillan Publishing Company, 1976.

Courtney, Alice E., and Lockeretz, Sarah Wernick. "A woman's place: an analysis of the roles portrayed by women in magazines advertisements." *Journal of Marketing Research* 8(1971):92–95.

Crandall, Vaughn, and Robson, Alice. "Children's repetition choices in an intellectual achievement situation following success and failure." *Journal of Genetic Psychology* 97(1960):161–168.

Cull, John G., and Hardy, Richard E. "Language meaning (gender shaping) among blind and sighted students." *The Journal of Psychology* 83(1973):333–334.

Daly, Mary. "After the Death of God the Father." Mimeographed. Pittsburgh, Pennsylvania: Know, Inc., n.d.

––––––. *The Church and the Second Sex.* New York: Harper and Row Publishers, 1968.

––––––. "Women and the Catholic Church." Pp. 124–138 in Robin Morgan (ed.), *Sisterhood is Powerful.* New York: Random House, 1970.

––––––. *Beyond God the Father.* Boston, Mass.: Beacon Press, 1973.

Daniels, Arlene Kaplan. "Feminist perspectives in sociological research." Pp. 340–380 in Marcia Millman and Rosabeth Moss Kanter (eds.), *Another Voice: Feminist Perspectives on Social Life and Social Science.* Garden City, New York: Anchor, 1975.

Darland, M. G., Dawkins, S. M.; Lovasich, J. L.; Scott, E. L.; Sherman, M. E.; and Whipple, J. L. "Application of multivariate regression studies of salary differences between men and women faculty." Presented to American Statistical Association annual meetings, 1973.

Davis, Elizabeth Gould. *The First Sex.* Baltimore, Maryland: Penguin Books, 1972.

De Crow, Karen. *Sexist Justice.* New York: Random House, 1974.

De Fleur, Melvin L. "Occupational roles as portrayed on television." *Public Opinion Quarterly* 28(1964):56–74.

DeStefano, Johanna S. "A study of developing perceptions of referents in selected English generic terms." Mimeographed. Columbus, Ohio: The Ohio State University, 1975.
_____. Personal communication. Columbus, Ohio: The Ohio State University, 1975.
Deutscher, Irwin. *Married Life in Middle Years.* Kansas City: Community Studies, 1959.
Diamond, J. Timothy. Personal communication, July 10, 1976.
Di Iorio, Judith. Personal communication, July 10, 1976.
Dizard, Jan E. "The price of success." Pp. 192–201 in Louise Kapp Howe (ed.), *The Future of the Family.* New York: Simon and Schuster, 1972.
Domhoff, G. William. *Who Rules America?* Englewood Cliffs, New Jersey: Prentice-Hall, 1967.
_____. *The Bohemian Grove and Other Retreats.* New York: Harper and Row, 1974.
Dunning, R. "Discrimination: women in sports." Unpublished manuscript, F 35 North Campus Way, Davis, Calif., 1972.
Durkheim, Emile. *Suicide.* Glencoe, Illinois: The Free Press, 1951.

Eckhardt, Kenneth. "Deviance, visibility, and legal action: The duty to support." *Social Problems* 15(1968):470–477.
Ehrlich, Carol. "The male sociologist's burden: the place of women in marriage and family texts." *Journal of Marriage and the Family* 33(1971):421–430.
Eichenlaub, John E. *New Approaches to Sex in Marriage.* New York: Dell, 1961.
Ellsworth, P. C.; Carlsmith, J. M.; and Henson, A. "The stare as a stimulus to fight in human subjects: a series of field experiments." *Journal of Personality and Social Psychology* IV(1972):302–311.
Epstein, Cynthia Fuchs. *Women's Place: Options and Limits on a Professional Career.* Berkeley, Calif.: The University of California Press, 1970.
_____. "Positive effects of the multiple negative; explaining the success of black professional women." Pp. 150–173 in Joan Huber (ed.), *Changing Women in a Changing Society.* Chicago, Ill.: The University of Chicago Press, 1973.
Erikson, Erik. *Identity, Youth and Crisis.* New York: Norton and Co., 1968.
Essig, Garth. "Hormones in men and women." Presentation to Sex Roles Seminar, Fall, Columbus, Ohio: The Ohio State University, 1974.
Etzioni, Amitai. "Sex control, science and society." *Science* 16(1968):1007–1010
Eyesenck, H. J. *The Effects of Psychotherapy.* New York: International Science Press, 1955.

Falk, Gail. "Sex discrimination in the trade unions: legal resources." Pp. 254–276 in Joe Freeman (ed.), *Women: A Feminist Perspective.* Palo Alto, Calif.: Mayfield Publishing Co., 1975.
Farmer, H. S., and Bohn, M. J. "Home career conflict reduction and the level of career interest in women." *Journal of Counseling Psychology* 17(1970):228–232.
Farrell, Warren T. "Women's and men's liberation groups: political power within the system and outside the system." Pp. 171–201 in Jane Jacquette (ed.), *Women in Politics.* New York: Wiley, 1975.
Federbush, Marcia. *Let Them Aspire.* (3rd edition with addenda.) Pittsburgh, Pennsylvania: Know Inc., 1973.
Felshin, Jan. *The American Woman in Sport.* Reading, Mass.: Addison-Wesley Publishing, 1974.
Festinger, Leon. *The Theory of Cognitive Dissonance.* New York: Harper and Row, 1957.
Fields, Rona M. *Public Education: Training for Sexism.* Philadelphia, Pennsylvania: Know Inc., n.d.
Filene, Peter. "Him/her/self/" Pp. 389–410 in Judy Blankenship (ed.), *Scenes from Life: Family, Marriage and Intimacy.* Boston, Mass.: Little-Brown and Co., 1976.
Firestone, Shulamith. *The Dialectic of Sex.* New York: Wm. Morrow and Co., 1971.

Fiske, Shirley. "Pigskin review: An American initiation." Pp. 241–258 in Marie Hart (ed.), *Sport in the Sociocultural Process*. Dubuque, Iowa: William C. Brown, 1972.

Flora, Cornelia Butler. "The passive female: her comparative image by class and culture in women's magazine fiction." *Journal of Marriage and the Family*. 33(1971):435–444.

Flora, Cornelia B., and Lynn, Naomii B. "Women and political socialization: considerations of the impact of motherhood." Pp. 37–53 in Jane S. Jaquette, *Women in Politics*. New York: Wiley Interscience, 1974.

Folb, Edith. "A comparative study of urban black argot." Occasional Papers in Linguistics, no. 1. University of California at Los Angeles. March, 1972.

Ford, Clellar S., and Beach, Frank A. *Patterns of Sexual Behavior*. New York: Harper & Row, 1951.

Franklin, Clyde W. Jr., and Walum, Laurel Richardson. "Toward a paradigm of substructural relations: an application to sex and race in the United States." *Phylon* 33(1972):242–253.

Frazier, Nancy, and Sadlek, Myra. *Sexism in School and Society*. New York: Harper and Row, 1973.

Freeman, Jo. *The Politics of Women's Liberation: A Case Study of an Emerging Social Movement and it's Relation to the Policy Process*. New York: David McKay Company, 1975.

Freud, Sigmund. *Civilization and it's Discontents*. London: Hogarth Press, 1930.

Freidan, Betty. *The Feminine Mystique*. New York: Dell, 1963.

Friedl, Ernestine. *Women and Men: An Anthropologist's View*. New York: Holt, Rinehart and Winston, 1975.

Friedlander, Beatrice et al. "Women in rock and roll." Unpublished Manuscript. Columbus, Ohio: The Ohio State University, 1973.

Fuchs, Victor. "Differences in hourly earnings between men and women." *Monthly Labor Review* 94(1971):9–15.

Gagnon, John. "Physical strength, once of significance." Pp. 169–178 in Deborah S. David and Robert Brannon (eds.), *The Forty-Nine Percent Majority: The Male Sex Role*. Reading, Mass.: Addison-Wesley Publishing Co., 1976.

Galbraith, John Kenneth. *Economics and the Public Purpose*. Boston: Houghton Mifflin, 1973.

Garfinkel, Harold. *Studies in Ethnomethodology*. Englewood Cliffs, N.J.: Prentice-Hall Inc., 1967.

Garland, Neal T. "The better half? the male in the dual professional family." Pp. 199–215 in Constantina Safilios-Rothschild (ed.), *Toward a Sociology of Women*. Lexington, Mass.: Xerox Publishing Co., 1972.

Gehlen, Frieda. "Women in Congress." *Transaction* 49(1969):36–40.

Gillespie, Dair L. "Who has the power? the marital struggle." *Journal of Marriage and the Family* 33(1971):445–58.

Gingold, Judith. "One of these days—pow right in the kisser." *Ms.* August (1976):51–52, 94.

Glazer-Malbin, Nona. "The captive couple: the burden of gender roles in marriage." In Don H. Zimmerman and D. Lawrence Wieder (eds.), *Social Problems in Contemporary Society*. New York: Praeger Publishers, 1976.

Gleser, Goldine C.; Gottschalk, Louis A.; and Watkins, John. "The relationship of sex and intelligence to choice of words: a normative study of verbal behavior." *Journal of Clinical Psychology* 15(1959):182–191.

Goffman, Irving. *The Presentation of Self in Everyday Life*. Garden City, New York: Doubleday and Co., Inc., 1959.

_____. *Asylums*. New York: Anchor, 1961.

_____. *Interaction Ritual*. New York: Anchor Books, 1967, pp. 47–95.

Gold, Sarah. "Equal protection for juvenile girls in need of supervision in New York State." *New York Law Forum* 17(1971):570–98.

Goldberg, Phillip. "Are women prejudiced against women?" *Transaction,* Vol. 5, No. 5 (1968), pp. 28–30

Goode, William H. *After Divorce.* Glencoe, Ill. The Free Press, 1956.

———. *The Family.* Englewood Cliffs, New Jersey: Prentice Hall, 1964.

———. *World Revolution and Family Patterns.* New York: The Free Press, 1963.

Gordon, Michael, and Shankweiler, Penelope. "Different equals less: female sexuality in recent marriage manuals." *Journal of Marriage and the Family* 33(1971):459–466.

Gordon, Nancy M.; Morton, Thomas E.; and Braden, Ina C. "Faculty salaries: is there discrimination by sex, race and discipline?" *American Economic Review* 64(1974):419–427.

Gosnell, Harold F. *Democracy: The Threshold of Freedom.* New York: Ronald Press, 1948.

Graham, Patricia A. "Women in academe." Pp. 720–40 in Athena Theodore (ed.), *The Professional Woman.* Cambridge, Mass.: Schenkman Publishing Co., 1971.

Grahame, Alma. "The making of a non-sexist dictionary." *Ms.* December (1973):12–14, 16.

Griffin, Susan. "Rape: the all-American crime." Andover, Mass.: Warner Modular Publications, Inc., 1973.

Grønseth, Erick. "The breadwinner trap." Pp. 175–191 in Louise Kapp Howe (ed.), *The Future of the Family.* New York: Simon and Schuster, 1972.

Gross, Edward. "Plus ca change . . . ? the sexual structure of occupations over time." *Social Problems.* 16(1968):198–208.

Grunden, Rickie Sue. "Toward a theory of feminine movement and the acquisition of sports skills." Unpublished Paper. Columbus, Ohio: The Ohio State University, 1973a.

———. "Changing roles of women in *Sports Illustrated* and *Tennis World.*" Unpublished Paper. Columbus, Ohio: The Ohio State University, 1973b.

Gumperz, John J., and Hymes, Dell. *Directions in Sociolinguistics.* New York: Holt, Rinehart and Winston, Inc., 1972.

Gutman, Jonathan. "Self-concepts and television viewing among women." *Public Opinion Quarterly.* 37(3):389–397.

Hall, Edward T. *The Silent Language.* Garden City, New Jersey: Doubleday, 1959.

———. *The Hidden Dimension.* New York: Doubleday, 1966.

Hall, Robert E. *Sex and Marriage.* New York: Planned Parenthood, 1965.

Hammel, Lisa. "Mothers carry women's lib message to grade school." *The New York Times Magazine,* January 1971, p. 8.

Hardin, Garrett. "Abortion—or compulsory pregnancy." Pp. 242–254 in Kenneth C. W. Kammeyer (ed.), *Confronting the Issues: Sex Roles, Marriage and the Family.* Boston, Mass.: Allyn and Bacon, Inc., 1975.

Harding, Esther. *The Way of All Women.* New York: Longmans, Green, 1933.

Harford, T. C.; Willis, C. H.; and Deabler, H. L. "Personality correlates of masculinity-femininity." *Psychological Reports* 21(1967):881–884.

Harris, Ann Sutherland. "The second sex in academe," *American Association of University Professors Bulletin* 56(1970):283–295.

Harrison, Barbara Gruzzi. *Unlearning the Lie: Sexism in the School.* New York: Liverights, 1973.

Hartley, Ruth E. "Sex-role pressures and the socialization of the male child." Pp. 7–13 in Joseph Pleck and Jack Sawyer (eds.), *Men and Masculinity.* Englewood Cliffs, New Jersey: Prentice-Hall, 1974.

Heidensohn, Frances. "The deviance of women; a critique and an enquiry." *British Journal of Sociology* 19(1968):160–175.

Heller, Joseph. *Something Happened.* New York: Knopf, 1974.

Henley, Nancy. "Power, sex and non-verbal communication." *Berkeley Journal of Sociology* 18(1973):1–26.

Henry, Alice. *Women and the Labor Movement.* New York: George H. Duran, 1923.

Herschberger, Ruth. *Adam's Rib.* New York: Harper and Row, 1948.

Hiltband, Maxine et al. "How the New York Times sees women." Unpublished Paper. Columbus, Ohio: The Ohio State University, 1974.

Hochschild, Arlie Russell. "The Sociology of feeling and emotion: selected problems." Pp. 280–307 in Marcia Millman and Rosabeth Moss Kanter (eds.), *Another Voice: Feminist Perspectives on Social Life and Social Science.* Garden City, New York: Anchor/Doubleday, 1975.

Hole, Judith, and Levine, Ellen. *The Rebirth of Feminism.* New York: Quadrangle Books, 1971.

Holmstron, Lynda Lytle. *The Two-Career Family.* Cambridge, Mass.: Schenkman Publishing Co., 1972.

Holmstrom, Lynda Lytle, and Burgess, Ann Wolbert. "Rape: the victim and the criminal justice system." Presented at the First International Symposium on Victimology. Jerusalem, September 2–6, 1973.

Horner, Martina. "Toward an understanding of achievement related conflicts in women." *Journal of Social Issues* 28(1972):157–175.

Horney, Karen. *Feminine Psychology.* New York: Norton and Company, Inc., 1967.

Huber, Joan. "Toward a socio-technological theory of the women's movement." *Social Problems.* 1976a.

_____. "The future of parenthood: implications of declining fertility." Cincinnati, Ohio: Paper presented at Pioneers for Century III, April 24, 1976b.

_____. Personal commucication, April 15, 1976.

Hudnell, Terese Connerton, and Dunham, Jan Michele. "Rape: a study of attitudes." Unpublished Paper. Columbus, Ohio: The Ohio State University, 1974.

Hutchins, Grace. *Women Who Work.* New York: International Publishers, 1952.

Hyman, Herbert, and Sheatsley, Paul. "Attitudes toward desegregation." Pp. 405–418 in John H. Kessel, George F. Cole, and Robert G. Seddling (eds.), *Micropolitics: Individual and Group Level Concept.* New York: Holt, Rinehart and Winston, 1970.

Iglitzin, Lynne B. "The making of the apolitical woman: femininity and sex-stereotyping in girls." Pp. 25–26 in Jane S. Jaquette, *Women in Politics.* New York: Wiley Interscience, 1974.

"J." *The Sensuous Woman.* New York: Lyle Stuart, 1969.

Jacklin, C.; Heupers, M.; Mischell, H.; and Jacobs, C. "As the twig is bent: sex role stereotyping in early readers." Unpublished paper. Department of Psychology, Stanford University, Palo Alto, Calif., 1972.

Jackson, Jacqueline I. "But where are the men?" *Black Scholar* Vol. 3 (1971), No. 4:30–41.

Jackson, Phil, and Lahadenne, Henriette. "Inequalities of teacher-pupil contacts." Pp. 123–34 in Melvin Silberman (ed.), *The Experience of Schooling.* New York: Holt, Rinehart and Winston, 1971.

Jaquette, Jane S. "Introduction: women in American politics." Pp. xiii–xxxiii in Jane S. Jaquette (ed.), *Women in Politics.* New York: Wiley Interscience, 1974.

Jennings, Kent, and Norman, Thomas. "Men and women in party elites: social roles and political resources." *Midwest Journal of Political Science* 12(4):469–492.

Johnson, Warren R. *Human Sexual Behavior and Sex Education.* Philadelphia, Pa.: Lea and Febiger, 1968.

Jordan, Joan. *The Place of American Women.* Boston: The New England Press, 1969.

Jung, Carl G. *Contributions to Analytical Psychology.* New York: Harcourt, Brace, Inc., 1928.

Kagan, Jerome. "Acquisition and significance of sex-typing and sex-role identity.: Pp. 137–

167 in M. L. Hoffman and L. W. Hoffman (eds.), *Review of Child Development Research.* Volume 1. New York: Russell Sage Foundation, 1964a.

_____. "The child's sex role classification of school objects." *Child Development* 35:1051–1056, (1964b).

Kanowitz, Leo. *Women and the Law: The Unfinished Revolution.* Albuquerque, New Mexico: The University of New Mexico Press, 1969.

Katz, David. "Faculty salaries, promotions and productivity at a large university." *American Economic Review* 63(1973):469–477.

Katzman, Natan. "Television soap operas: what's been going on anyway?" *Public Opinion Quarterly* 36(1972):200–212.

Kemener, B. J. "A Study of the Relationship between the Sex of Student and the Assignment of Marks by Secondary School Teachers." Ph.D. dissertation, East Lansing, Mich.: Michigan State University, 1965.

Key, Mary Ritchie. *Male/Female Language.* Metuchen, New Jersey: The Scarecrow Press, 1975.

Kinsey, Alfred C. et al. *Sexual Behavior in the Human Female.* New York: Simon and Schuster, 1948.

Kirschner, Betty Frankle. "Introducing students to women's place in society." Pp. 289–292 in Joan Huber (ed.), *Changing Women in a Changing Society.* Chicago, Illinois: The University of Chicago Press, 1973.

_____. "The two-location family." Paper presented to Sex-Roles Seminar, Columbus, Ohio: The Ohio State University, April 26, 1976.

Klein, Dorie. "The etiology of female crime: a review of the literature." *Issues in Criminology* 8(1973):3–30.

KNOW. *Sesame Street and Sex-Role Stereotypes* (revised). Pittsburgh, Penn.: Know, Inc., 1970.

Knowles, Louis, and Prewitt, Kenneth. *Institutional Racism.* Englewood Cliffs, New Jersey. Prentice-Hall, 1969.

Kochman, Thomas. "The kinetic element in black idiom." Pp. 160–69 in Thomas Kochman (ed.), *Rappin' and Stylin' Out.* Urbana, Illinois: University of Illinois Press, 1972.

Koedt, Anne. "The myth of the vaginal orgasm." Pp. 284–89 in Sue Cox (ed.), *Female Psychology: The Emerging Self.* Chicago: Science Research Associations, Inc., 1976.

Kohen, Andrew I. "Women and the economy: a bibliography and review of the literature on sex differentiation in the labor market." Columbus, Ohio: The Ohio State University, Center for Human Resources Research, 1975.

Kohlberg, Lawrence. "A cognitive-developmental analysis of children's sex-role concepts and attitudes." Pp. 82–166 in Eleanor Maccoby (ed.), *The Development of Sex Differences.* Stanford, Calif.: Stanford University Press, 1966.

Korda, Michael. *Male Chauvinism: How It Works.* New York: Random House, 1973.

Korner, A. F. "Neonatal startles, smiles, erection, and reflex sucks as related to state, sex, and individuality." *Child Development* 40(1969):1039–1053.

Kramer, Cheris. "Women's speech: separate but unequal?" Pp. 43–56 in Barrie Thorne and Nancey Henley (eds.), *Language and Sex: Difference and Dominance.* Rowley Mass.: Newbury House, 1975.

Labov, William. "Rules for ritual insults." Pp. 265–314 in Thomas Kochman (ed.), *Rappin' and Stylin' Out.* Urbana, Ill.: University of Illinois Press, 1972.

Lake, Alice. "Are we born into our sex-roles or programmed into them?" *Woman's Day* January, 1975, pp. 24–25.

Lakoff, Robin. *Language and Woman's Place.* New York: Colophon Books, 1975.

Lancaster, Jane Beckman. "In praise of the achieving female monkey," Pp. 5–9 in *The Female Experience.* Del Mar, California: Communications Research Machines, Inc., 1973.

Lane, Robert E. *Political Life.* Glencoe, Ill.: The Free Press, 1959.

Lang, Theo. *The Difference between a Man and a Woman.* New York: Bantam Books, 1971.

Lansing, Marjorie. "The American woman: voter and activist." Pp. 5–24 in Jane S. Jaquette (ed.), *Women in Politics.* New York: Wiley Interscience, 1974.

LaRue, Linda J. M. "Black liberation and woman's lib." *Transaction* 61(1970):59–64.

Laws, Judith Long. "A feminist review of marital adjustment literature: the rape of the locke." *Journal of Marriage and the Family* 33(1971):483–516.

Lear, Martha Weinman. "You'll probably think I'm stupid." *The New York Times Magazine.* April 11, 1976.

LeMasters, E. E. "Folklore about parenthood." Pp. 295–303 in Judy Blankenship (ed.), *Scenes from Life: Views of Family, Marriage and Intimacy.* Boston, Mass.: Little, Brown and Co., 1976.

Lenski, Gerhard E. *Power and Privilege: A Theory of Social Stratification.* New York: McGraw-Hill Publishing Co., 1966.

Lepper, Mary M. "A study of career structures of federal executives." Pp. 109–130 in Jane S. Jaquette (ed.), *Women in Politics.* New York: Wiley Interscience, 1974.

Lerner, Richard M. "Some female stereotypes of male body build-behavior." *Perceptual and Motor Skills* 28(1969):363–366.

Leslie, Gerald R. *The Family in Social Context.* (Chapter 6.) New York: Oxford, 1967.

Lester, Julius. "Being a boy." Pp. 270–276 in Deborah S. David and Robert Brannon (eds.), *The Forty-Nine Percent Majority: The Male Sex Role.* Reading, Mass.: Addison-Wesley Publishing Co., 1976.

"Letters to the editor." *The Lantern.* Columbus, Ohio: The Ohio State University. October 17, 1970.

Levin, Ira. *The Stepford Wives.* New York: Random House, 1972.

Lewis, Michael. "State as an infant-environment interaction: an analysis of mother-infant interactions as a function of sex." *Merrill-Palmer Quarterly of Behavior and Development* 18(1972):95–121.

Lipmen-Blumen, Jean, and Tickameyer, Ann R. "Sex roles in transition: a ten year perspective." Pp. 297–337 in Alex Inkeles (ed.) *Annual Review of Sociology,* Vol. 1. Palo Alto, California: Annual Reviews, Inc., 1975.

Lloyd, Cynthia B. "The division of labor between the sexes: a review." Pp. 1–24 in Cynthia B. Lloyd (ed.), *Sex, Discrimination and the Division of Labor.* New York: Columbia University Press, 1975.

Lopez, Lisa. "A study of rape." Unpublished Paper. Columbus, Ohio: The Ohio State University, 1974.

Lowi, Theodore J. *The Politics of Disorder.* New York: Basic Books, 1971.

Lydon, Susan. "The politics of orgasm." Pp. 197–205 in Robin Morgan (ed.), *Sisterhood is Powerful.* New York: Random House, 1971.

Lyles, Thomas. "Grouping by sex." *National Elementary Principal* 46(1966):38–41.

Lynn, Naomi. "Women in American politics: an overview." Pp. 364–385 in Jo Freeman (ed.), *Women: A Feminist Perspective.* Palo Alto, Calif.: Mayfield Publishing, 1975.

MAC (Men Against Cool). "Men against Cool." Mimeo, Chicago, Ill., 1970.

Maccoby, Eleanor. "Women's intellect." Pp. 24–39 in Seymour Farber and Robert Wilson (eds.), *The Potential of Women.* New York: McGraw-Hill, 1963.

―――. *The Development of Sex Differences.* Stanford, California: Stanford University Press, 1966.

Maccoby, Eleanor, and Jacklin, Carol Nagy. *The Psychology of Sex Differences.* Stanford, California: Stanford University Press, 1974.

MacDougald, Duncan, Jr. "Language and sex." In Albert Ellis and Albert Abarbanel (eds.), *The End of Behavior.* London Hawthorne Books, 1961.

Macklin, E. D. "Heterosexual cohabitation among unmarried college students." *The Family Coordinator* 21(1972):463–472.

Markie, Gerald E., and Nam, Charles B. "The impact of sex predetermination on fertility." Presented at the annual meetings of the Population Association of America: April 1973.

Marshall, Hannah, and Knafl, Kathleen. "Professionalizing motherhood: la leche league and breast feeding." Presented at the American Sociological Association, New York, August 26–30, 1973.

Marx, Karl. *Early Writings.* Translated and edited by T. B. Bottomore. New York: McGraw-Hill Book Co., 1964.

Masters, William H., and Johnson, Virginia E. *Human Sexual Response.* Boston: Little, Brown, 1966.

McClelland, David C. *The Achieving Society.* Glencoe, Ill.: Free Press, 1961.

McClelland, D. C., and Watt, N. F. "Sex role alienation in schizophrenia." *Journal of Abnormal Psychology* 73(1968):226–39.

McGhee, Paul, and Grodzitsky, Phyllis. "Sex-role identification and humor among preschool children." *Journal of Psychology* 84(1973):189–193.

McNeil, John. "Programmed instruction versus visual classroom procedures in teaching boys to read." *American Educational Research Journal* 1(1964):113–120.

Mehrabian, A. *Nonverbal Communication.* Chicago: Aldine-Atherton Press, 1972.

Mencken, H. L. *The American Language,* 4th Edition and two supplements. Abridged and edited by Raven I. McDavis. New York: Knopf, 1963.

Miller, S. M. "The making of a confused middle-class husband." Pp. 374–381 in Judy Blankenship (ed.), *Scenes from Life: Views of Family, Marriage, and Intimacy.* Boston, Mass.: Little, Brown and Co., 1976.

Millet, Kate. *Sexual Politics.* New York: Doubleday and Co., 1970.

Millman, Marcia, and Kanter, Rosabeth Moss. *Another Voice: Feminist Perspectives on Social Life and Social Science.* Garden City, New York: Anchor/Doubleday, 1975.

Mills, C. Wright. *The Sociological Imagination.* New York: Oxford University Press, 1959.

Minton, Cheryl; Kagan, Jerome; and Levine, Janet A. "Maternal control and obedience in the two year old." *Child Development* 42(1971):1873–94.

Mischel, W. *Personality and Assessment.* New York: Wiley, 1968.

Mitchell-Kernan, Claudia. "Signifying, loud-talking and marking." Pp. 315–336 in Thomas Kochman (ed.), *Rappin' and Stylin' Out.* Urbana, Ill.: The University of Illinois Press, 1972.

Money, John, and Ehrhardt, Anke A. "Rearing of a sex-reassigned normal male infant after traumatic loss of the penis." Pp. 46–51 in Jack Petras (ed.), *Sex: Male/Gender: Masculine.* Port Washington, New York: Alfred Publishing Co., 1975.

Morris, Demond. *Intimate Behavior.* New York: Random House, 1971.

Morrison, Toni. "What the Black woman thinks about woman's lib." *The New York Times.* (August 15):64.

Moss, E. A. "Sex, age and state as determinants of mother-infant interaction. *Merrill-Palmer Quarterly of Behavior and Development* 13(1967):19–36.

Mulligan, Linda. "Women's role options and priorities: self-esteem as a correlate." Unpublished Paper. Columbus, Ohio: The Ohio State University, 1975.

Mussen, P. H. "Some antecedents and consequents of masculine sex typing in adolescent boys." *Psychological Monographs* 75(1961), No. 506.

Nagel, S. S., and Weitzman, L. J. "Women as litigants." *The Hastings Law Journal* 23(1962):171–198.

Ness, Evaline. *Sam, Bangs and Moonshine.* New York: Holt Rinehart and Winston, 1967.

Newsweek. September 24, 1973, p. 84.

Newton, Niles. "Trebly sensuous woman." Pp. 22–25 in *The Female Experience.* Del Mar, California: Communication Research Machines, 1973.

"No comment." *Ms.* April 1974, p. 96.

"No girls (or lady teachers) please." *Nation's Schools* 83(1969):68–69.

NOW (National Organization for Women). "Bill of rights adopted at NOW's first national conference." Washington, D.C. Also Pp. 512–514 in Robin Morgan (ed.), *Sisterhood is Powerful.* New York: Vintage Press, 1967.

O'Connor, Lynn. "Male dominance: the nitty-gritty of oppression." *It Ain't Me, Babe.* 1(1970):9–11.

O'Hara, Robert. "The roots of careers." *Elementary School Journal* 62(1962):277–280.

Oppenheimer, Valerie Kincade. "Demographic influence on female employment and the status of women." *American Journal of Sociology* 78(1973):184–199.

Ounsted, C., and Taylor, David C. *Gender Differences: Their Ontongeny and Significance.* Edinburgh and London: Churchill Livingston, 1972.

Pederson, F. A., and Robson, K. S. "Father participation in infancy." *American Journal of Orthopsychiatry.* 39(1969):466–72.

Pleck, Joseph H. "Psychological frontiers for men." *Rough Times* 6(1973):14–15.

Pollak, Otto. *The Criminality of Women.* Philadelphia, Pennsylvania: The University of Pennsylvania Press, 1950.

Poloma, Margaret M. "Role conflict and the married professional woman." Pp. 197–198 in Constantina Safilios-Rothschild (ed.), *Toward a Sociology of Women.* Lexington, Mass.: Xerox Publishing Co., 1972.

Poloma, Margaret M., and Garland, Neal T. "The myth of the egalitarian family: familial roles and the professionally employed wife." Pp. 741–761 in Athena Theodore (ed.), *The Professional Woman.* Cambridge, Mass.: Schenkman Publishing Co., 1971.

Polatnick, Margaret. "Why women don't rear children: a power analysis." *Berkeley Journal of Sociology* 18(1975):45–86.

Rappoport, Rhona, and Rappoport, Robert N. "The dual-career family: a variant pattern and social change." Pp. 216–244 in Constantina Safilios-Rothschild (ed.), *Toward a Sociology of Women.* Lexington, Mass.: Xerox Publishing Co., 1972.

Reckless, Walter, and Kay, Barbara. *The Female Offender.* Report to the President's Commission on Law Enforcement and the Administration of Justice. Washington, D.C.: U.S. Government Printing Office, 1967.

Reuther, Rosemary Radford. *New Woman/New Earth: Sexist Ideologies and Human Liberation.* New York: The Seabury Press, 1975.

Rheingold, Joseph. *The Fear of Being a Woman.* New York: Grune and Stratton, 1964.

Rickles, Nathan K. "The angry woman syndrome." *Archives of General Psychiatry* 24(1971).

Roberts, Barbara. "Psychosurgery: the final solution to the women problem?" *The Second Wave* (Number 1, 1972).

Roby, Pamela. "Structural and internalized barriers to higher education." Pp. 121–140 in Constantina Safilios-Rothschild (ed.), *Toward a Sociology of Women.* Lexington, Mass.: Xerox Publishing Co., 1972.

Rodman, H. "The textbook world of family sociology." *Social Problems* 12(1965).

Rosen, Ruth. "Sexism in history or, writing women's history is a tricky business." *Journal of Marriage and the Family.* 33(1971):541–544.

Rosenkantz, Paul; Vogel, Susan; Bee, Helen; and Broverman, Donald. "Sex-role stereotypes and self-concepts in college students." *Journal of Consulting and Clinical Psychology* 32(1968):287–295.

Rosenthal, Robert, and Jackson, Lenore. "Pygmalion in the classroom: an excerpt." Pp. 115–240 in Melvin Silberman (ed.), *The Experience of Schooling.* New York: Holt, Rinehart and Winston, 1971.

Rossi, Alice. "Equality between the sexes." Pp. 98–143 in Robert Jay Lifton (ed.), *The Woman in America.* Boston: Houghton-Mifflin, 1964.

_____. "Sex equality: the beginnings of an ideology." Pp. 344–353 in Constantina Safilios-Rothschild (ed.), *Toward a Sociology of Women.* Lexington, Mass.: Xerox Publishing Co., 1972a.

_____. "Women in science: why so few?" Pp. 141–153 in Constantina Safilios-Rothschild (ed.), *Toward a Sociology of Women.* Lexington, Mass.: Xerox Publishing Co., 1972b.

Runciman, Walter Garrison. *Relative Deprivation and Social Justice: A Study of Attitudes to Social Inequality in Twentieth Century England.* Berkeley, Calif.: University of California Press, 1966.

Ryan, Patricia, and Schirtzinger, Marie. "A look at women in religion: Catholicism and Judaism." Unpublished paper. Columbus, Ohio: The Ohio State University, 1974.

Saario, Terry; Jacklin, Carol; and Tittle, Carol. "Sex role stereotyping in the public schools." Harvard Educational Review 43(1973):386–416.

Sachs, Jacqueline. "Cues to the identification of sex in children's speech." Pp. 152–171 in Barrie Thorne and Nancy Henley (eds.), *Language and Sex: Difference and Domination.* Rowley, Mass.: Newbury House, 1975.

Sachs, Jacqueline; Lieberman, Philip; and Erickson, Donna. "Anatomical and cultural determinants of male and female speech." Pp. 74–83 in Roger W. Shuy and Ralph W. Fasold (eds.), *Language Attitudes: Current Trends and Prospects.* Washington D.C.: Georgetown University Press, 1973.

Safilios-Rothschild, Constantina. "Family sociology or wives' family sociology?" *Journal of Marriage and the Family* 31(1969):290–301.

Sandler, Bernice. Material presented for the record to the committee on the Judiciary, House of Representatives, 92nd Congress. Hearings of Equal Rights for Men and Women, March 31, 1971.

Saxton, Lloyd. *The Individual, Marriage and the Family.* Belmont, California: Wadsworth Publishing, 1968.

Scanzoni, Letha, and Scanzoni, John. *Men, Women and Change: A Sociology of Marriage and Family.* New York: McGraw Hill, 1976.

Scheff, Thomas J. *Being Mentally Ill: A Sociological Theory.* Chicago: Aldine, 1966.

Scheflen, A. E. *Body Language and the Social Order.* Englewood Cliffs, N.J.: Prentice-Hall, 1972.

_____. *How Behavior Means.* Garden City, New York: Doubleday-Anchor, 1974.

Schneider, Joseph, and Hacker, Sally. "Sex role imagery in the use of the generic 'man' in introductory texts: a case in the sociology of sociology." *American Sociologist* 8(1973):12–18.

Schulz, Muriel R. "The semantic derogation of women." Pp. 64–75 in Barrie Thorne and Nancy Henley (eds.), *Language Sex: Difference and Domination.* Rowley, Mass.: Newbury House, 1975.

Scully, Diana, and Bart, Pauline. "A funny thing happened on the way to the orifice: women in gynecology textbooks." Unpublished Paper. Chicago, Ill.: University of Illinois at Chicago Circle, 1972. Abbreviated version pp. 283–288 in Joan Huber (ed.), *Changing Women in a Changing Society.* Chicago: University of Chicago Press, 1973.

Sears, R. R. "Development of gender role." Pp. 133–62 in F. A. Beach (ed.), *Sex and Behavior.* New York: Wiley, 1965.

Seaver, W. Burleigh. "Pygmalion is alive and working in Chicago." *Psychology Today* (May, 1974):102–103.

Seeman, Jeanette. "The hidden curriculum: gender stereotyping in sixth grade mathematics books: 1963–1974." Unpublished Paper. Columbus, Ohio: The Ohio State University, 1974.

Sexton, Patricia. "Are schools emasculating our boys?" *Saturday Review* 48(1965):57.

Shaw, Gary. *Meat on the Hoof*. New York: Dell Publishers, 1972.

Sheehy, Gail. *Passages: Predictable Crises of Adult Life*. New York: E. P. Dutton, 1976.

Sherfey, Mary Jane. "A theory of female sexuality." Pp. 220–230 in Robin Morgan (ed.), *Sisterhood is Powerful*. New York: Random House, Vintage Books, 1966.

Shortridge, Kathleen. "Working poor women." Pp. 242–253 in Jo Freeman (ed.), *Women: A Feminist Perspective*. Palo Alto, Calif.: Mayfield Publishing Co., 1975.

Shostak, Arthur B. "Blue-collar work." Pp. 98–106 in Deborah David and Robert Brannon (eds.), *The Forty-Nine Percent Majority: The Male Sex Role*. Reading, Mass.: Addison-Wesley Publishing Co., 1976.

Shulman, Alix. "Organs and orgasms." Pp. 292–303 in Vivian Gornick and Barbara Moran (eds.), *Women in Sexist Society: Studies in Power and Powerlessness*. New York: New American Library, 1972.

Shuster, Janet. "Grammatical forms marked for male and female in English." Unpublished paper. Chicago: University of Chicago, 1973.

Simon, Rita. *The Contemporary Woman and Crime*. Rockville, Maryland: National Institute of Mental Health, Center for Studies of Crime and Delinquency, 1975.

Skolnick, Arlene. *The Intimate Environment: Exploring Marriage and the Family*. Boston: Little, Brown and Co., 1973.

Sommer, Robert. *Personal Space: The Behavioral Basis of Design*. Englewood Cliffs, N.J.: Prentice-Hall, 1969.

Spaulding, Robert. "Achievement, creativity and self-concept correlates of teacher-pupil transactions." *Elementary School Journal* 63(1963).

Spence, Janet T.; Helmreich, Robert; and Stapp, Joy. "Ratings of self and peers on sex role attributes and their relation to self-esteem and conceptions of masculinity and femininity." *Journal of Personality and Social Psychology* 32(1975):29–39.

Stein, Peter J. "The decision to remain single." Pp. 414–420 in Judy Blankenship (ed.), *Scenes from Life: Views of Marriage, Family and Intimacy*. Boston: Little, Brown and Co., 1976.

Stoll, Clarice Stasz. *Female and Male*. Dubuque, Iowa: William C. Brown, Co., 1974.

Stoller, R. J. "Effects of parents' attitudes on core gender identity." *International Journal of Psychiatry* 4(1967):57.

Sussman, Marvin. "Marriage contracts: social and legal consequences." Plenary Address presented at the 1975 International Workshop on Changing Sex Roles in Family and Society, July 17, 1975.

Swacker, Marjorie R. "The sex of speaker as a sociolinguistic variable." Pp. 76–83 in Barrie Thorne and Nancy Henley (eds.), *Language and Sex: Difference and Dominance*. Rowley, Mass.: Newbury House, 1975.

Szasz, Thomas. *The Myth of Mental Illness*. New York: Harper & Row, 1961.

――――. *The Manufacture of Madness*. New York: Harper & Row, 1970.

Thorne, Barrie. "Women's self-help: a new medical concept." Discussion presented at the meetings of the North Central Sociological Society, Windsor, Canada, May 3, 1974.

Thorne, Barrie, and Henley, Nancy. *Language and Sex: Difference and Dominance*. Rowley, Mass.: Newbury House, 1975.

Thomas, W. I., and Znaniecki, Florian. *The Polish Peasant in Europe and America*. Boston: Gorham Press, 1918. 2nd Edition. New York: Knopf, 1927.

Thompson, Wayne N. *Quantitative Research in Public Address and Communication*. New York: Random House, 1967.

Tiedt, Iris M. "Realistic counselling for high school girls." *The School Counsellor* 19(1972):354–6.

Tiger, Lionel, and Fox, Robin. *The Imperial Animal.* New York: Holt, Rinehart and Winston, Inc., 1971.

Tittle, C. K.; McCarthy, K.; and Steckler, J. F. "Women and educational testing: a selective review of the research, literature and testing practices." Unpublished manuscript. City University of New York: Office of Teacher Education, 1973.

Tresemer, David. "Fear of success: popular but unproven." Pp. 58–62 in *Psychology Today* (eds.), *The Female Experience.* Del Mar, Calif.: Communications Research Machines, Inc., 1973.

_____. "Assumptions made about gender roles." Pp. 308–339 in Marcia Millman and Rosabeth Moss Kanter (eds.), *Another Voice: Feminist Perspectives in Social Life and Social Science.* Garden City, New York: Anchor/Doubleday, 1975.

Trudgill, Peter. "Sex, covert prestige and linguistic change in urban British English of Norwich." *Language in Society* 1(1972):179–95.

Tumin, Melvin M. *Social Stratification: The Forms and Functions of Inequality.* Englewood Cliffs, New Jersey: Prentice Hall, 1967.

Vanderbilt, Amy. *Amy Vanderbilt's Etiquette.* Garden City, New York: Doubleday and Co., Inc., 1972.

Vogel, Susan; Broverman, Inge; and Gardner, Jo-Ann. *Sesame Street and Sex-Role Stereotypes.* (Revised). Pittsburgh, Pa.: Know, 1970.

Walley, D. *What Boys Can Be.* Kansas City: Hallmark, n.d.

_____. *What Girls Can Be.* Kansas City: Hallmark, n.d.

Walum, Laurel Richardson. "The origins of the women's movement." Lecture. Columbus, Ohio: The Ohio State University, 1970.

_____. "A content analysis of La Leche League newsletters." Unpublished paper. Columbus, Ohio: The Ohio State University, 1973.

_____. "The changing door ceremony: some notes on the operation of sex-roles in everyday life." *Urban Life and Culture* 2(1974a):506–515.

_____. "The etiquette of bondage." *Newsday.* Long Island, New York (May, 1974b).

_____. "Teaching/learning about social organization through ethnomethodology." Presented to Teacher's Corps Members Training Institute, Richmond, Va. July, 1975.

Walum, Laurel Richardson, and Franklin, Clyde, Jr. "Structural components of wives' working." Report prepared for Center for Human Resources, Columbus, Ohio: Ohio State University, 1972.

Walum, Laurel Richardson, and Milder, N. David. "Female roles and protest activity: the meat boycott of 1973." Presented to the American Sociological Association Annual Meeting. New York, August, 1974c.

Watson, John S. "Operant conditioning of visual fixation in infants under visual and auditory reinforcement." *Developmental Psychology* 1(1969):508–516.

Weber, Max. *From Max Weber.* Edited by Hans H. Gerth and C. Wright Mills. New York: Oxford University Press, 1946.

Weisstein, Naomi. "Kinder, kuche, kirche as scientific law: psychology constructs the female." Pp. 205–220 in Robin Morgan (ed.), *Sisterhood Is Powerful.* Random House: New York, 1971.

Weitzman, Lenore J., and Rizzo, Diane. "Images of males and females in elementary textbooks." New York: National Organization for Women's Legal Defense and Education Fund, 1974.

Weitzman, Lenore J.; Eifler, Deborah; Hokada, Elizabeth; and Ross, Catherine. "Sex-role socialization in picture books for preschool children." *American Journal of Sociology* 77(1972):1125–1150.

Wells, Audrey, and Smeal, Eleanor Curti. "Women's attitudes toward women in politics: a survey of urban registered voters and party committeewomen." Pp. 54–72 in Jane S. Jaquette, *Women in Politics*. New York: Wiley Interscience, 1974.

Werner, Emmy E., and Bachtold, Louise M. "Personality characteristics of women in American politics." Pp. 75–84 in Jane S. Jaquette, *Women in Politics*. New York: Wiley Interscience, 1974.

Westoff, Charles; Potty, Robert G.; Sage, Phillip C.; and Mishler, E. *Family Growth in Metropolitan America*. Princeton: Princeton University Press, 1961.

Williams, Mary. "A biology primer for feminists philosophers." Unpublished paper. Department of Philosophy and Biology, Columbus, Ohio: The Ohio State University, 1975.

Willis, Frank N., Jr. "Initial speaking distance as a function of the speakers' relationship." *Psychonomic Science* 6(1966):221–222.

Wilmore, Jack H. "They told you, you couldn't compete with men and you, like a fool, believed them. Here's hope." *Womensports.* (June, 1974):40–43.

Wilson, Everett K. *Sociology: Rules, Roles and Relationships*. Homewood, Ill.: Dorsey Press, 1971.

Women on Words and Images. *Dick and Jane as Victims*. Princeton, New Jersey, 1972.

Wood, Marion. "The influence of sex and knowledge of communication effectiveness on spontaneous speech." *Word* 22(1966):112–137.

Yarrow, L. J.; Rubenstein, J. C.; and Pederson, F. A. "Dimensions of early stimulation: differential effects on infant development. Paper presented at the meetings of the Society for Research in Child Development, 1971.

Yinger, Milton J. *Religion, Society and the Individual*. New York: The Macmillan Co., 1957.

Zimmerman, Don H., and West, Candace. "Sex roles, interruptions and silences in conversations." Pp. 105–129 in Barrie Thorne and Nancy Henley (eds.), *Language and Sex: Difference and Dominance*. Rowley, Mass.: Newbury House, 1975.

Index